READING
SHAKESPEARE'S
DRAMATIC LANGUAGE

A GUIDE

THE ARDEN SHAKESPEARE

*Second Series

READING
SHAKESPEARE'S
DRAMATIC LANGUAGE

A GUIDE

Edited by Sylvia Adamson, Lynette Hunter,
Lynne Magnusson, Ann Thompson
and Katie Wales

The Arden website is at
http://www.ardenshakespeare.com

The general editors of the Arden Shakespeare have been
W. J. Craig and R. H. Case (first series 1899–1944),
Una Ellis-Fermor, Harold F. Brooks, Harold Jenkins and
Brian Morris (second series 1946–1982)

Present general editors (third series)
Richard Proudfoot, Ann Thompson and David Scott Kastan

This edition of *Reading Shakespeare's Dramatic Language – A Guide,*
first published 2001 by The Arden Shakespeare

Editorial matter © 2001 Sylvia Adamson, Lynette Hunter,
Lynne Magnusson, Ann Thompson and Katie Wales

Thomson Learning
Berkshire House
168–173 High Holborn
London WC1V 7AA

Typeset by LaserScript, Mitcham, Surrey

Printed in Singapore by Kin Keong

British Library Cataloguing in Publication Data
A catalogue record for this book is available from the British Library

Library of Congress Cataloguing in Publication Data
A catalogue record has been requested

ISBN 1–903436–29–X (pbk)

NPN 9 8 7 6 5 4 3 2 1

CONTENTS

CONTRIBUTORS

Sylvia Adamson, Professor of Linguistics and Literary History, University of Manchester, UK

William C. Carroll, Professor of English Literature, Boston University, College of Liberal Arts, Massachusetts, USA

Keir Elam, Professor of English Drama, University of Florence, Italy

Lynette Hunter, Professor of the History of Rhetoric, University of Leeds, UK

David Scott Kastan, Professor of English and Comparative Literature, Columbia University, New York, USA

Roger Lass, Distinguished Professor of Historical and Comparative Linguistics, University of Cape Town, SA

Peter Lichtenfels, theatre director, and Senior Lecturer in Acting and Theatre at Manchester Metropolitan University, UK

Lynne Magnusson, Professor of English Language and Literature, Queen's University, Canada

Pamela Mason, Shakespeare Institute, University of Birmingham, UK

Walter Nash, Emeritus Professor of English Language, University of Nottingham, UK

Terttu Nevalainen, Professor of English Philology, University of Helsinki, Finland

Ann Thompson, Professor of English Language and Literature, King's College, London, UK

Katie Wales, Professor of English Language, University of Leeds, UK

George T. Wright, Regents' Professor of English, Emeritus, University of Minnesota, USA

ABBREVIATIONS FOR WORKS
BY SHAKESPEARE

References to Shakespeare's works are to the Arden Shakespeare, except where a particular textual point necessitates
quotation from a different edition. In such cases the line
reference for the quotation is enclosed in square brackets.

For the following works, references are to the Arden third
series (Arden 3) editions:

AC	*Antony and Cleopatra*
H5	*King Henry 5*
JC	*Julius Caesar*
KL	*King Lear*
LLL	*Love's Labour's Lost*
MW	*The Merry Wives of Windsor*
Oth	*Othello*
Son	*Shakespeare's Sonnets*
TC	*Troilus and Cressida*
Tem	*The Tempest*
Tit	*Titus Andronicus*
TNK	*The Two Noble Kinsmen*

For the following works, references are to *The Arden
Shakespeare Complete Works* (1998):

AYL	*As You Like It*
CE	*The Comedy of Errors*
Cor	*Coriolanus*
Cym	*Cymbeline*

Ham	*Hamlet*
1H4	*King Henry IV Part 1*
2H4	*King Henry IV Part 2*
1H6	*King Henry VI Part 1*
2H6	*King Henry VI Part 2*
3H6	*King Henry VI Part 3*
H8	*King Henry VIII*
Luc	*The Rape of Lucrece*
MA	*Much Ado About Nothing*
Mac	*Macbeth*
MM	*Measure for Measure*
MND	*A Midsummer Night's Dream*
MV	*The Merchant of Venice*
Per	*Pericles*
R2	*King Richard II*
R3	*King Richard III*
RJ	*Romeo and Juliet*
Tim	*Timon of Athens*
TN	*Twelfth Night*
TS	*The Taming of the Shrew*
VA	*Venus and Adonis*
WT	*The Winter's Tale*

PREFACE

The Arden Shakespeare has always been conscious of a broadly based readership, and in this book we offer a range of different approaches to interest those studying and teaching Shakespeare's work in schools, colleges and universities, as well as those producing his plays in the theatre and those reading for pleasure.

Each chapter has been specifically commissioned for the volume, and the collection is designed to be accessible, interdisciplinary and rooted in practical examples. The main features of the collection are its combination of discussions from literary criticism, rhetoric, performance and the history of language, and its focus on the more frequently studied Shakespearean texts.

While our main purpose is to make Shakespeare's language and his uses of language more accessible to modern readers, in the process we aim also to provide an introduction to recent changes in the way his language and style are studied. The contributors to the collection represent some of the important trends in contemporary scholarship: the resurgence of interest in rhetorical practices, from Renaissance ideas to contemporary conversation theory; the impact of theatre studies, with their emphasis on language's relation to the physical realities of the stage space and the actor's body; and the revival of the historical impulse in language study and in literary criticism. The combination of approaches is intended to equip readers with ways of reading a language that sometimes seems startlingly similar to our own and sometimes dauntingly different.

The volume is organised in three parts. Part I looks at language from a literary perspective, offering strategies from practical criticism, from an understanding of rhetoric, and from contemporary English language studies and the theatre. It provides a historical approach to issues of oral and written presentation, to the structure of poetry and word-play, and to social and theatrical contexts. Part II looks at literature from a linguistic perspective; it takes us into Shakespeare's verbal toolbox, describing the sounds, words and grammar of Elizabethan English, as well as the rich repertoire of regional and social varieties that Shakespeare heard around him and that we can still hear today in the voices of his characters. Part III acts as a resource centre for the collection as a whole, with a guide to further reading and an extensive A–Z of Renaissance literary and rhetorical devices, explained and illustrated from Shakespeare's own practice, often with modern examples alongside to show that figures of speech are still a living force, though their names may have changed or been forgotten.

Through its interdisciplinary collaborations, the collection as a whole attempts to provide an informed and engaging understanding of dramatic language in the Early Modern period and a practical guidebook for all those interested in reading and performing Shakespeare today.

NOTE ON THE TEXT

Rhetorical and critical terms which are explained in the A–Z are in **bold** print at their first occurrence within a chapter. Other technical terms are introduced in ***bold italic*** print.

Part I

THE LANGUAGE OF SHAKESPEARE'S PLAYS

INTRODUCTION

In Part I we attempt to explore a number of issues that come to the fore when we read Shakespeare's dramatic language today, and to offer our readers a range of approaches to the written and spoken language of the Renaissance period. We aim to enable students in particular to undertake close reading and analysis of the language of Shakespeare and his contemporaries with greater skill and confidence; thereby, we believe, enhancing enjoyment as well as understanding of these texts.

Chapter 1 provides an entry point for the modern reader by exploring the way Shakespeare uses the language of everyday life within a continuum that allows it to move from the literal to the slightly heightened to the very heightened. The four chapters which follow explore elements of style in Shakespeare's dramatic language, referring explicitly to expectations of the audience in the Early Modern period. Building on critical practices from both the Renaissance and modern day, this group discusses the special demands that dramatic form makes on language. Topics covered include the word-play of pun and parody, the power of rhetoric, the counterpoint of metre and rhythm, and particularly the idea of decorum as a principle guiding stylistic choices.

The chapters on larger language actions – description, narrative, persuasion and dialogue – draw variously from current conversation theory, and from both Renaissance and modern language practices in rhetoric and more general techniques for telling stories and histories. They look at how these relate to power and manipulation, to relating words to reality through direct, indirect and contradictory strategies, and to the importance of interaction in social language and dialogue.

The three chapters engaging with issues of character, theatre language and performance also extend the range of critical approaches. The study of 'openings' focuses on the immediacy of the dramatic moment and the contract that is established between the actor and the audience; and drawing on theatre practice and performance theory, both of the remaining chapters introduce vocabulary that allows for discussion of the actor's body and breath, and the impact they have on speaking, silence and action.

1

HEIGHTENED LANGUAGE

Ann Thompson

Compared with the kind of language we might expect to find in a modern newspaper, magazine or popular novel, Shakespeare's language strikes us as complex, elaborate and at times difficult to understand. Remarkably, it still works well enough in the theatre: audiences at the reconstruction of 'Shakespeare's Globe' in London, many of whom have never been to the theatre before, let alone to a play by Shakespeare, seem to have little difficulty grasping the gist of what is going on and responding appropriately to individual speeches and exchanges of dialogue. Programmes at the Globe do provide synopses of the plays, but these are quite minimal and those who read them are boldly exhorted 'to follow the story as the original audience would have done, [and] let the actors themselves guide you'. The international success of Baz Luhrmann's 1996 film of *Romeo and Juliet*, which retained Shakespeare's dialogue while setting the story in a modern location ('Verona Beach'), also testifies to the continuing ability of ordinary people (including many young people) to follow the language in a performance context.

But if you were to sit one of those playgoers or filmgoers down in front of a copy of one of Shakespeare's plays and ask him or her to comment on the language of a particular passage, or even to provide a paraphrase or 'translation' of it, problems would arise. Speaking very broadly, we could identify three reasons for this. First would be precisely the absence of the performance context: a good actor who understands the language can convey its sense through facial and vocal expression, intonation and gesture. Second is the fact that Shakespeare's language is four hundred years old and a great deal has changed between 1600 and 2000, including the meaning and usage of many individual words; while the gist may be graspable, the detail can be obscure or impenetrable. Third is the relatively recent problem that most people today lack the analytical tools and vocabulary to discuss language in any but the most general terms; to a large extent we have lost the terminology people used in 1600 and we have failed to agree on an alternative set of terms. Several of the contributions to this book aim to promote a better under-standing of the earlier terminology, while others offer different strategies for talking and writing about language.

In the remainder of this chapter introducing Part I, I shall start the ball rolling by arguing for a considerable degree of continuity between Shakespeare's dramatic language and everyday modern language, and I shall attempt to demonstrate that it is possible at least to begin to analyse Shakespeare's language without using the traditional vocabulary of rhetorical analysis or the terminology of discourse studies, although both – along with the vocabulary of theatre and performance studies – can be enormously interesting and useful, as other chapters in Part I will show. I want to introduce the idea of 'heightened language' as one such basic concept and use it as a jumping-off point for some of the debates that will follow: how does an author 'heighten', 'work up' or intensify language and how does an auditor or reader identify, describe and explore those effects?

In my experience as a teacher, I have often found that students can readily identify points at which Shakespeare's language is (a) difficult or (b) particularly striking or impressive, but they struggle to describe these linguistic phenomena in any detail, sometimes resorting to calling the language 'flowery' (a term which can be used either positively or negatively) or simply 'effective' (which seems to beg the question). Editors and commentators can help with some kinds of difficulty by providing glosses and paraphrases, but even they often fail to explain the precise source of the difficulty by offering simply a 'translation' without analysing the complexity of the language.

I think it is also the case that the importance that we have given in recent years to metaphor, and our association of **metaphor** with the popular notion of 'imagery', have in themselves given rise to certain distortions. The search for 'images' tends to emphasize (a) the novel and (b) the visual: we look for what is striking or original on the one hand and for mental pictures on the other; we ignore or undervalue what is familiar or conventional or what is non-visual. This approach may be more appropriate to Metaphysical poetry, where we find ingenious metaphors like John Donne's famous comparison of himself and his lover to the two legs of a pair of compasses in his poem 'A valediction: forbidding mourning', but it is not always helpful in relation to dramatic language, which has after all to make sense to auditors and cannot afford to be too obscure if it is going to keep them following what is going on. Moreover, they already have visual work to do (in reality in the theatre, in their imagination as readers) so another layer of picture-making can become problematic. And the tendency to privilege 'running' or repeated images has encouraged a rapid attention shift away from linguistic style towards larger patterns of meaning: it implies that we are only interested in the micro-level of language in so far as it can be seen as contributing to macro-level meanings such as 'themes'.

I want to begin by suggesting that Shakespeare's language is in some ways very like everyday language, and that there is a kind of continuum which allows it to 'rise' from the colloquial level to the 'slightly heightened' and then to the 'very heightened'. (For a more specifically Renaissancecentred view of 'levels' of language, see Chapter 3 by Sylvia Adamson; here, I am using 'heightened' to refer primarily to metaphorical language.) I put the words 'rise' and 'heightened' in scare-quotes because I do not want to imply a value judgement: it is obvious if one thinks of King Lear's devastating lines addressed to his dead daughter Cordelia, 'O thou'lt come no more, / Never, never, never, never, never' (*KL* 5.3.306–7), that language does not have to be metaphorical to be maximally effective (see, for example, Chapter 4 by George T. Wright for strategies that discuss the effectiveness of rhythm). The continuum can be explored, initially at least, by focusing on the basic distinction between the literal and the figurative use of words, defining 'figurative' in the broadest sense to include any meaning other than the literal. 'Figurative' language includes metaphorical language but also includes a range of other 'heightening' strategies (see, for example, Chapter 5 by Walter Nash on puns and parody). I am not proposing the literal/figurative distinction as one which could or should be a governing concept in this kind of analysis; I have found however that it can be a useful way to start talking about 'Shakespeare's dramatic language', and to illustrate how this can happen I shall explore some aspects of the 'heightening' (and 'lowering') of language in one scene in *Richard III*.

The scene is the fourth one in the play, Act 1 scene 4. It takes place in the Tower of London where George, Duke of Clarence, brother of the reigning King Edward IV, has been imprisoned. In the opening scene of *Richard III*, Richard, Duke of Gloucester, another, younger brother of Edward IV (later to become Richard III), has encountered Clarence on his way to the Tower and has pretended to sympathize with his plight, but at the end of 1.3 we have seen Richard hiring two murderers to kill Clarence as part of his plan to become king himself. The 'Keeper' or jailer begins 1.4 by asking Clarence how he is:

KEEPER

Why looks your Grace so heavily today?

CLARENCE

O, I have pass'd a miserable night,
So full of fearful dreams, of ugly sights,
That, as I am a Christian faithful man,
I would not spend another such a night
Though 'twere to buy a world of happy days,
So full of dismal terror was the time.

(1.4.1–7)

Most readers will probably agree that the language of this passage is not particularly difficult. Challenged to comment on its style, however, they may not know what to say apart from the negative points that it lacks 'images' and **alliteration**. What happens when we try to distinguish between literal and figurative language? What is the first word in the passage that is not used in a strictly literal sense? The word 'heavily' might attract attention: the Keeper is not asking Clarence why he has suddenly put on weight but is enquiring about his attitude of worry or unhappiness. 'Heavily' in this context is figurative or metaphorical at a very 'low' level and has obvious continuities with everyday expressions such as 'depressed' and 'weighed down' when used of the mind or spirit. It reminds us that ordinary, colloquial language can be regularly figurative or metaphorical in ways we scarcely notice. Similarly, in lines 5–6 the words 'spend' and 'buy' are used figuratively – we do not literally 'spend' nights or 'buy' days – but again we can easily overlook the 'heightening', partly because these terms are part of the very familiar nexus of metaphors, still current in our own culture, whereby 'time is money'. And once we have started thinking about time metaphors, we might go back to 'passed' – 'I have passed a miserable night' – and notice that this equally familiar metaphor involves a kind of spatialization whereby time is envisaged as a place or landscape through which we pass. (For further discussion of these 'everyday' metaphors, see Lakoff and Johnson, as listed below.)

Encouraged by the Keeper to go on, Clarence 'heightens' his language somewhat in a vivid description of his dream in which he is on a sea voyage crossing to France during a storm with his brother Richard who pushes him overboard and causes him to drown. This speech could be called both 'descriptive' (see Chapter 6 by William C. Carroll) and 'narrative' (see Chapter 7 by David Scott Kastan). Clarence exclaims:

> O Lord! Methought what pain it was to drown:
> What dreadful noise of waters in my ears;
> What sights of ugly death within my eyes!
> Methoughts I saw a thousand fearful wrecks;
> Ten thousand men that fishes gnaw'd upon;
> Wedges of gold, great anchors, heaps of pearl,
> Inestimable stones, unvalu'd jewels,
> All scatter'd in the bottom of the sea.

> (21–8)

While this passage is twice distanced from literal reality – (a) by the fact that it is a description of a dream; (b) by the fact that one cannot, literally, describe what it is like to die by drowning – it is notable that the language nevertheless remains close to the literal, the 'heightening' being attributable to such devices as exaggeration of scale ('a thousand fearful wrecks', 'ten thousand men', 'inestimable stones', 'unvalu'd jewels') and the use of lists and parallel terms rather than to the use of metaphor. For the audience or reader at this point, Clarence's words can also be read ironically, reminding us that we already know that Richard is indeed planning to kill him, and the historically well informed will know that his fate is to be drowned in a barrel of wine.

But then there is a further 'heightening' when Clarence describes how his dream continued his experience after death:

O, then began the tempest to my soul:
I pass'd, methought, the melancholy flood,
With that sour ferryman which poets write of,
Unto the kingdom of perpetual night.

(44–7)

Here, the quasi-literal storm of the voyage-narrative becomes 'the tempest to my soul', a metaphorical expression for mental or spiritual disorientation and anguish. It is interesting that Shakespeare, a Christian writer depicting Christian characters for a Christian audience, draws on a vision of the afterlife taken from pagan sources here: 'the melancholy flood' is the river Styx and the 'sour ferryman' Charon; the 'poets' who write about them are Romans who wrote in Latin, notably Virgil and Seneca. Later in his account Clarence describes seeing 'a shadow like an angel' (53) and 'a legion of foul fiends' (58) which made him think he was 'in hell' (62) and caused him to pray to God for forgiveness (69–72), thus seamlessly combining pagan and Christian versions of the afterlife.

This device of alluding to other stories 'which poets write of' is a very common way for Shakespeare to 'heighten' or enrich his own work, and it is often necessary for editors to explain the allusions to modern readers who are not familiar with the standard range of tragic, romantic and religious narratives known to Shakespeare and to some if not all of his audience. The phenomenon of allusion to other texts, sometimes called 'intertextuality', is of course still familiar today, notably in popular cinematic genres: horror films, for example, regularly rely on the ability of their audience to recognize motifs repeated from previous films in the same genre.

Clarence sleeps again at this point in the scene and, after a brief speech by Brackenbury, Lieutenant of the Tower, we get the stage direction, '*Enter the two* Murderers', and the language returns quite explicitly (and wittily) to the literal level: 'What would'st thou, fellow? And how cam'st thou hither?' asks Brakenbury, to which the First Murderer replies 'I would speak with Clarence, and I came hither on my legs' (85–7). There then ensues a grimly comic dialogue between the two murderers, who debate whether to kill Clarence in his sleep or wake him up before killing him. They speak in prose, like many lower-class characters in Shakespeare, and unlike the socially superior characters who have preceded them (see Chapter 13 by Katie Wales in Part II), but that is not to say their language is devoid of 'heightening'. The Second Murderer has twinges of conscience, but the First reminds him of the promised reward and asks 'Where's thy conscience now?' (125), imagining 'conscience' as an object rather than as an abstraction. On being told it is 'in the Duke of Gloucester's purse', he asks, 'When he opens his purse to give us our reward, thy conscience flies out?' (126–8) and provokes an extended rejection of 'conscience':

> I'll not meddle with it; it makes a man a coward. A man cannot steal but it accuseth him; a man cannot swear but it checks him; a man cannot lie with his neighbour's wife but it detects him. 'Tis a blushing, shamefaced spirit, that mutinies in a man's bosom. It fills a man full of obstacles; it made me once restore a purse of gold that by chance I found. It beggars any man that keeps it; it is turned out of towns and cities for a dangerous thing; and every man that means to live well endeavours to trust to himself, and live without it.

> (132–42)

The 'heightening' devices here are simple ones still found in everyday language: personification (conscience is now seen as being like a human being) and repetition (the same words and structures are repeated in repetitive patterns), but the speech is a self-conscious set-piece or *tour de force* and could be seen as a kind of rehearsal on Shakespeare's part for Falstaff's later and more famous rejection of 'honour' (*1H4* 5.1.127–41).

Clarence wakes while the Murderers are still talking and calls 'Where art thou, Keeper? Give me a cup of wine' (160). The Second Murderer replies 'You shall have wine enough, my lord, anon' (161), alluding ironically to the plan they have just made to 'throw him into the malmsey-butt in the next room' (153–4). He has switched into blank verse now, adjusting his language to that used by Clarence, and the rest of the scene is in verse with both Murderers using relatively formal language. (For further discussion of how speakers influence each other, see Chapter 9 by Lynne Magnusson.) To take one example of this shift, when Clarence warns the Murderers that God will take vengeance on them if they murder him, they reply:

2 MURDERER
　　And that same vengeance doth He hurl on thee,
　　For false forswearing, and for murder too:
　　Thou didst receive the sacrament to fight
　　In quarrel of the House of Lancaster.
1 MURDERER
　　And like a traitor to the name of God
　　Didst break that vow, and with thy treacherous blade
　　Unrip'st the bowels of thy sovereign's son.

(197–203)

In alluding to biblical injunctions and in enumerating the crimes that Clarence has committed (and that Shakespeare has dramatized in the *Henry VI* plays), as well as in speaking verse, they have strictly speaking moved 'out of character' at this point, 'heightening' their language in a way inappropriate for men of their ostensible class and level of education. They also violate Elizabethan linguistic propriety by using the familiar 'thee' and 'thou' forms instead of the polite 'you' which ordinary people might be expected to use towards a member of the royal family, though the distinction was beginning to break down during this period. (See Sylvia Adamson's discussion of this point in Part II, Chapter 14.) These 'violations' of rules are however not unusual in Shakespeare, who is prepared to sacrifice this kind of naturalistic consistency for the immediate needs of a particular situation.

It is of course highly implausible that in real life murderers would pause to 'reason with' their victim (as they themselves put it at 159) for over a hundred lines of blank verse before finally striking a blow (at 266). What is happening here is that the drama itself has come to centre on linguistic competence: will Clarence be able to talk them out of doing their job or will they be able to counter him at every turn? In this section of the scene, as in the confrontations between Isabella and Angelo in *Measure for Measure* and Antony's speeches at Caesar's funeral in *Julius Caesar* (discussed by Lynette Hunter in Chapter 8), characters' lives and the outcome of the plot are seen to depend quite literally on 'words, words, words' (*Ham* 2.2.192).

Shakespeare's theatre itself was very dependent on words, by comparison with modern forms of dramatic and cinematic performance; plays were performed in natural daylight with no scenery and minimal props, so the language was required to do the kind of work which can now be done by stage design, artificial lighting and special effects. It is even possible to feel in a modern production or film that Shakespeare's language becomes redundant: why are these actors taking so long to tell us that it is dawn (*RJ* 2.3 and 3.5), or that it is dark (*Mac* 2.1), or that there is a storm going on (*KL* 3.1 and 3.2), when we can see and hear it all before they tell us? It is perhaps not surprising that some of the most successful modern representations of the plays are those that dare to be minimal, allowing full scope to the language, rather than those that overwhelm it with lavish sets and effects.

In the absence of videotapes, recordings, reviews or even good eyewitness accounts of Shakespeare's plays, we too are dependent in a different way on the words of the texts: they are all we have to go on. Of course, as the chapters by Pamela Mason, Peter Lichtenfels and Keir Elam demonstrate, the words evoke gestures, actions, relationships; they establish a contract with the audience; they allow us to reconstruct what an original performance might have been like, and to imagine a wide range of subsequent performance possibilities. Our hope is that this book will help its readers to attend more closely to what Shakespeare does with words, to understand something of the linguistic context of those words, and to find their own words for engaging in informed discussion of the issues. All of these things can be done in a number of different ways, as we hope to demonstrate. In the next chapter, Lynne Magnusson offers a general introduction to Shakespeare's dramatic style in terms of the Renaissance art of rhetoric, providing a context for some of the more specialized chapters that follow.

FURTHER READING

Lakoff, George and Mark Johnson, *Metaphors We Live By* (Chicago and London: Chicago University Press, 1980)

> Lakoff and Johnson argue that metaphor is an inevitable and inescapable element in everyday conceptualization and verbalization, not a 'literary' embellishment. They identify broad categories of structural metaphors ('time is money'), orientational metaphors ('more is up') and ontological metaphors ('the mind is a machine') which influence the ways in which we perceive, think and act as well as speak and write. They do not discuss elaborated or heightened uses of language, but their approach is thought provoking for students of literature and implicitly illustrates the extent to which some of Shakespeare's most complex metaphors are grounded in everyday language.

McDonald, Russ (ed.), *Shakespeare Reread: The Texts in New Contexts* (Ithaca, N.Y., and London: Cornell University Press, 1994)

> Some of the ten essays in this volume were conceived as contributions to a conference session on 'Close Reading Revisited', which would have

been an equally appropriate title. Contributors, who include Stephen Booth, Barbara Hodgdon, Pat Parker and Helen Vendler, address issues of textual analysis in relation to current contextual (social, historical, political) ways of reading. There is no consistent ideological stance, but all the approaches are challenging and theoretically sophisticated.

Thompson, Ann and John O. Thompson, *Shakespeare, Meaning and Metaphor* (Brighton: Harvester Press, 1987)

This book applies non-literary research on metaphor to a number of Shakespearean texts – *Troilus and Cressida, King Lear, Hamlet*, Sonnet 63 – and more generally to Shakespeare's use of metaphors from the domain of printing. The approaches used are drawn from philosophy, psychology, linguistics and anthropology, and the authors argue that they can illuminate Shakespearean usage even though they do not address it directly but focus on everyday language. In turn the approaches themselves are tested and illuminated by the range and complexity of Shakespearean examples.

Wright, George T., 'Hendiadys and *Hamlet*', *PMLA* (*Publications of the Modern Language Association of America*) (1981), 96, 168–93

Wright discusses the importance of the 'doubling' scheme of hendiadys ('They drank from cups and gold' is a classic example) as both a frequent local effect in *Hamlet* (and other plays of Shakespeare's middle period) and a reflection of the play's thematic concern with doubleness, disjunction, misleading parallels and false relationships. This essay has become a classic example of the significance of a particular rhetorical device to a single text.

2

STYLE, RHETORIC AND DECORUM

Lynne Magnusson

This chapter is meant to provide some resources for talking about Shakespeare's dramatic style. Questions about style are questions about the choice-making implicit in a writer's language: how does the particular wording or phrasing of any utterance stand out among options potentially available in the language of the period? and what may have governed the choice of one stylistic possibility over others? I will consider, first, how the Elizabethan emphasis on rhetoric provided Shakespeare with a wide range of stylistic options and encouraged his showmanship in language. Second, I will consider what functions language is called upon to perform to create a play's world and its characters, and how Shakespeare's stylistic choices are governed partly by decorum, the fit between language and situation.

What, above all, set the youthful Shakespeare in the 1590s on a course that would make him the most widely admired both of canonical and of popular authors in English was his astonishing aptitude with language. He could turn words and sentences into dazzling performances. What especially fostered his talents for verbal risk-taking and display and created an audience that took pleasure in performative language was a renewed emphasis in sixteenth-century education on rhetoric. Rhetoric is an art developed in ancient times by the Greeks and Romans to give public speakers – whether senators, citizens, or lawyers – systematic techniques for persuading their audiences. The Roman orator, Marcus Tullius Cicero –

or 'Tully', as Shakespeare's characters call him – was probably the single most influential name among classical rhetoricians in Shakespeare's time. Reading Cicero's writings encouraged Renaissance schoolboys to place the highest value on well-developed communication skills, to celebrate eloquence as the core of their humanity and the base on which to build up workable social communities and just governments. What could be more inspiring than Cicero's sales pitch for rhetoric?

> [T]here is to my mind no more excellent thing than the power, by means of oratory, to get a hold on assemblies of men, win their good will, direct their inclinations wherever the speaker wishes ... For the one point in which we have our greatest advantage over the brute creation is that we hold converse one with another, and can reproduce our thought in word ... To come ... to the highest achievements of eloquence, what other power could have been strong enough either to gather scattered humanity into one place, or to lead it out of its brutish existence in the wilderness up to our present condition of civilization as men and as citizens, or, after the establishment of social communities, to give shape to laws, tribunals, and civil rights? ... [M]y assertion is this: that the wise control of the complete orator is that which chiefly upholds not only his own dignity, but the safety of countless individuals and of the entire State.[1]

This optimism about eloquent wisdom echoes throughout Renaissance writings. It is caught up in how educators of the day taught Latin; it is also caught up in how the English court and its increasingly learned councillors imagined a civilized state. Although for the ancients the techniques of rhetoric served primarily to train orators to speak persuasively in council chambers, public ceremonies and legal courts, Shakespeare would have encountered the techniques updated not only to typical political (and commercial) situations of his own time but also to almost all the imaginable forms of written and literary composition. Rhetorical eloquence was understood both as equipment for business and living and as equipment for poetry and plays.

All of Shakespeare's plays draw on the resources of rhetoric, but none capitalizes on the word rage of the 1580s and 1590s like the stylish *Love's Labour's Lost.* Here, showing off with words is the main game, both for the writer and his characters. For this reason, the play is a good place to start to build some skill in spotting the figures of speech that expanded Shakespeare's stylistic options, and I will draw on it for my initial examples. But it is also important to understand that rhetoric is not just about style or figures of speech, so let's begin by considering where style fits in the larger picture provided by rhetoric. The historical tradition of rhetoric encompasses almost everything you might want to know in order to write and argue effectively in virtually any situation. What Renaissance writers thought of as the Ciceronian pattern of rhetoric divided its knowledge into five parts: *invention*, *disposition*, *style*, *memory* and *delivery*. *Invention* is a particularly important category, which offers tools for generating and developing ideas. Students of rhetoric might be encouraged, for example, to start from *commonplaces*, and to play variations upon these familiar shared ideas. This may sound like opposite advice from today's strategies for awakening one's individual creativity, but think of Shake-speare's sonnets, so often praised for their original genius, and how the first seventeen work, basically, by varying an entirely conventional idea: a beautiful man should have children to pass on his beauty. There's little difference between this and the preoccupying clichés of our day – for example, that an attractive woman should maintain her looks with exercise and diet. *Invention* provides strategies for reworking and develop-ing materials like these commonplaces, including *topics* – or precepts for varying – and a large arsenal of argumentative tactics (see also Chapter 8). One of the guiding principles here is *copia*, a facility much admired in Shakespeare's time for using language to amplify and vary any idea or expression. For example, the leading character in *Love's Labour's Lost* develops a long and virtuoso speech by finding all the inventive ways he possibly can to overturn one of the play's commonplaces: that women distract men from serious study. Berowne and his youthful friends, urged on by the King of Navarre, have signed on to a vow to withdraw from the world's pleasures, women included, in order to pursue a reclusive three-year plan of study. The whole action of the play turns on their embarrassing violations of their vow, brought on, especially, by a group of visiting ladies, with whom the men fall in love. So Berowne's speech helps to save their dignity by bringing out how women's eyes might be a proper object of study: 'From women's eyes this doctrine I derive: / … They are the books, the arts, the academes, / That show, contain and nourish all the world' (4.3.324–7). It's like building arguments for the contrary to the 'thin' commonplace to show that fat is indeed beautiful.

Rhetoric is not just a method of composition but also a subject matter in *Love's Labour's Lost*, with characters admiring or critiquing the 'sweet smoke of rhetoric' (3.1.60) or the 'great feast of languages' (5.1.35–6) in one another's talk. Most of the five parts get some sort of explicit attention, except perhaps *disposition*, which treats the effective arrangement and organization of speeches. *Memory* and *delivery*, parts of rhetoric often given slighter treatment in handbooks but clearly transferrable to theatrical performance, get mentions. A boy sent by the lords to make a speech to the ladies receives instruction in both: we hear how 'well by heart' he had learned his message and how the lords rehearsed him in 'action and accent': 'Thus must thou speak, and thus thy body bear' (5.2.99–100). Those performing skits and masques within the play often encounter a scoffing audience, and it is again in terms of a key rhetorical term that the effect of audience contempt is imagined: it 'will kill the speaker's heart / And quite divorce his *memory* from his part' (5.2.149–50; italics added). Yet there is no doubt that it is *style* that gets the lion's share of the attention, reflecting both the Elizabethans' special accent on this part of rhetoric and what most fired Shakespeare's imagination.

Holofernes, the schoolteacher character, captures the play's special excitement with stylistic devices and figures of speech when he responds to the showy language of his friend, 'What is the figure? What is the figure?' (5.1.59). In developing a stylistic rhetoric, treatises often divided figures of speech in two types: *tropes*, or figures of thought, which 'translate' words from their normal sense or usage, and *schemes*, or figures of sound, which create ornamental patterns with words through repeating or transforming letters, syllables, or words. Everyone knows that Shakespeare is a master of *tropes* like metaphor, but, apart from alliteration ('The preyful Princess pierced and pricked a pretty pleasing pricket', 4.2.56), the *schemes* that are the main show pieces in this play are less well known. That is not to say we don't use them any more. Virtually no political speech, advertisement, children's poem or popular song today is without some of these verbal devices of repetition, because they work to make things memorable, but most of us don't have names or systematic strategies for exploiting their effects.

Let's take a sampling of schemes of repetition on display, together with their rarefied and colourful names:[2]

✦ *To know* the thing I am forbid *to know*

(1.1.60)

(**epanalepsis** – repeating word(s) at the beginning and end of a unit, such as a line, phrase, clause or sentence)

✦ If you are armed *to do* as sworn *to do*

(1.1.22)

(**epistrophe** – repeating word(s) at the end of a series of clauses)

✦ Let fame, that all hunt after in their *lives*,

Live registered upon our brazen tombs

(1.1.1–2)

(**anadiplosis** – repeating word(s) ending one line or other unit at the start of the next; also illustrates **polyptoton** – repeating words derived from the same root, but having different endings or forms)

✦ And as it is *base* for a soldier to *love*, so am I in *love* with a *base* wench

(1.2.56–8)

(**antimetabole** – repeating words in converse order)

✦ *Light* seeking *light* doth *light* of *light* beguile

(1.1.77)

(**diacope** – repeating a word with one or few between; also
antanaclesis – a type of pun which repeats a word with shifting sense)

As we can see from this final example, puns, which highlight multiple meanings of words, are related to the patterned schemes of repetition. Pun strings abound in this play, often with one character's word returned by the other with a shifted sense (**asteismus**):

KATHERINE

you are a *light* [i.e. loose in morals] wench.

ROSALINE

Indeed, I weigh not you, and therefore *light* [i.e. weighing little].

(5.2.25–6)

Shakespeare experiments with a different type of verbal patterning in schemes of word construction. Rhetorical handbooks had names for schemes providing elegant variation by adding a syllable at the beginning of a word (*prosthesis*) or at the end (*proparalepsis*), but Shakespeare seems to do them one better with the pompous Armado's 'enfreedoming' (3.1.121), which builds on to both the beginning and end of the clear and simple verb 'to free'.

Indeed, Armado is a character created by taking to extremes the age's love affair with copia, the attitude expressed by the scholarly Erasmus that 'there is nothing more admirable or more splendid than a speech with a rich copia of thoughts and words overflowing in a golden stream'.[3] One recommended way to produce this abundant supply of words was to vary an expression by using synonyms (**synonymia**). As Armado comments to the person he is promising to 'enfreedom', 'Thou wert immured, restrained, captivated, bound' (3.1.121–2). The play cues us to the fact that Shakespeare expects us to see some of the language as overblown by introducing Armado's style, by way of a letter of his that the King reads out, as a source of mockery and entertainment for the lords. The dramatist is fully aware of how stultifying consistently overblown language can be, and, as the letter is read out, he makes the situation all the more amusing by contrasting Armado's synonym-like variations with the simple word repetition of the lower-class worker he is criticizing:

KING   [*reading*] *There did I see that low-spirited swain, that*
    base minnow of thy mirth –
COSTARD   Me?
KING   *That unlettered small-knowing soul* –
COSTARD   Me?
KING   *That shallow vassal*–
COSTARD   Still me?

(1.1.239–45; original italics)

But the dividing line between a 'fine surplus' of style and 'too much' is a big issue in this comedy, for the heroes are themselves berated for their overly fine words by the ladies they woo. Berowne is set the full-year-long test of trying with his words to make the 'speechless sick' respond and smile before his beloved Rosaline will consent to marry him. That is, he is set the task not of producing a golden stream of *copia* but instead of finding a language that is seemly and fitting for the people involved and the situation of speech. It is again the art of rhetoric that provides the term for this more functional virtue of language – ***decorum***.

What applies here to Berowne – the need to attend to stylistic function as well as stylistic display – seems also to have applied to the young dramatist who created him. The

worship and cultivation of eloquence won't in itself make a
good speaker or a great dramatist, because elaborate speech
does not suit all occasions. One of the most powerful
sequences in *King Lear*, when Lear stubbornly refuses to take
in the information given him about who placed his messenger
in the stocks, uses absolutely plain and simple speech, giving
the effect of grown men reduced to a child-like argument:

KENT
                    It is both he and she,
    Your son and daughter.
LEAR   No.
KENT   Yes.
LEAR   No, *I say.*
KENT   *I say,* yea.
LEAR   No, no, they would not.
KENT   Yes, they have.

                                                    (2.2.203–10)

    (but note too the **anadiplosis** – Shakespeare understands that schemes
    of repetition turn up for emphasis even in the most mundane quarrels)

A dramatic language cannot be merely an exhibitionist style,
all on one level. The dramatist must give voices to a world and
all its varied businesses. For dramatic language to represent a
world and its businesses, the style will be varied: kings, earls,
townspeople, merchants, ploughmen and kitchen help will all
speak differently, and merchants (for example) will shift their
speech depending on whether they address physicians or tavern
maids. We too shift our speech with person and occasion
(think, for example, of asking your boss to extend an urgent
deadline versus telling your friend she can't borrow your car),
but social differences expressed in language were even more
strongly marked in Elizabethan times. Shakespeare had to be
like a verbal chameleon, able not only to mimic in his writing
all the street lingos around him, but able to tune in, at least
through imagination, to the registers of conversational

situations and formal occasions he could never have been part of. This ability to make us hear a plurality of real-world voices shows up even in relatively early plays. Think of the brief opening sequence in *The Taming of the Shrew*:

✦ I'll feeze ['do in', beat] you, in faith.

(Induction 1.1)

(colloquial aggression of drunken tinker against tavern hostess)

✦ You will not pay for the glasses you have burst?

(Induction 1.6)

(business-like directness of aggrieved hostess)

✦ Huntsman, I charge thee, tender well my hounds.

(Induction 1.15)

(self-confident order issued to subordinate by a lord)

✦ An't please your honour, players [are come]
    That offer service to your lordship.

(Induction 1.76–7)

(deference of the subordinate to his master)

It is clear, then, that dramatic style must be guided by decorum and that part of Shakespeare's wonderful inventiveness is in discovering the languages to fit a wide range of situations and relationships. At the same time, had Shakespeare conformed completely to decorum as interpreted by Renaissance theorists of literature and drama his language would not have been as fully dramatic as it in fact is. In *The Art of English Poesy*, George Puttenham uses the word 'decencie' to translate the classical concept of decorum:

> our speech asketh one maner of *decencie*, in respect of the person who speakes: another of his to whom it is spoken: another of whom we speake: another of what we speake, and in what place and time and to what purpose.[4]

Caught up here with the important principle of situated speech is a principle of social regulation, an emphasis on what is 'proper' in different relationships and situations. Paradoxically, Shakespeare's realization of a fully dramatic language depends also on his recognition of the potentially anti-dramatic pull of 'decencie' or decorum. If kings in kingly situations always speak like kings and servants always defer to them, if women always maintain the silence or modesty in speech considered in Renaissance times to be fitting to them, then everyone stays in their places. There's no conflict, nothing going wrong, no negotiation of new roles, or transformations – all elements at the heart of drama. Blatant indecorum can make for exciting drama, and Shakespeare knows how to exploit it in many different ways. The basic situation, for example, of *The Taming of the Shrew* illustrates indecorum: Katherine, the 'shrew' of the title, is hard for her father to marry off because her speech style is improper. Loud, aggressive, crude, unruly, matching wits and temperamental words with men, she is far from exhibiting the restrained speech considered 'decent' for a gentlewoman. 'Asses are made to bear,' she tells her suitor, 'and so are you' (2.1.200). Although, as we have seen, *copia* or fullness of speech was a quality Renaissance schoolboys were taught to revere, all the praise for modest and silent women meant that the reverse was true for girls and women. Hence all of Shakespeare's talkative women – Rosalind in *As You Like It*, Beatrice in *Much Ado About Nothing*, and others – are, in a way, created out of an imaginative, and perhaps forward-looking, use of indecorum.

For dramatic language where decorum rubs up against indecorum, let's look at the talk in *The Merchant of Venice* between the overspent aristocrat Bassanio and the Jewish merchant and moneylender Shylock:

SHYLOCK   Three thousand ducats, well.
BASSANIO   Ay, sir, for three months.
SHYLOCK   For three months, well.
BASSANIO   For the which, as I told you, Antonio shall be bound.

SHYLOCK　Antonio shall become bound, well.

BASSANIO　May you stead me? Will you pleasure me? Shall I know your answer?

SHYLOCK　Three thousand ducats for three months, and Antonio bound.

BASSANIO　Your answer to that?

SHYLOCK　Antonio is a good man.

BASSANIO　Have you heard any imputation to the contrary?

SHYLOCK　Ho no, no, no, no: my meaning in saying he is a good man, is to have you understand me that he is sufficient, – yet his means are in supposition: he hath an argosy bound to Tripolis, another to the Indies, I understand moreover upon the Rialto, he hath a third ... but ships are but boards, sailors but men; there be land-rats, and water-rats, water-thieves, and land thieves (I mean pirates), and then there is the peril of waters, winds, and rocks. The man is notwithstanding sufficient, – three thousand ducats: I think I may take his bond.

BASSANIO　Be assur'd you may.

SHYLOCK　I will be assur'd I may; and that I may be assur'd, I will bethink me ...

(1.3.1–29)

Decorum is at work here to match style to each of the speakers. Even in asking for a loan, Bassanio speaks the aristocratic language of liberal, open-handed courtesy, although a liberality he expects everyone else to extend to him. He talks as if with the assumption that one person will 'stead' (help out) another, that if you 'pleasure' (gratify, do a turn for) me today I'll do the same for you tomorrow. Furthermore, Bassanio speaks with all the self-confidence of a man entirely used to being taken at his word, expecting no one to doubt his 'Be assur'd'. His style is 'proper' to him: it bespeaks his class with all its prerogatives. Most Londoners in Shakespeare's day would have had less occasion to meet a

Jewish merchant than a Bassanio, Jews having been expelled and kept out of England for three centuries, but with his language Shakespeare tries to capture the cultural and occupational difference of Shylock. The careful and practical consideration of details and risk levels, the commercial language that almost forecasts word urns in modern-day insurance policies like 'all perils', the cautious sizing up of a man's words and assets suggested by Shylock's repeating of what Bassanio says – the language 'fits' or, indeed, creates the speaker. But this decorum of language and speaker is not the whole verbal drama of the encounter here. We find also Shakespeare's ingenious exploitation of *anti-decorum* in the 'misfit' between the language and the person addressed. Our attention is drawn to a collision of languages, signalled most strongly by the way Shylock picks up words and phrases Bassanio uses, like 'be assur'd', and repeats them with a different sense and accent. Unexpectedly perhaps, this example takes us back to the rhetorical schemes of repetition that we had first discussed as eloquent ornamentation. Through the repetition – including even a showy antimetabole in the last line quoted – Shakespeare tells us that the two men speak different languages, inhabit alien cultures. The mismatched dialogue calls into question whether any pre-existing 'decorum' could cover the tense and exciting cross-cultural encounter at the play's centre. Here, without question, schemes of repetition are not primarily ornamental but have a clear dramatic function in bringing out the plurality of the play's voices.

Shakespeare's invention of a fully dramatic language, then, strikes a fine and imaginative balance between the love and embellishment of words for their own sake and the functional matching of words to situations. In this chapter I have talked about stylistic function mainly in relation to the characters and worlds represented in a play, but a more comprehensive account of dramatic language would need to bring in other questions about the tasks language must accomplish in the theatre. For example, however great the attraction of dazzling verbal displays, the dramatist must use language in such a way as to carry the plot forward efficiently and to address his audience's need for comprehensibility. Furthermore, language must work in the theatre in concert with the enacted spectacle and the actor's voice and body, so that what we see will at times flesh out the bare bones of a speech and what is said will at times transform our perception of what we see. These and other uses of language will be discussed in later chapters, including especially those on narrative, description, metre, theatrical language and bodily meanings.

NOTES

1 Marcus Tullius Cicero, *On the Making of an Orator* ('De oratore'), trans. E.W. Sutton and H. Rackham, 2 vols (Cambridge, Mass.: Harvard University Press, 1959), 1.23–7.

2 Italics are added in these and all subsequent examples, unless otherwise stated. See also the A–Z of Rhetorical and Critical Terms.

3 Desiderius Erasmus, *On Copia of Words and Ideas* ('De utraque verborum ac rerum copia'), trans. Donald B. King and H. David Rix (Milwaukee, Wis.: Marquette University Press, 1963), 11.

4 George Puttenham, *The Art of English Poesy* (1589), introduction by Baxter Hathaway (reprinted Kent, Ohio: Kent State University Press, 1957), 270.

FURTHER READING

Elam, Keir, *Shakespeare's Universe of Discourse: Language-Games in the Comedies* (Cambridge: Cambridge University Press, 1984)

Elam makes use of modern theories taken from linguistics and semiotics alongside Renaissance approaches to language in an analysis of the dialogue of Shakespearean comedy (with particular attention to *Love's Labour's Lost*). He demonstrates that the apparently highly stylized exchanges between characters on Shakespeare's stage are to a large extent governed by the same rules and conventions as everyday conversation.

Hibbard, G.R., The Making of Shakespeare's Dramatic Poetry (Toronto, Buffalo and London: University of Toronto Press, 1981)

Hibbard argues that Shakespeare's early love for fine poetry and sensuous description is at odds with the requirements of a truly dramatic style, which must be responsive to the demands of the theatre and to the pressure to push the action forward. The book also examines how Shakespeare incorporates, critiques, parodies and transforms older dramatic styles inherited from playwrights of the 1580s and early 1590s. It traces a development to a flexible and fully theatrical language through Shakespeare's early plays to *Henry IV*, a process, he argues, that involves Shakespeare's self-conscious and constructive criticism, not only of the dramatic writings of others but also of his own earlier stylistic experiments.

Joseph, Sister Miriam, *Shakespeare's Use of the Arts of Language* (New York and London: Hafner, 1966)

Although written many years ago, this work is still a mine of information about the different elements of language in the Renaissance, and what commentators at the time had to say about them. Mainly concerned with Shakespeare's plays, but providing some material written by his contemporaries, Joseph works through the persuasive effects of grammar, argument, logic, pathos and ethos. Every device is illustrated with examples from the plays, and her index allows us to locate devices used by particular plays.

3

THE GRAND STYLE

Sylvia Adamson

There is an upstart crow, beautified with our feathers, that with his tiger's heart wrapped in a player's hide, supposes he is as well able to bombast out a blank verse as the best of you.

Robert Greene's attack on Shakespeare, 1592

THE THREE STYLES

To understand the importance of 'heightened language' to Shakespeare and his contemporaries, we need to place it in the context of the general theory of style that was being taught in Renaissance schoolrooms and textbooks (as outlined by Lynne Magnusson in Chapter 2). A useful starting point is Thomas Wilson's *Art of Rhetoric.* First published in 1553, Wilson's was the most popular and influential handbook of its kind and Shakespeare almost certainly read it, either at school in Stratford-upon-Avon or during his literary apprenticeship in London, where a new edition came out in 1585. In the excerpt below, Wilson, like other Renaissance rhetoricians, identifies 'three manner of styles':

(1)

the great or mighty kind, when we use great words, or vehement figures; the small kind, when we moderate our heat by meaner [i.e. more middling] words, and use not the most stirring sentences; the low kind, when we use no metaphors nor translated words, nor yet use any amplifications, but go plainly to work, and speak altogether in common words.[1]

The grouping of styles into three basic types – a high or grand style, a middle style and a low or plain style – had been a central plank of literary theory since classical times and strong traditions had developed of linking each type of style with specific genres and characters. In drama, the grand style had become the default style for histories and tragedies, the middle style for comedies, the low style for such interludes as the sheep-shearing scene in *The Winter's Tale* or the tavern scenes in the *Henry IV* plays; the grand style was for princes and generals, the middle style for lovers and merchants, the low style for rustics and plebeians. Traditionally too, genre and character types were closely connected. This is why the aristocratic onstage audience for the play-within-a-play at the end of *A Midsummer Night's Dream* don't expect the 'rude mechanicals' to succeed in the grand style of tragedy – and they don't. Indeed, it would have been a remarkably subversive gesture on Shakespeare's part if they had, because the decorum that matched speakers with styles reflected a social doctrine as well as a literary convention. In medieval and Renaissance society, the high style was the language of court diplomacy, the form of speech appropriately used by and to the nobility, and preserving their stylistic monopoly was often seen as a necessary part of maintaining existing social hierarchies. This viewpoint is reflected – and sometimes ironically reflected on – in the plays themselves. Lynne Magnusson (Chapter 9, pp. 136–7) draws attention to the polite 'high' style with which Goneril veils her threat to strip Lear of his royal retinue (*KL* 1.4.238–40), and there's a similar moment in *The Winter's Tale*, where King Leontes, even in the act of disowning his wife, shrinks from addressing her by the 'base title' that her (supposed) adultery has deserved, for fear that:

(2)
       barbarism (making me the precedent)
   Should a like language use to all degrees,

   And mannerly distinguishment leave out
   Betwixt the prince and beggar

(2.1.84–7)

By using beggar's language to a Queen, he argues, he would set
a precedent for the enemies of civilization to overturn all
proper distinctions between the different classes of society
(thus jeopardizing the princely privileges of his own rank).

   Alongside these literary and social interpretations of the
three styles, a rather different way of looking at them had
grown up in the course of the sixteenth century. It was
inspired by the Renaissance discovery (or recovery) of the
link between rhetoric and forensic oratory, a link perhaps
most influentially expounded in Cicero's *Orator* (one of the
lost classical works that came to light again in the fifteenth
century). Cicero interprets the three styles primarily as
forensic tools, alternative strategies for winning debates in the
law court or the senate house: 'the simple style for proving,
the middle style for pleasing, the vehement style for moving'.[2]
The attractions of this view for a dramatist are obvious:
instead of passively reflecting social rank or literary genre,
style is given a dynamic role in shaping audience response.
Forensic orators, like protagonists in a play, compete for the
allegiance of their auditors and canny style-selection (rather
than argument or evidence) is what determines the outcome.
Shakespeare, who is thought to have read a translation of
Cicero's *Orator* in the mid-1590s, shows his interest in
forensic oratory by staging such contests directly in two plays
written shortly afterwards: *The Merchant of Venice*, with its
courtroom confrontation between Shylock and Portia, and
Julius Caesar, where Brutus and Antony compete for the
sympathy of the crowd in the Roman Forum (see Chapter 8,
pp. 124–8).

   The forensic model of style does not always stack neatly on
top of the social and literary models. High-born characters

may adopt low styles for particular persuasive purposes, or speakers may switch from one style to another as their objectives change (from 'proving', say, to 'pleasing'). Even so, rhetoricians agreed that mastery of the grand style remained the orator's greatest achievement, because the grand style doesn't simply influence its auditors' verdicts or votes, it has the power to change their view of the world. As Cicero says in the *Orator*: 'it storms the feelings – implants new ideas and roots out the old'.[3] For this reason, it is often associated with powerful natural forces: torrents, storms and particularly thunder, the traditional image for the voice of God.

Before Shakespeare, the acknowledged master of 'thundering' verse was Christopher Marlowe, who, in *Tamburlaine* (1587?), transferred the forensic grand style triumphantly to the popular stage and the poetic drama. What made the play particularly famous – or notorious – was its full-frontal challenge to the socio-stylistic *status quo* defended by Leontes in example 2 above. In the character of Tamburlaine, Marlowe took a shepherd (traditionally a low-style speaker) and gave him the ability to 'threaten the world with high-astounding terms', a weapon that enables him to root out old monarchies and establish his own empire in their place. As I have already indicated, Shakespeare did not follow Marlowe down this politically dangerous path. But he did challenge him for the mastery of the grand style, a step that was felt to be equally audacious in threatening the *status quo* of the theatrical world. In the first recorded comment on Shakespeare's work, Greene attacks him as a kind of literary Tamburlaine, an 'upstart' actor-turned-author, whose 'shake-scene' talents are endangering the livelihood of his social superiors, the university-educated playwrights such as Marlowe (and Greene himself). Thirty years later, in the obituary verses prefixed to the First Folio, Ben Jonson paints the same picture, though turning the insult into eulogy: Shakespeare has far outshone 'Marlowe's mighty line', and his power to 'shake a stage' has secured him a place among the great founders of European tragedy, alongside 'thundering Aeschylus' himself.

AN IDENTIKIT OF THE GRAND STYLE

Examples of the grand style in action – in narrative, description, persuasion, dialogue – will be found in other chapters in this volume. The aim of this chapter is to provide a guide to its typical linguistic forms, with the exception of its verse form (which is described by George T. Wright in Chapter 4). In this section, I want to look rather closely at a single representative example, matching its features to the blueprint given by Wilson in example 1. The passage I've chosen is almost a copybook illustration of all the grand-style functions reviewed above. In terms of its dramatic context, it combines everything a Renaissance audience would have associated with the grand style: the genre is tragedy, the scene one of tempest and tempestuous passion; a kingly speaker addresses powers even greater than himself and undertakes a mighty act of persuasion – to bring about the destruction of the world.

(3)

LEAR

> You sulphurous and thought-executing fires,
> Vaunt-couriers of oak-cleaving thunderbolts,
> Singe my white head! And thou, all-shaking thunder,
> Strike flat the thick rotundity o'th'world,
> Crack nature's moulds, all germens spill at once
> That make ingrateful man!

(KL 3.2.4–9)

The linguistic features that Wilson directs us to look for in such a passage are:

✦ great words
✦ vehement figures

✦ metaphors (also known as 'translated words')
✦ stirring sentences
✦ amplifications.

'Great words'

To Wilson and his readers, 'great words' meant words that were simultaneously long and strange: typically Latinisms, archaisms and novel compounds (how these words were formed is explained by Terttu Nevalainen in Chapter 15). The prestige of the first group – words borrowed from Latin – was a straightforward reflection of the contemporary prestige of Latin literature and culture. In some accounts we find the social model of the three styles being mapped on to a hierarchy of cultures (high / middle / low = Latin / French / English) and from there on to the different layers in the word stock. George Puttenham, for example, in his *Art of English Poesy* (1589), draws a three-way contrast between polysyllabic Latinisms, disyllabic French borrowings and monosyllabic native English words. Other commentators saw the native monosyllables as the rude mechanicals of the society of words, useful for performing the necessary grammatical work of the sentence (e.g. *and*, *if*, *of*, *the*) but too vulgar for important roles. Thomas Nashe likened them to the small change in your purse and John Dryden was later to call them 'village words which give a mean idea of the thing'. Latinate words were felt to give a grander idea of things, partly because of their greater length and partly because the more complex stress patterns of polysyllabic words made them sound more musical to Renaissance ears (listen to the rhythm of 'polysyllabic Latinate', for instance, and compare it with 'long strange'). Lear's speech, like any other in the grand style, includes a number of Renaissance Latinisms (the dates are those of the earliest uses recorded in the OED): *sulphurous* (1530), *ingrateful* (1547), *rotundity* (1589), *germen* (1605), the last probably coined by Shakespeare in this very line (from Latin *germen*, 'a seed').

Some of Shakespeare's contemporaries thought that an equal strangeness could be achieved by resurrecting native English words that had passed out of common use. Archaizing was in any case a method of heightening approved by classical rhetoricians, and Ben Jonson was echoing his Latin mentor, Quintilian, when he argued that archaisms 'lend a kind of Majesty to style' because their age gives them 'authority' while their disuse gives them 'a kind of grace-like newness'.[4] Shakespeare is not such a notable archaizer as, say, Edmund Spenser, but there is one striking instance in this passage: *spill*, which he normally uses for shedding blood or losing liquid, appears here with its original Anglo-Saxon sense of 'destroy', a sense that by 1605 was somewhere between old-fashioned and obsolete.

Both borrowed and native forms could be used in compounds, the third major source of 'great words', represented in example 3 by *thought-executing, vaunt-couriers, oak-cleaving, all-shaking*. Some of Shakespeare's compounds – such as *all-shaking* in this group – are modelled on classical originals, but many more are new creations. Their value is twofold: they combine the strangeness of new words with the excitement of new thoughts by prompting us to recognize a concept or property which previously we had only been able to express by roundabout description (e.g. Angelo's 'snow-broth' blood, *MM* 1.4.58; Macbeth's 'air-drawn' dagger, *Mac* 3.4.61). Many compounds have a certain rich mystery about them too, since it's not always clear what roundabout descriptions they might correspond to. In the present group, '*thought-executing* fires' has caused editors some problems. One suggests 'acting as quick as thought', another asks: 'is Lear calling on lightning to destroy thought, or to carry out his wishes, or both?' (See also Chapter 15, p. 240)

'Vehement figures', 'metaphors', 'translated words'

No one would deny that 'vehement' is an appropriate description of Lear's language in example 3. One of the sources of this effect is its grammatical structure – the repeated alternation of vocative (*you fires . . . thou thunder . . .*) and imperative (*singe . . . strike*). Vocative and imperative are the direct grammatical expression of the speech acts of summoning and commanding, which are speech acts closely associated with the grand style if only because they are typical acts of kings and rulers. Lear does rather a lot of summoning and commanding in the play, but the effect is heightened here because his addressees are not, as elsewhere, servants or daughters but cosmic powers who control the universe. He is, of course, imagining himself as one of their victims ('singe my white head'), but in language, at least, he is also their controller. It is he who ordains their destructive acts in the sequence of imperatives: *singe, strike, crack* and *spill.*

The other main figures of speech in the passage follow as a natural consequence of its grammar of command: they are **apostrophe** (the figure of direct address) and ***prosopopoeia*** (the form of **metaphor** that attributes human characteristics to animals or inanimate objects). Prosopopoeia is always implicit in the use of apostrophe since whatever is addressed (whether skylarks, urns or thunderbolts) is by the very fact of being addressed made equivalent to a human interlocutor. But in example 3 the humanizing of nature is made explicit by another metaphor in which the flashes of lightning are likened to the vanguard of an invading army (*vaunt-couriers*, from the French *avant-coureurs*, 'scouts' or 'heralds'). Metaphor has been valued in most kinds of literature for its ability to make us see one thing (e.g. a storm) in terms of another (e.g. a battle), but prosopopoeia was a form of metaphor particularly prized in the grand style because it demonstrates the orator–poet's godlike power to breathe life into dead things.

'Stirring sentences'

In Wilson's usage, as in Elizabethan English more generally, *sentence* is more likely to refer to a thought or proposition than to a type of grammatical construction. But in example 3 both are sufficiently 'stirring'. Lear's thought encompasses the destruction of the world and he expresses it in the grammatical form that Cicero and Quintilian had thought the most powerful of the orator's weapons – the ***periodos*** (periodic sentence). Quintilian had argued that 'it is in verbs that the real strength of a discourse resides'[5] and the periodic construction was designed to give verbs their maximum impact by delaying them. The periodic sentence is in effect a mini-drama, where the hearers' expectations are roused, held in suspense and finally satisfied. For maximum suspense, Quintilian had advised making the main verb the last word of the sentence. This is more difficult to achieve in English than in Latin because it is liable to distort normal English word order but Shakespeare manages it for one of the climaxes of Antony's speech in the Forum:

(4)
  And in his mantle muffling up his face,
  Even at the base of Pompey's statue,
  Which all the while ran blood, great Caesar *fell*.

  (*JC* 3.2.185–7; my italics)

More common is the kind of delay he gives us in the first sentence of example 3. This could have been written as in 5 below, which is a more natural word order but (as a comparative reading will show) one with far less dramatic impact:

(5)
                              Singe my white head
  You sulphurous and thought-executing fires,
  Vaunt-couriers of oak-cleaving thunderbolts.

Lear's second sentence also follows Quintilian's advice to make sentences 'rise and grow in force' but it takes a different route. Again verbs are the key words, but here they're arranged in a simple list-like sequence of clauses with the effect of climax coming from the fact that each verb is a degree more violent in meaning than the one before: *strike – crack – spill* (i.e. 'destroy').

'Amplifications'

Amplification is, and was, an ambiguous word. It could mean devices for making a form of expression longer and more elaborate; or it could mean devices for making a topic imaginatively larger or, as Marlowe put it, 'high-astounding'. Generally, though, in oratorical grand style the two kinds of amplifying go together, as in the figures that Lear draws on in example 3. **Synonymia** (restatement by the use of synonyms) was the most widely practised method of amplifying. Quintilian defines its aims as 'to make the sense stronger and more obvious' and its forms as: 'words of the same meaning are grouped together' or 'thoughts of similar content'.[6] Other chapters in this volume give examples of the first of the cases, synonymia of the word (see Chapter 6, p. 97, and Chapter 2, p. 23); Lear draws on the second, equally common type, synonymia of the phrase. His speech is a set of verbal variations on the theme of 'destroy the world', which, by detailing different aspects of that event, enhance our sense of its all-embracing enormity.

The amplifying figure of **epitheton** is also well represented. Described by Puttenham as 'the qualifier',[7] it can take the form of an appositive descriptive phrase (the second line of example 3, qualifying *fires* in the first line, is an epithet of this sort); but its best-known form is the adjective attached to a noun (as in '*white* head' or '*ingrateful* man'). The natural affinity between the adjective and the grand style shows in the fact that the six lines of example 3 yield seven adjectives and five of the seven belong to the class of 'great words': three compounds (*thought-executing, oak-cleaving, all-shaking*) and two Latin-isms (*sulphurous, ingrateful*). Most are used to enhance the dimensions of the storm itself, especially our sense of it as an active agent (*executing, cleaving, shaking*), but some sound the keynotes of Lear's inner turmoil: *white* reminds us of the pathos of old age (cf. 'a head / So old and white as this', 3.2.23–4), *ingrateful* of the events that have driven him to the verge of madness (cf. 'monster ingratitude!', 1.5.37; 'filial ingratitude', 3.4.14).

DETECTING BOMBAST

For modern readers, brought up to distrust public oratory and to relish the terse and downbeat in literature, the grand style has proved something of a problem. Indeed it was not without its critics in Shakespeare's time and it is to this period that we owe the term still used to describe an unreal or excessive heightening of language: *bombast* – originally the name for the cotton wool used to pad out clothing and make the wearer seem larger or more impressively shaped. But at four hundred years' distance it's difficult to know whether and where Elizabethan ideas of bombast coincide with our own. As Walter Nash reminds us (Chapter 5, pp. 83–4), the distinction between parody and the real thing is sometimes in the ear of the beholder (or the intonation of the actor). It is easy enough, even for modern readers of *2 Henry IV* and *Henry V*, to distinguish Ancient Pistol's 'swaggering' rant from Tamburlaine's 'high-astounding terms'. But what of characters who fulfil the literary and social criteria traditionally associated with the grand style: princes, generals and tragic heroes? With speakers such as these, how can we tell the grand from the merely grandiose?

Let's look first at two test cases from *Troilus and Cressida*. In example 6 below Agamemnon, the 'noble general' of the

Greeks, persuades his despondent allies to continue the war against Troy, arguing that the setbacks in their seven-year campaign should be regarded as knots in a piece of wood, or trials of stamina imposed by the gods. In example 7, from the closing scene of the play, Troilus, representing the other camp in the war, responds to the death of the Trojan champion, Hector.

(6)

> Checks and disasters
> Grow in the veins of actions highest reared,
> As knots, by the conflux of meeting sap,
> Infects the sound pine, and diverts his grain
> Tortive and errant from his course of growth ...
> Why then, you princes,
> Do you with cheeks abashed behold our works,
> And think them shames which are indeed naught else
> But the protractive trials of great Jove
> To find persistive constancy in men?

(1.3.5–9, 17–21)

(7)

> But march away.
> Hector is dead. There is no more to say.
> Stay yet. – You vile abominable tents,
> Thus proudly pitched upon our Phrygian plains,
> Let Titan rise as early as he dare,
> I'll through and through you!

(5.11.21–6)

Most modern readings and productions of this play interpret it as a satire rather than straightforward tragedy, and Shakespeare often encourages that reading by bringing onstage Thersites, whose role is to debunk the high claims of other protagonists. But Thersites is not present to comment on these two speeches. Instead what allows us to interpret examples 6 and 7 as bombast rather than the authentic grand style is the combination of two factors: (1) an overheightening – hyper-inflation we might call it – of the language and (2) a perceptible mismatch between word and action. Agamemnon and Troilus both fail the reality test.

In example 6, linguistic hyper-inflation appears in Aga-memnon's choice of 'great words'. His pine-knot **simile** contains five Latinisms in three lines – *conflux, infect, divert, tortive, errant.* That in itself is not unusual in an age so intoxicated with Latin. But it's worth noting that all five are placed in key positions for the meaning, and their effect for most members of a contemporary audience, as for us, could only be to make the meaning obscure: *divert* and *errant* (in the sense intended here) were relatively recent coinages (both are included in a contemporary dictionary of 'hard words') while *tortive* and *conflux* may even have made their English début in this very passage. What is particularly striking is that when Agamemnon uses the figure of synonymia it is only in order to gloss one Latinate hard word with another – *tortive* and *errant.* If this makes us suspect that his great words are designed to impress rather than to inform, then our suspicion might be confirmed by his second argument, where he redescribes the situation by replacing the plain English 'shames' with the Latinate *protractive trials* and *persistive constancy.* This is the rhetorical figure known as ***paradiastole*** (restatement in other terms). Used in courtly high style as a device of flattery or in forensic oratory as a method of extenuating the defendant's crime ('that wasn't *murder*, it was *justifiable homicide*'), paradiastole is a device which increasingly came under suspicion in Shakespeare's time. Henry Peacham, for instance, in *The Garden of Eloquence* (1593), describes it as being used 'to cover vices with the mantles of virtues'.[8] Elsewhere in *Troilus and Cressida*, Ajax argues that Achilles' supporters are covering his vices with the mantle of sickness when they call his bad behaviour *melancholy* (i.e. modern

English 'depression') rather than *pride* (2.3.85–6). In the case of Agamemnon's paradiastole in example 6, the extenuating terms themselves show a degree of hyper-inflation: *protractive* and *persistive* may, like *tortive*, have been invented for this occasion and the three together provide an unusually dense clustering of the *-ive* suffix (see Chapter 15, p. 247), which some commentators have suggested is a marker of unusual heightening in Shakespeare's coinages. Moreover, the high words are not matched by deeds. The action of the play, a catalogue of failure and dishonour, tends to support the diagnosis that the Greeks' situation merits the term *shames* rather than *persistive constancy*.

In its dramatic context – this is Agamemnon's first appearance in the play – the effect of example 6 is to characterize him either as a pompous nonentity, divorced from the rude realities of military stalemate, or as a crafty politician, who uses rhetoric for purposes of deceit, disguising unpalatable facts so as to cheer the troops and prolong a *shame*-ful war.

In sharp contrast to this, the excerpt from Troilus' last speech (example 7) begins with the abandonment of words. With Hector's body as the mutely eloquent witness of the brutality of war and the futility of heroism, 'there is no more to say'. The rhyme *away/say* prepares us to hear this as one of Shakespeare's curtain-closing couplets (see Chapter 4, p. 63), very similar to the despairing couplets of Kent and Edgar which precede the 'dead march' at the end of *King Lear*. But unlike Edgar, Troilus instantly decides that there is more to say after all and he goes on to say it at some length. As with Agamemnon's speech, linguistic hyper-inflation is very evident here, this time in the form of heavy **alliteration**:

Thus *p*roudly *p*itched u*p*on our *P*hrygian *p*lains

Alliteration, being associated with native English poetry rather than classical models, was regarded with some suspicion by

Renaissance writers and though they nonetheless used it for serious purposes (it contributes, for instance, to the emphatic ending of example 3: 'That *m*ake ingrateful *m*an'), they also deplored its overuse, parodically described by Sir Philip Sidney as '*r*hymes *r*unning in *r*attling *r*ows'.[9] Excessive alliteration was a popular marker of the would-be grand style that comes to grief. This is one of the things that turns Quince's tragic Prologue into comedy:

(8)
   Whereat with *b*lade, with *b*loody *b*lameful *b*lade,
   He *b*ravely *b*roach'd his *b*oiling *b*loody *b*reast

(MND 5.1.146–7)

Troilus is not, of course, made a figure of fun like Quince, but it seems likely that we're intended to interpret his 'rattling row' of *p*s as linguistic excess.

There is also a consistent mismatch between language and reality in example 7 that makes even the orthodox features of the grand style ring hollow. Apostrophe and prosopopoeia give life to the tents, which by the figure of **metonymy** stand for the Greeks inside them. There is no doubt that tents are thematically important in the play, and to the Trojans they are the visible symbol that their land is under enemy occupation. Even so, to insult a tent as Troilus does here ('you vile abominable tents') comes uncomfortably close to Pyramus–Bottom's denunciation of the (all-too-human) Wall in Quince's farcical production: 'O wicked wall … / Curs'd be thy stones' *(MND* 5.1.178–9). Personifying the sun as Titan only in order to challenge him to rise early seems equally pointless, and the culmination of Troilus' threats, the revenge he promises to inflict on these hapless tents at sunrise, remains vague because he neglects Quintilian's advice that the orator should conclude with a strong main verb. As it is, we have to infer whether he means 'I'll [go] through and through you', which risks sounding weak, or 'I'll [run my sword] through and through you', which risks sounding silly. What we may well infer is that he doesn't quite know *what* he will do. Most tellingly of all, the threatened action is not only unspecified but in the end it is postponed, Troilus concluding that '*hope* of revenge shall hide our inward woe' (5.11.31; my italics). Again it seems that the grand style (or its bombastic counterfeit) is as much as anything a form of comfort food.

AUTHENTICATING THE GRAND STYLE

My third test case is a more complex and controversial example. Othello, like Agamemnon, is described by other characters as a 'noble general' (2.2.11). Like Agamemnon he often uses a very grand style indeed, in which he is liable to produce synonymia that couples Latinate with Latinate, as in 'circumscription and confine' (1.2.27). As Pamela Mason points out (Chapter 10, pp. 147–9), even before we hear Othello's speech for ourselves, we have been primed by Iago to interpret it as 'bombast circumstance / Horribly stuffed with epithets of war' (1.1.12–13). Iago sees eloquence as self-aggrandizement and deceit or, in his words, 'bragging and . . . fantastical lies' (2.1.221). Part, at least, of his aim in plotting against Othello is to strip away the 'noble' exterior and show him up as no more than an 'erring Barbarian' (1.3.356). By the first scene of Act 4 this goal seems to have been achieved: Othello physically falls down and linguistically falls apart. The typical syntax and verse form of the grand style disintegrate, leaving oaths, disordered strings of nouns and, finally, silence (4.1.35–43). When he regains the power of action, it is to strike Desdemona (4.1.239); when he regains the power of speech, he uses it to commit the 'barbarism' that even Leontes draws back from by calling Desdemona a 'whore' (4.2.73, 91). As is made clear by the ample comments of Lodovico (4.1.264–82) and Emilia (4.2.117–40), both action and word are to be interpreted as quite unusually shocking. Anticipating

Leontes' argument in example 2, Emilia points out that
Othello has violated the rules of ordered society and made
himself equal to 'a beggar in his drink' (4.2.122).

The question has been raised whether Othello recovers from
this moral and linguistic collapse. This is a question both
about the character and about the grand style itself. Can either
survive the discovery of the 'barbarian' within? Critical debate
on this issue has largely focused on Othello's last long speech.
How should we respond to it? Is it, as some critics have
argued, evidence that he recovers his original dignity as the
'noble general' – one of the defining types of the grand-style
speaker? Or is it, as other critics have felt, a hollow self-
dramatization – like Troilus'? Are we here too seeing a beaten
man 'cheering himself up', as T.S. Eliot put it? Probably the
question is answered afresh in each production or each
reading of the play. But it's worth noting the form of language
that Shakespeare gives Othello for his attempted self-
rehabilitation. The speech ends with these lines:

(9)
> And say besides that in Aleppo once,
> Where a malignant and a turbanned Turk
> Beat a Venetian and traduced the state,
> I took by th' throat the circumcised dog
> And smote him – thus!   *He stabs himself.*
> (5.2.350–4)

Here Othello offers a piece of his own history. It's like (and
may even be part of) the life story which first moved
Desdemona's pity and love (1.3.130–70) and which Iago
dismissed as 'bragging and ... fantastical lies' (2.1.221). It is
marked as grand-style oration by its epithets (*malignant,
turbanned, circumcised*); by its sonorous foreign names
(*Aleppo, Venetian*); by the metaphor (which identifies the
Turk both with Iago and with Othello); by the delaying clauses
of lines 351–2 that create a syntactic suspense before the final

verb; and by the final verb itself, *smote*, already a semi-archaism in Shakespeare's time, strongly associated with the language of the Bible and in particular with the avenging actions of a wrathful God. There is no doubt that Othello is enhancing his stature by the implied comparison (in the tradition of Tamburlaine, who explicitly called himself 'the scourge of God'). But what blocks us from reading example 9 as 'bombast circumstance' is the final action, which proves in the most graphic way possible that the deed matches the word. The double meaning in Lodovico's response – 'O bloody *period*!' (354; my italics) – recognises that the climactic rhetoric of the grand style periodos has here been turned into climactic action. (In fact, as explained on pp. 232–4, Othello's speech culminates on a word that *requires* the accompaniment of an action.) Stylistically, too, though the language is very grand by modern standards, there is no foregrounded excess to its grandeur. On the contrary, the Latinate *traduced* is carefully balanced by the native *beat*, the four-syllable *circumcisèd* is joined to the monosyllabic *dog*, the biblical *smote* is preceded by the commonplace *took*.

It is perhaps, above all, this counterpointing of exotic and homely that is the hallmark of the authentic grand style in Shakespeare. We hear the same music if we return to our prototype example of the style, Lear's address to the storm in example 3. Contrary to what we might expect from Wilson's description in example 1, Lear's speech clearly demonstrates that the 'common words' of English are not excluded from the grand style, nor are they just the thread on which its 'great words' are strung. Rather, they make a distinct contribution to its design and character. A native adjective can be used to domesticate a borrowed noun (in 3 the newly imported abstract noun *rotundity* is made both comprehensible and concrete by being joined with the common native adjective *thick*); or a Latinate adjective can find an emphatic cadence in a native noun (Lear's *ingrateful man* follows the same pattern as Othello's *circumcised dog*). On the larger scale, too, sonorous and simple may divide the domain of the sentence between them. In 3, the 'great words' of Lear's opening noun phrases, which invoke cosmic powers, modulate into the four native monosyllables of the verb phrase, which, equally powerfully, depict their human effects: 'Singe my white head!'

Notes

1　Thomas Wilson, *The Art of Rhetoric* (1585 version), ed. G.H. Mair (Oxford: Clarendon Press, 1909), 169.

2　Cicero, *Orator*, ed. H.M. Hubbell (London: William Heinemann, 1971, revised edn), 356.

3　Cicero, *Orator*, ed. H.M. Hubbell (London: William Heinemann, 1971, revised edn), 376–7.

4　Ben Jonson, *Timber: or, Discoveries Made upon Men and Matter*, in *Works*, vol. 8, ed. C.H. Herford, P. Simpson and E. Simpson (Oxford: Clarendon Press, 1947), 622.

5　Quintilian, *Institutio Oratoria*, vol. 3, ed. H.E. Butler (London: William Heinemann, 1976), 2.520 (my translation).

6　Quintilian, *Institutio Oratoria*, vol. 3, ed. H.E. Butler (London: William Heinemann, 1976), 2.470–3.

7　George Puttenham, *The Art of English Poesy*, ed. G.D. Willcock and A. Walker (Cambridge: Cambridge University Press, 1936), 176–7.

8　Henry Peacham, *The Garden of Eloquence* (1593) ed. W.G. Crane (Gainesville, Fla.: Scholars' Facsimiles and Reprints, 1954), 169.

9　John Hoskins, *Directions for Speech and Style* (*c.* 1599), ed. H.H. Hudson (Princeton, N.J.: Princeton University Press, 1935), 15–16.

Further reading

Adamson, S.M., 'The literary language', in R. Lass (ed.), *The Cambridge History of the English Language, Vol. 3, 1476–1776* (Cambridge: Cambridge University Press, 1999), 539–653

> This chapter offers an introduction to the Renaissance theory and practice of rhetorical richness (*copia*), including an extensive account of the linguistic make-up of the grand style. The discussion is not

restricted to Shakespeare, but enables the reader to place Shakespeare's style in its literary–historical context.

Houston, J.P., *Shakespearean Sentences: A Study in Style and Syntax* (Baton Rouge and London: Louisiana State University Press, 1988)

A discussion of the chronological development of Shakespeare's style in terms of the changing relations in it between colloquial and Latinate sentence structures. The opening chapter provides an introduction to Shakespeare's use of inverted word-orders, and later chapters, notably 4 and 6, consider the role of such constructions in creating the grand style.

Hussey, S.S., *The Literary Language of Shakespeare* (London and New York: Longman, 1992, 2nd edition)

Of the several books devoted to Shakespeare's language this is probably the most accessible introduction for the literary reader, and the second edition takes account of recent work on rhetoric. In contrast to Houston, Hussey's primary focus is on vocabulary rather than syntax, but he too offers an account both of the range of Shakespeare's styles and of their chronological development. The book concludes with a reading of four plays: *Henry V*, *As You Like It*, *Macbeth* and *The Winter's Tale*.

McAlindon, T., *Shakespeare and Decorum* (London: Macmillan, 1973)

An attempt to relate the concept of 'the three styles' to the analysis of character and action. Arguing that 'the doctrine of decorum was as much a part of moral as of rhetorical tradition', McAlindon aims to show how deeply it affected Shakespeare's 'understanding and representation of human behaviour'. The book includes detailed discussions of *Richard II*, *Hamlet*, *Othello*, *Macbeth* and *Antony and Cleopatra*.

4

SHAKESPEARE'S METRE SCANNED

George T. Wright

I

Most plays in Shakespeare's time were written in verse because audiences evidently enjoyed hearing a lively pulsing rhythm from the actors on the stage. When they went to comedies, they heard many lines that rhymed, even in catchy, tumbling doggerel couplets, which Shakespeare used sometimes in his early plays:

(1)
> 'Twas Í won the wáger, though yóu hit the whíte,
> And béing a wínner, God gíve you good níght!
>
> > (*TS* 5.2.187–8)

But by the time Shakespeare began to write plays, the usual form for most of the lines in heroic tragedies or histories and even in comedies was **blank verse** – unrhymed ***iambic pentameter***. Pentameter meant that there were five metrical units, or feet; iambic, that each foot was usually composed of a relatively unstressed syllable (usually marked ˘) followed by a stronger one (´).

iambic foot	thĕ óx
iambic pentameter	Thĕ óx hăth thérefŏre strétch'd hĭs yóke ĭn váin
	(*MND* 2.1.93)

The model for this metrical pattern was a Latin verse that measured the syllables mainly by their length or duration –

the strong ones took twice as long to say as the weak ones. But a version of this Latin metre based on stress, not on duration or quantity, turned out to be an ideal pattern for English verse of this time. The main advantage of a five-foot line of verse is that it cannot divide into equal halves; if it tries to, the first half-line of five syllables has only two of the five strong stresses, the second has three. (See example 7 below.) So the verse cannot become singsong, as lines of four or six feet easily do in English. Shakespeare wrote four-stress verse now and then, especially for the song-like speeches of fairies or witches:

(2)

    Up and down, up and down,
    I will lead them up and down

                                       (*MND* 3.2.396–7)

(3)

    Double, double, toil and trouble;
    Fire burn, and cauldron bubble

                                       (*Mac* 4.1.10–11)

But the five-foot line is different. Because it doesn't divide into equal halves, it sounds more like ordinary spoken English:

(4)

    The more I hate, the more he follows me.

                                       (*MND* 1.1.198)

(5)

    O Hamlet, thou hast cleft my heart in twain.

                                        (*Ham* 3.4.158)

This capacity of the line of language to sound like the English that everyone spoke, only a bit grander and more eloquent, was seized on by playwrights of the 1590s and 1600s to make the talk in their verse plays come to life. In this project, Shakespeare led the way.

He wasn't the first to use a strong heroic line. Christopher Marlowe, born the same year as Shakespeare, had been especially successful in developing a powerful verse line for his heroic plays about Tamburlaine and for dark dramas of sin and retribution like *Doctor Faustus* and *The Jew of Malta*. His 'mighty' lines are so-called because each one seems a strong statement that stands by itself, linked grammatically to the others but syntactically separate, and metrically quite regular, with decisive stresses frequently falling on emphatic mono-syllables.

(6)
> I hold the Fates bound fast in iron chains,
> And with my hand turn Fortune's wheel about,
> And sooner shall the sun fall from his sphere
> Than Tamburlaine be slain or overcome.

(Tamburlaine, Part I, 1.2.174–7)

In his heroic poem *Hero and Leander*, too, Marlowe used mighty rhymed couplets to regale his audience with a fast-moving erotic narrative. Shakespeare's non-dramatic poems (*Venus and Adonis* and *The Rape of Lucrece*) build up differently. They are written in stanzas, and stanzas move more deliberately as they tell their stories or explore the emotions of their characters. They edge the narrative forward, stanza by stanza (sixty or seventy syllables at a clip), and in this they resemble a play that moves ahead by dividing its forward movement among different speakers.

Like other contemporaries, Shakespeare wrote plenty of long speeches for some characters, but as he learned his craft he tended to limit their length and make his drama less out of one-long-speech-answering-another than out of quicker and defter exchanges between two or more characters. Some speeches are long, but many exchanges are shorter, and the verse of one character often dovetails into the verse of another, so that they even share the same verse lines. Notice here how directly Macbeth's first speech answers Banquo's question, and how Banquo's final half-line picks up Macbeth's metre as well as his language:

(7)

BANQUO

The earth hath bubbles, as the water has,
And these are of them. – *Whither are they vanish'd?*

MACBETH

Into the air; and what seem'd corporal melted,
As breath into the wind. Would they had stay'd!

BANQUO

Were such things here as we do speak about?
Or have we eaten on the insane root
That takes the reason prisoner?

MACBETH

Your children shall be kings.

BANQUO

                                You shall be King.

                                    (1.3.79–86; italics added)

The same deftness is to be found in the skill with which, in individual speeches, Shakespeare has one line's variant metrical pattern answer another's. Instead of making each verse line sound like the previous one, he keeps varying their interior structure. In theory, iambic pentameter may seem to call for every line to sound like examples 8 and 9, with a stronger stress on every second syllable:

(8)

A rush, a hair, a drop of blood, a pin

                                    (*CE* 4.3.71)

(9)

That, when the brains were out, the man would die

                                    (*Mac* 3.4.78)

(10)

    Titania wak'd, and straightway lov'd an ass

(MND 3.2.34)

But in practice it doesn't work out that way. In fact, another great advantage of writing this kind of verse is that there are so many possibilities of variation. A poet can reverse the stress pattern of the first two syllables:

(11)

    Slow in | pursuit; but match'd in mouth like bells

(MND 4.1.122; italics added in examples 11–22)

(12)

    Not that | I think you did not love your father

(Ham 4.7.110)

In such lines, the initial swerve away from the iambic, usually called a **_trochee_** (´˘), came to seem an enlivening metrical variation, especially when the rest of the line reverts to the familiar pattern. This trochaic swerve can also come in mid-line, or at both the beginning and at mid-line:

(13)

    But that I know | *love is* | begun by time

(Ham 4.7.111)

(14)

    Met we | on hill, in dale, | *forest* |or mead

(MND 2.1.83)

The syllables that usually call for stress in English poetry as in English speech are monosyllabic nouns, verbs, adjectives, adverbs, and the primary-stressed syllables of longer words. But this is only a general rule, and sometimes one or more of a line's strong beats will fall on a so-called minor syllable – say, a pronoun, preposition, conjunction, unemphatic verb, or a syllable of a longer word that normally receives only secondary stress:

(15)

For Brutus *is* an honou*r*able man

(JC 3.2.83)

(16)

To go in person *with* me *to* my house

(CE 5.1.234)

(17)

My mistress *with* a monster *is* in love

(MND 3.2.6)

In these lines you don't come down hard on those weaker strong syllables but say them naturally. This kind of variation gives what is usually known as a **pyrrhic foot** (˘˘), but the lighter beat doesn't radically affect our sense of an alternating rhythm through the syllables of the line.

In another variation usually called a **spondee** (˘´), he can place a strong syllable in a weak position in the line:

(18)

The way to dusty death. | *Oùt, oút,* | *brief can*dle!

(Mac 5.5.23)

In such a line, the strong syllable in weak position does not displace the metrical stress from another strong syllable in the strong position that follows the weak one. The two are often marked ˘´ to show that the first syllable receives a kind of intermediate stress but the second retains its place as one of the five major beats in the line.

Finally, he can do several of these things at once:

(19)

Féll ĭn | the weeping brook. Her clothes | *sprèad wíde*

(Ham 4.7.175)

(20)

Cháuntĭng | *faìr hýmns* | *tŏ thĕ* | *còld frúit* | less moon

(MND 1.1.73)

Even when apparently major and minor words are next to one another, normal speech and regular metre may stress the minor one. This often happens, for example, with phrasal verbs, where the particle that completes the phrasal verb looks like a preposition but isn't:

(21)
   Scàrf úp the tender eye of pitiful Day

(*Mac* 3.2.47)

(22)
   If music be the food of love, *plày ón*

(*TN* 1.1.1)

(23)
   Will I *sèt úp* my everlasting rest

(*RJ* 5.3.110)

Another grammatical point worth remembering: Depending on the context, the word *not* may or may not deserve to be stressed; the metre will make clear whether Shakespeare's actors stressed it. In example 12 the need to stress it will be apparent to anyone, but usually when the word appears in unstressed position its negative idea is easily conveyed without undue emphasis. In lines like the following, some modern actors (like television news readers) frequently stress *not* or other negatives unnecessarily and in the process wrench the metre badly:

(24)
   You wóuld | nǒt thén | have parted with the ring

(*MV* 5.1.202)

(25)
   He máy | nǒt, ǎs | unvalu'd persons do,
   Carve for himself

(*Ham* 1.3.19–20)

(26)

   Brĭng mĕ | nŏ móre | reports; let them fly all

(Mac 5.3.1)

Another way Shakespeare can vary the sound of a line is to have its phrasing break at different places, not only after the fourth syllable (common in verse before Shakespeare and frequent in Shakespeare, too – see examples 4, 10, 11, 13 and 20 above) but after the third (5), fifth (7: 1, 2), sixth (9, 18, 19), seventh (27: 1) or eighth (22), and maybe more than once (8, 14). (This mid-line break in phrasing is sometimes called by the Latin term **caesura**, though in Latin verse the placement of the caesura is not variable, as in English, but fixed.)

When several of these different lines combine to make a speech, they may all be iambic pentameter, but the sound of that basic pattern is different in every line because the phrases that make up each line are differently constructed. The first four lines in example 27, for instance, break their phrasing (either minimally or decisively) after the seventh, after the fourth, after the sixth and after the fifth syllables, a variety that surely increases the expressiveness of the passage.

(27)

   Life's but a walking shadow, a poor player,
   That struts and frets his hour upon the stage
   And then is heard no more. It is a tale
   Told by an idiot, full of sound and fury,
   Signifying nothing.

(Mac 5.5.24–8)

Here the last line seems to be only a half line, but this is one more way of varying the music. As Shakespeare comes to write more and more lines in blank (unrhymed) verse, the mid-line breaks between phrases fall more often in the second half of the line, so it becomes natural for the lines to be **enjambed** – that is, for phrases to spill over from one line to the next without punctuation or noticeable pause, and even for the sentences or clauses to run more and more from mid-line to mid-line, as they do in this speech of Hamlet's:

(28)
> Sir, in my heart there was a kind of fighting
> That would not let me sleep. Methought I lay
> Worse than the mutines in the bilboes. Rashly –
> And prais'd be rashness for it: let us know
> Our indiscretion sometime serves us well
> When our deep plots do pall, and that should learn us
> There's a divinity that shapes our ends,
> Rough-hew them how we will

(5.2.4–11)

This easy commerce between the sentence and the line makes for a more natural English, although in the theatre the verse is harder to hear as verse because it is harder to tell where the lines begin and end. But if we listen closely, we can hear two currents running: the iambic pentameter line of (usually) ten syllables, with its predominant weak–strong repetitive pattern, and, at the same time, the unfolding sentence, with its developing syntactical pattern. And, as in the next example (29), the line and the sentence often refuse to finish together until we get to the end of a speech or a scene.

Or if one character's speech ends in mid-line, it often happens that another speaker completes the line, a habit reminiscent of the way people in actual life keep finishing each other's sentences. If the actors are attentive to the way their speeches are metrically completing each other, we can actually hear in the theatre how those long individual speeches that defined and dominated Marlowe's theatre have given way to duets, trios, or even larger ensembles. There are famous verse duets between Romeo and Juliet, Lorenzo and Jessica (in *The Merchant of Venice*), Othello and Iago, and Macbeth and Lady Macbeth. Here is one trio from Macbeth. Macduff has just

learned that his wife and children have been slaughtered by
Macbeth.

(29)
MACDUFF
  My children too?
ROSS
                    Wife, children, servants, all
  That could be found.
MACDUFF
                        And I must be from thence!
  My wife kill'd too?
ROSS
                I have said.
MALCOLM
                            Be comforted.
  Let's make us med'cines of our great revenge,
  To cure this deadly grief.
MACDUFF
  He has no children. – All my pretty ones?
  Did you say all? – O hell-kite! – All?
  What, all my pretty chickens, and their dam,
  At one fell swoop?
MALCOLM
  Dispute it like a man.
MACDUFF
                    I shall do so;
  But I must also feel it as a man

(*Mac* 4.3.211–21)

Some lines here are short, but that appears not to have worried
Shakespeare. But even the short ones, on stage, may not sound
short because they may combine with other short ones to form,
or seem to form, full ones. Is 'To cure this deadly grief' meant to
be heard alone, or is it completed by 'He has no children', a
phrase that seems both to complete a line that began with the

previous phrase and to begin a line that will be completed by 'All my pretty ones?' The same is true a few lines later with 'Dispute it like a man.' Such phrases may be called *squinting*: they look both ways, they can be heard both ways, and what matters in the theatre is not how the lines appear on the page or in the prompt-book but how the ear hears them from the stage.[1]

II

Variety in Shakespeare's verse appears not only within single speeches, but also within and between scenes, and from the early plays to his last. As Shakespeare grew more assured in his command of his medium, his verse lines became more daring, more run-on, and more surprising in the ways they combined with each other and with the patterns of English syntax. The lines of an early play such as *The Comedy of Errors* can easily be heard to sound out their five beats, and, because they often rhyme, we can easily tell where they begin and end.

(30)

> To me she speaks, she moves me for her theme;
> What, was I married to her in my dream?
> Or sleep I now and think I hear all this?
> What error drives our eyes and ears amiss?

(2.2.180–3)

Like other playwrights of the 1590s, Shakespeare wanted his audience to enjoy the dialogue of rhyme, where one line answers another and the playgoers, in on the game, can anticipate hearing it happen. Even when the characters speak blank verse, in this early play the lines are almost always endstopped and easy to hear as lines:

(31)

> The clock hath strucken twelve upon the bell;
> My mistress made it one upon my cheek;

> She is so hot because the meat is cold;
> The meat is cold because you come not home;
> You come not home because you have no stomach;
> You have no stomach having broke your fast …

(1.2.45–50)

Just a few years later, in *A Midsummer Night's Dream*, we can hear the play's verse music altering somewhat. Rhymed couplets are still prominent, especially in the lovers' comic exchanges, but for some of the more problematical and sensitive parts of the play (e.g. Theseus' fifth-act theory of the imagination, and Hippolyta's response to it), Shakespeare uses a more supple blank verse, running the phrases over the line endings in a way that seems appropriate to the more puzzling human experience they are discussing:

(32)

> The poet's eye, in a fine frenzy rolling,
> Doth glance from heaven to earth, from earth to heaven;
> And as imagination bodies forth
> The forms of things unknown, the poet's pen
> Turns them to shapes, and gives to airy nothing
> A local habitation and a name.

(5.1.12–17)

The bumbling artisans speak either prose or very bad verse, and the fairies often speak shorter, rhymed lines, presumably to suggest the more magical world of song they come from. But Shakespeare's art is by no means as schematic as this makes it sound. On the whole, when quarrels grow serious (even between fairies), or when the characters are concerned with perplexing issues like love, imagination, death, hounds' voices or the strangeness of dreams (for the courtly characters, not Bottom), Shakespeare usually prefers to use unrhymed verse. Not that seriousness is cast aside when rhyme enters or when briefer lines take the stage: the issues still are important, and significant points may be made (they may even be made in prose). Blank verse may be cheerful in tone, festive, even jubilant, but there is a grain in it, an edge, that lends itself to suggestions of fuller and deeper meanings than rhymed couplets can usually carry. In couplets the rhyme seems again and again to affirm the form, and the form of the world, whereas in blank verse that absence of corresponding sounds at the ends of successive or alternate lines implies an openness in the universe we are visiting. Rhyme – especially rhymed couplets – gives that world a surer foundation, a frame on which the audience, if not the characters, can count, so that when the lovers explore their confusions about the causes and the condition of love, their rhyming helps to assure the audience that the dangers are under control, that magic herbs and our sense of the fitness of things will straighten out these amusing mix-ups sooner or later. In the meantime we can hear the full lines as lines, the rhymes as rhymes, the prose as prose. The shifts are clear and intelligible; it is the characters, not the audience, who are baffled.

By the time we get to *Hamlet*, the metrical balance has shifted very far from the rhymed couplets that seemed so natural and reassuring at the beginning of Shakespeare's career. In the darkened perspective from which we view the apparently prosperous kingdom of Denmark, no one (except the Players) ever speaks more than four lines of consecutive rhymed couplets, and then only to end a scene or a distinct part of a scene. Most of the play's verse is blank (92 per cent) – troubled, enjambed, suspect, often desperate – and more than a quarter of the play is in prose. This is a world whose order is in doubt, caught between the imperatives of a ruthless state and the demands of justice and revenge; and Hamlet's 'antic disposition' (his pretending to be a little mad) is reflected in the play's astonishing verse, by turns smooth, elegant, graceful (as long as things seem under control), but full of self-interruptions, line breaks late and frequent, and other forms of metrical disorder when Claudius' authority or Hamlet's plan of vengeance is in tatters. Through all the wreckage of order the verse persists, still audible, still the design that guides the anxious audience through to the violent, poisonous, unpromising end.

The verse of *Macbeth* is almost a mirror image of that of *A Midsummer Night's Dream*. The short-line couplets are here, but spoken by witches instead of fairies. Instead of lovers answering each other's iambic pentameter couplets, we find here a single intense married pair so attuned that they frequently help each other speak full verse lines:

(33)

LADY MACBETH

  Did not you speak?

MACBETH

                    When?

LADY MACBETH

                        Now.

MACBETH

                            As I descended?

LADY MACBETH

  Ay.

MACBETH

  Hark! Who lies i' th' second chamber?

LADY MACBETH

  Donalbain.

MACBETH

  This is a sorry sight.

                                                  (2.2.16–18)

In *Macbeth*, blank verse is central, dominant, mighty and – more than problematical – tragic. Its weight is impressive, unrelenting, mysterious, and its power to reveal anxious and disturbed states of mind is crucial (a power of which *A Midsummer Night's Dream* made only sparing use). There is little prose in *Macbeth* and few rhymed full-line couplets (mainly to signal the ends of scenes). But the variety of *Macbeth* is mainly *within* its iambic pentameter. Certainly its prose scenes and the witches' rhymed chants make effective contrasts with the predominant blank verse, but the blank verse itself achieves an intensity here that Shakespeare hardly surpassed anywhere else.

How does he do it? First, by the resourceful use of metrical variations deployed in sentences that freely exceed the metrical lines, as we have seen above in 7, 27, 28 and 29. But the metrical personalities of Macbeth and Lady Macbeth are as distinctive as the choral voice of the witches. Macbeth's metre is often manly, downright, open, the beats falling on plain monosyllables, even when the words express fear: 'So foul and fair a day I have not seen' (1.3.38); 'the time has been, / That, when the brains were out, the man would die' (3.4.77–8); 'There would have been a time for such a word' (5.5.18). His longer speeches, on the other hand, are full of backings and shiftings, of subtle motions with and against the patterned line('Whó căn | be wise, amaz'd, | témperăte, | ănd fúrĭoŭs, / Lóyăl | and neu | trăl, ĭn | a mo | měnt? Nó màn', 2.3.105–6), or

(34)

> Béttĕr | bĕ wĭth | the dead,
> Whom we, to gain *our* peace, have sent to peace,
> Thăn ŏn | the tor | tŭre ŏf | the mind to lie
> In rest | lĕss ĕcstăsy. | Dúncăn | ĭs ĭn | his grave;
> Áftĕr | lìfe's fĭt | ful fever he | slèeps wéll,
> Tréasŏn | has done | *hìs* wórst: | nor steel, | nŏr póisŏn,
> Málĭce | domestic, | foreign lev | y̆, nóthĭng,
> Can touch | *hìm* fúrthĕr!

(3.2.19–26; italics added)

Here the usual variations – trochaic, pyrrhic, spondaic (all shown above) – are amplified by a series of 'emphatic' pronouns that are mainly not in stress positions but that underscore the perverse contrast Macbeth is making between the happy condition of the king he has murdered and his own and Lady Macbeth's continuing misery. These pronouns (*our, his* and *him*) gain what may be called a *contrary stress*: the voice rises in pitch to say them, then falls immediately, and the next syllable still receives one of the major beats in the line. Effects like these help an alert actor to convey Macbeth's deeply disturbed mind.

Lady Macbeth, in contrast, often uses short phrases, forceful half-lines that combine with others to make up telling whole ones: 'Nought's had, all's spent' (3.2.4); 'He is about it' (2.2.4); 'Give me the daggers' (2.2.53); 'What's done is done' (3.2.12); 'What's done cannot be undone' (5.1.69); and the extended bursts of clipped phrases out of which Macbeth and his wife, in their high moment of murder, make tense verse lines out of the tersest phrases:

(35)
    Have done to this.
                    If we should fail?
                                    We fail

                                            [1.7.59]

She often uses expressive spondees to give great force to her overwhelming ambition or incipient remorse: *unsex, top-full, make thick, fell purp(ose), keep peace, thick Night, keen knife, Hold, hold* (1.5.40–53), and 'Nought's had, all's spent'. Yet, despite these formidable spondees, her language is usually quick in movement, focusing on syllables that call for special emphasis. The metre is still easily audible, but the focal syllables make sure we don't just pound evenly on all five strong syllables of the line:

(36)
                    What *beast* was't then
    That made you *break* this enterprise to me?

When you *durst* do it, *then* you were a *man*;
And, to be *more* than what you were, you would
Be so much *more* the man. Nor time, nor place,
Did *then* adhere, and yet you would *make both*:
They have made them*selves*, and that their fitness *now*
*Does un*make *you*.

> (1.7.47–54; italics added here and in examples 37–40)

This remarkable conversational fluency, which is hardly to be matched by any other character in Shakespeare, keeps clinching its points by focusing on key syllables, as people are likely to do under the stress of strong emotion.

Changes in Shakespeare's verse style continued to the end of his career. In particular, the patterning of sound in his last plays becomes increasingly complex, with adventurous displays of repeated words and word elements (syllables, vowel and consonant sounds), rewordings of ideas, self-interruptions, stresses falling on minor words, and line endings that cut into grammatical phrases in surprising ways:

(37)

How, *dare not*? *do not*? *Do* you know, and *dare not*?

> (*WT* 1.2.377)

(38)

                         A callat
Of boundless tongue, who *late* hath *beat* her husband,
And now *baits* me! This *brat* ...

> (*WT* 2.3.90–2)

(39)

A devil, a bor*n devil, o*n whose *nature*
Nurture can *never* stick; o*n* who*m m*y p*a*ins
Hu*m*anely t*a*ke*n* – *all, all lost*, quite *lost*!

> (*Tem* 4.1.188–90)

(40)

> Oh, if thou couch
> But *one* night *with* her, every hour in't *will*
> Take hostage *of* thee *for* a hundred *and*
> Thou shalt remember nothing more than *what*
> That banquet bids thee *to.*

(*TNK* 1.1.182–6)

Despite the word-play and the forcing of sense over the line endings, the syntax remains conversational, and the metre offers an audibly reliable but eccentric guide to the structured verse. The turmoil within essentially ordered lines can be taken to exemplify, in harmony with these last plays' exploration of tragic separations, losses and reconciliations, the enduring gift of richly unfolding life. It is there in the plot, and it is there in the metrically varied speeches that carry each play forward, line by line and scene by scene.

Note on Shakespeare's English

The lines cited above sometimes show differences between Shakespeare's grammar and ours: 'Met we' (14), 'durst' (36: 49). He uses some old forms of words: 'strucken' (31: 1), 'whither' for 'where' (7: 80), and 'Methought' (28: 5). He frequently compresses or elides words, making two syllables into one, as we can tell from the punctuation either of his own compositor or of modern editors: 'i' th' (33: 17), 'was't' (36: 47). To fit the metre, forms like 'I have' (29: 213) were often elided then as now, and words like 'corporal' (7: 81) and 'prisoner' (7: 85) had two syllables, not three; 'heaven', as in 32: 13, often but not always was monosyllabic.

The standard ten-syllable line often had a feminine or double ending – i.e. an extra unstressed syllable at the end which did not affect the metre substantially. See 7: 80, 81; 12: 18; 28: 4, 6, 9 and others. Finally, most lines follow normal

English word order, but inversion of the normal order is not unusual, as we see in 14, 17, 30: 180, 182 and 32: 12.

NOTE

1 For a variety of reasons, mainly having to do with the complexities of play production in Shakespeare's time and the author's evident lack of interest in supervising the publication of his plays, many lines and passages do not follow the patterns described above. There are long lines, short lines, and lines with extra syllables or missing syllables; many of these look intentional, but some do not. For a fuller description of the verse, see my *Shakespeare's Metrical Art* (Berkeley: University of California Press, 1988).

FURTHER READING

McDonald, Russ, 'Reading *The Tempest*', *Shakespeare Survey*, 43 (1990), 15–28

> This is one of a series of excellent articles the author has written on Shakespeare's late verse style. McDonald is full of telling observations, beautifully described and illustrated, about Shakespeare's remarkable verbal techniques and his handling of repetitive vowel and consonant patterns, as well as his metrical dexterity. This essay is especially insightful in revealing the verbal patterning in *The Tempest* and showing how it serves the thematic purposes of that play.

Spain, Delbert, *Shakespeare Sounded Soundly: The Verse Structure and the Language* (Santa Barbara: Capra Press, Garland-Clarke Editions, 1988)

> The author calls this *A Handbook for Students, Actors, and Directors*; it is intended especially for inexperienced actors who have trouble speaking Shakespeare's lines with a firm sense of their metrical patterning. Spain sympathetically recognizes the difficulties and offers sensible, clear and accurate advice about how to handle them. This is a very unpretentious, helpful guide to Shakespeare's verse practice.

Tarlinskaja, Marina, *Shakespeare's Verse: Iambic Pentameter and the Poet's Idiosyncrasies* (New York: Peter Lang, 1987)

> A Russian linguist now living in the United States, Tarlinskaja adopts a rigorously scientific approach to metrical study. She analyses vast numbers of verse lines and makes extensive use of statistical charts and

tables in order to frame precise generalizations about Shakespeare's metrical practice. By studying the correlation between positions 1–10 in the iambic line and lexical and phrasal stress, she measures changes in Shakespeare's verse style over the years and his differences from other poets and dramatists. Her book is difficult to read, but she is sensitive to the rhythms of verse, and her work deserves much more attention than it has received from literary metrists.

Wright, George T., *Shakespeare's Metrical Art* (Berkeley: University of California Press, 1988)

Wright's aim is 'to describe the metrical system Shakespeare uses, particularly in his plays – the basic forms of his iambic pentameter line, its relation to other patterns (such as short lines, long lines, and prose), its changes over his career, and ... the expressive gestures and powers the system provides for Shakespeare and his dramatis personae'. Also included are discussions of the verse art of other Renaissance poets and playwrights, from Chaucer and Wyatt to Sidney, Spenser, Marlowe, Donne, Webster, Middleton and Milton.

5

PUNS AND PARODY

Walter Nash

If the due response to a pun is a groan, we must groan along o'
Shakespeare, because his plays are full of them, the good, the
bad and the baffling. In the theatre, perhaps, we do not mind
them or notice them so much, because there the skill of the
players and the sprightly business on stage carry us over the
intricacies of the text; but reading is another matter. Reading
demands that we should understand the words in particular as
well as the message in general. Reading says, take your time;
think about it.

Now 'thinking about it' presupposes an intuition of some
kind of value, beyond the merely picturesque, in a rhetorical
figure. What does the Shakespearean pun *do*? Does it
illuminate an exchange, or a scene? Does it typify a character,
reinforce an action? More generally, does it invoke some aspect
of contemporary culture and society? Reflect the aesthetic
tastes of a time? Presume acquaintance with, say, the sounds
and lexicon of Tudor–Stuart English? Require knowledge of
the commonplaces of learning and letters in Shakespeare's
day?

Such questions bring us down, inevitably, to particular
instances: what's the point? – what's the pun? – some puns
being more obviously or more subtly pointed than others.
Suppose, then, that we draw up a brief catalogue, a case of
some seven samples, taken randomly from scenes in which an
action apparently 'hangs' for a moment on an episode of
punning. What might we learn?

A CASE OF SAMPLES

SAMPLE 1: *JULIUS CAESAR* 1.1.5–29

The scene is Rome. The crowds are out to cheer Caesar's triumphant entry into the city. The tribunes Flavius and Murellus are trying to clear the streets, but the working folk, in cheeky holiday mood, are disposed to resist the officials' angry demands of 'what trade art thou? Answer me directly' (12). They do not answer directly. A cobbler teasingly describes himself as 'a mender of bad souls' (14), and begs the exasperated Murellus 'be not out with me', adding 'yet if you be out ... I can mend you' (16–7). To Flavius he declares 'all that I live by, is with the awl' (22), and further, 'I am, indeed sir, a surgeon to old shoes; when they are in great danger, I recover them' (24–5).

Comment

The pun on *all/awl* needs no footnote, nor does the play on *sole/soul*, with which the cobbler justifies his 'safe conscience' (13–14). More opaque perhaps, is the quibble on the meanings of *to be out*, as (a) 'to be angry' and (b) 'to have a hole in one's shoe'. There is a further pun on *recover*, in the senses 're-sole' and 'restore to health'. The shoe-surgeon additionally commends himself: 'As proper men as ever trod upon neat's leather have gone upon my handiwork' (26–7). 'As ever trod upon neat's leather' is an Elizabethan catch-phrase, here given particular point in its application to shoe-mending. Well: this is a play about murder and civil war, and here its first thirty lines are devoted to a thorough working of the tough old shoe-leather joke.

SAMPLE 2: *ROMEO AND JULIET* 1.1.1–4

Verona – as the Preface has established – and two serving men, Samson and Gregory, as proper lads as ever trod upon neat's leather. They are proud of being rather more than common drudges in the service of a great house. 'Gregory, on my word,' says Samson, 'we'll not carry coals'. To which Gregory replies, po-faced, 'No, for then we should be colliers'. Samson persists, 'I mean, and we be in choler, we'll draw' (meaning, 'draw our swords'). 'Ay,' says Gregory, 'while you live, draw your neck out of collar'. The badinage goes on for another thirty lines; then after that, with the entry of two of Montague's men, for thirty more, until swords are drawn; and this word-play, ending in sword-play, is the beginning of the play proper, a properly romantic sort of play.

Comment

Gregory pretends not to see the point of Samson's expression 'we'll not carry coals', which means 'we are not trash, we are men of honour'. This same expression occurs in *Henry V* 3.2.45–6, in a long speech by the character simply called 'Boy'. Reviewing the characters of the old Eastcheap mob, the Boy says of Nym and Bardolph 'in Calais they stole a fire-shovel. I knew by that piece of service the men would carry coals'.

There is an elaborate – or perhaps laboured – quibble on *colliers, choler* (anger), and *collar* (that is, the hangman's noose). The play on these words, together with *colour* in various senses, is a Shakespearean stand-by. See, for example, *1H4* 2.4.315–21, when Bardolph (the above-mentioned looter of fire-shovels), points to a face marred with fiery skin eruptions, and asks Prince Hal, 'My Lord, do you see these meteors? ... What think you they portend?' It is an invitation to read his disposition, as a hot-blooded fighting man. The Prince answers, with apparent intent to insult: 'Hot livers, and cold purses'. 'Hot' and 'cold' are two of the medieval 'complexions' (the other two being 'moist' and 'dry') symptomatic of a 'humour', or temperament. *Hot liver* can be glossed from a line in *The Rape of Lucrece* ('To quench the coal which in his liver glows', 47) as meaning 'lust';

and since *purse* in Elizabethan slang was one of several words meaning what nervous lexicographers define as 'the female pudend', the sense of *cold purses* may be paraphrased as 'the (loveless) embraces of whores', and Bardolph's scaly blotches consequently diagnosed as symptoms of venereal disease. 'Choler, my lord,' Bardolph protests, adding 'if rightly taken' (that is, 'if properly interpreted', the Prince having read them in the most improper terms). But Hal retorts: 'No, if rightly taken, halter', where *taken* puns on 'understood' and 'arrested'. Should Bardolph the robber ever be caught in the act (*rightly taken*), his *choler* will portend a *collar* namely the hangman's noose, or 'halter'. For other examples of the choler/collar/colour joke, see *2H4* 5.5.86–9 (Falstaff and Justice Shallow); *TN* 1.5.6 (Clown and Maria).

SAMPLE 3: *LOVE'S LABOUR'S LOST* 4.1.107–13

The scene is a royal deer-park, with a hunting party of courtiers armed with bows and arrows. A messenger comes with a letter for Lady Rosaline, from an admirer. One of the attendant gentlemen, Boyet, is inquisitive, and pesters Rosaline with 'Who is the suitor? Who is the suitor?' [107]. She replies, at first, 'Why, she that bears the bow' (108), and then explains this with 'Well then, I am the shooter', which prompts Boyet to ask, coyly, 'And who is your deer?' (113).

Comment

In Elizabethan English, it seems, the initial *s* of *suitor* was pronounced as *sh* – whence the silly-billy pun, *suitor/shooter*. Rosaline puts off Boyet's inquiry about the *suitor*, with the retort that she, of course, is the *shooter* – she carries a bow, does she not? But he persists, with the same question in a reverse slant, 'And who is your deer?', punning on 'deer' and 'dear'. This, like a similar quibble on 'hart' and 'heart', is standard pun-stuff, always handy when love is the theme and hunting the **metaphor**. (See, for example, *AYL* 3.2.242–3, Celia – describing the arrival in Arden of Rosalind's beloved Orlando: 'He was furnished like a hunter'. Rosalind: 'O ominous! he comes to kill my heart'.)

S AMPLE 4: *1 H ENRY IV* 2.4.217–37

Falstaff and Prince Henry, in the Boar's Head Tavern, after a bungled robbery at Gadshill, when Falstaff and co. have run away. Falstaff claims to have been attacked by 'three misbegotten knaves in Kendal green', in the dark. The Prince and his companion, Poins, want to know how Falstaff could distinguish colour by night. 'Come, tell us your reason,' the Prince insists; 'What sayest thou to this?' (229–30). And is seconded by Poins, 'Come, your reason, Jack, your reason?' Falstaff retorts:

> What, upon compulsion? Zounds! and I were at the strappado, or all the racks in the world, I would not tell you on compulsion. Give you a reason upon compulsion! If reasons were as plenty as blackberries I would give no man a reason upon compulsion, I.

(232–7)

Comment

The comic pun is on *reasons* and *raisins*, similarly pronounced in Elizabethan English. It is so very Falstaffian, so ingenious, and so funny in its nimble lameness. He is on the defensive, at first with his grandiose bluster about strappados and racks, and then with this fruity little, unheroic, spur-of-the-moment pun, disarming in its dottiness. (Those blackberries figure again, in the same scene, in Falstaff's burlesque of courtly discourse: 'Shall the blessed sun of heaven prove a micher, and eat blackberries?', 2.4.403–4.)

Sample 5: *Twelfth Night* 2.5.2–3

Pranks in the Lady Olivia's household. The stately and sour Malvolio is about to fall victim to an elaborate hoax devised by Maria, who has planted where he must find it a love-letter purportedly from the lady Olivia. Fabian, one of the company of comic servants, exclaims: 'Nay, I'll come. If I lose a scruple of this sport, let me be boiled to death with melancholy.'

Comment

Here is a pun not apparent to the eye. It depends on the homophony ('like-soundedness') in Elizabethan pronunciation of *boil* and *bile*. 'Bile' in Greek is *khole*, whence *mela(n) khole*, melancholy, signifying 'black bile', one of the constitutional/ psychological 'humours' of medieval medicine. This is indeed a learned pun, surprisingly so, perhaps, for the person who speaks it. It points, however, to a recurrent theme in the play, that of melancholy which is dispelled by 'sport' in the form of music, dancing, fooling, fellowship, in the end by true love. There is a good deal of melancholy in *Twelfth Night*. Olivia is melancholy in her mournful withdrawal. Malvolio is melancholy in his killjoy pride of place. Orsino is melancholy in his self-indulgent fantasies of being in love. Even the valiant Viola is beset by melancholy. Only the crazy backstairs gang are untouched. 'Sport' is the prescription – and it is surely not by chance that Fabian implies this with the word *scruple*, an apothecary's measure.

Sample 6: *Twelfth Night* 2.5.85–9

The 'sport' proceeds. Malvolio, observed from the shelter of the spreading box tree, finds the planted letter and thinks he recognizes the handwriting: 'By my life, this is my lady's hand. These be her very C's, her U's, and her T's; and thus makes she her great P's'. Andrew Aguecheek, dumbbell in residence, is puzzled: 'Her C's, her U's, and her T's? Why that?'

Comment

Even Andrew, with ears to hear like the rest of us, can recognize the scurrilous pun, innocently perpetrated by Malvolio, in 'thus makes she her great P's'. Like the rest of us, however, he is baffled by C's, U's and T's. His 'Why that?' suggests that these letters, thus 'spelt out' by Malvolio, imply something that has made the chorus in the shrubbery giggle. Some editors have 'why that –', suggesting a dawning recognition of what the letters might betoken. ('Why, that spells – !') If a mischievous spelling is intended, the letters spell out the word *cut*, which in the context might bear two meanings, one in itself sufficiently vulgar, the other potentially obscene. The vulgar sense, derived from horse-coping slang for a gelding, is 'dupe', or 'ineffectual fool'. Sir Toby uses the word in some such meaning at 2.3.183–4, encouraging Andrew in his hopeless pursuit of Olivia, 'Send for money, knight; if thou hast her not i' th' end, call me cut'. The lurking obscenity is 'female pudend'; it keeps the same company as words like *nick* and *mark* (for examples of which see *H5* 3.4.30–3, where the French princess innocently mouths English scurrilities, and *LLL* 4.1.129–38, one of the smuttiest passages in Shakespeare).

Sample 7: *Much Ado About Nothing* 2.3.42–56

Don Pedro, Prince of Aragon, asks his servant Balthazar to sing 'that song again' – with the practical effect of suspending the action for a moment while the actor playing Benedick takes up his station behind a theatrical bush. Balthazar is a self-deprecating artist, unwilling 'to slander music' (44) with a repeat performance. 'Nay pray thee, come,' says Don Pedro,

'Or if thou wilt hold longer argument, / Do it in notes' (51–3). Still Balthazar resists: 'Note this before my notes; / There's not a note of mine that's worth the noting' (53–4). Don Pedro grows impatient: 'Why, these are very crotchets that he speaks! / Note notes, forsooth, and nothing!'

Comment

The protracted punning on *notes, notes, noting, nothing* (pronounced 'notn', or 'nutn') is the kind of quibbling that led Dr Johnson, who groaned at all puns and particularly disliked Shakespeare's, to complain of 'frigidity', meaning a repetitive working of the text without the drive of real inspiration. (Quintilian condemns bad rhetoric as *frigidus*; the Aristotelian word is *psychros*, 'cold'.) There is a dramatic excuse for this loitering play of notes and nothing, however, since the audience must have time to observe Benedick observing the others, while the others pretend not to be observing him.

A further pun, on *crotchets*, in the twin sense of 'musical note' and 'whim', 'fancy', invites a general comment on Elizabethan aesthetics, in language and music, that may not come amiss as we close our case of samples. More than once in Shakespeare we find characters expressing pleasure in the sheer multivalency of language. Thus the Clown in *Twelfth Night*, commending Viola's skill in equivocation: 'To see this age! A sentence is but a chev'ril [kid leather] glove to a good wit – how quickly the wrong side may be turned outward!' (3.1.11–12). Language, like kid leather, is wonderfully flexible. Then again, in *Romeo and Juliet*, as Mercutio vies with Romeo in the sport of words: 'O here's a wit of cheveril, that stretches from an inch narrow to an ell broad' (2.4.83–4). Word-play is a humane art, he tells him: 'Now thou art sociable . . . now art thou what thou art, by art as well as by nature' (89–90).

The art of word-play, as practised by Benedick, is cumulative, figure building on figure. So also with music.

The Elizabethan composer, Thomas Morley, describes the compositional method that begins with a *point*, a brief melodic phrase. The musician 'taketh a point at his pleasure and wresteth and turneth it as he list, making either much or little of it as shall seem best in his own conceit.'[1] The *point*, thus worked, makes a section of a musical argument; further sections are added, to construct a *fancy*. This is not at all unlike the management of figures – puns, metaphors, images – in Shakespeare's dramatic language. There is an aesthetic of reiterations that a critic like Dr Johnson would find displeasing because it seemed to be going nowhere. Its insidious fascinations are implied by the anonymous Elizabethan lutenist who wrote:

> Fain would I change that note
> To which fond love hath charmed me
> Long, long to sing by rote,
> Fancying that that harmed me

The 'note' – the 'point' – proceeds 'by rote', by cumulative repetition, into the 'fancy' of an imprisoning structure. Even so do puns, metaphors, images, becoming fantastical – 'so full of shapes is fancy' (*TN* 1.1.14) – by and by become frigid.

SO WHAT DO THE PUNS *DO*?

Let us at this point remind ourselves of an important distinction between *puns as heard* and *puns as read*. Shakespeare's jokes were *scripted* to be *spoken* to be *heard*. They were of course deliberately constructed by him, and no doubt he thought critically about these constructions and their function in his text. That he disapproved of comic actors who would not stick to the script we may infer from Hamlet's instruction to the players – 'let those that play your clowns speak no more than is set down for them' (3.2.39–40); but he cannot have expected every member of his audience to pick up every sally quickfired from the apron stage of a lively theatre, and that may explain the presence in his word-play of an element of *redundancy*, meaning the construction of much wit to ensure the perception of a little. He can never have been quite sure how much would be perceived. Perhaps there was always a percentage of quips that missed the mark, or went down sadly on a wet Wednesday afternoon at the Globe. Perhaps there were times when the 'raisin' joke or the 'boiled' business won appreciative chuckles one day and died in silence the next. Such are the working conditions of a man of the theatre, who cannot have wholly anticipated his translation ('O Bottom! Thou art translated', *MND* [3.1.108–9]) into a man of the library. We are lucky; we have texts, and editors to instruct us in the complexities of the *pun as read*, though at times the ingenuity of commentators may remind us of Hamlet: 'Do you see yonder cloud that's almost in shape of a camel? ... Methinks it is like a weasel ... Or like a whale?' (3.2.377–83).

The mechanisms of the pun are quite simple; they turn on **homophony**, likeness of sound with difference of meaning, or **homonymy**, difference of meaning with similarity/identity of form, or sometimes both together. This primary device then has a rich potential yield of the troubled significance we denote with such words as *ambiguity, ambivalence, duality* or *equivocation,* or worse, *duplicity.* Like metaphor, puns may throw sidelights on shady matters; also like metaphor, they may deceive; or they can at once deceive and enlighten. This is of the very nature of creative language.

The puns sometimes occur as significant singletons, marking with emphasis the humour, the pathos, the tragedy even, of a dramatic event. Mercutio's announcement of his own death – 'Ask for me tomorrow and you will find me a grave man' (*RJ* 3.1.98–9) is such an instance. Elsewhere they come in squads, whether in bouts of wit-wrestling (a kind of 'rapping'), or as emblems of a dramatic psychology, for example in *Henry V* 3.7, where the French lords on the night before Agincourt are portrayed as boastful, bored and bitchy, their arrogance and dissension vented in a parade of sarcastic quibbles. (Then go to 4.3, the English camp on the morning of the battle, with the English nobles in pious fellowship, and King Henry making his 'band of brothers' speech. The telling contrast of attitudes – shallow French, solid English – appears in the language; the French are frivolous and profane in their word-play, the English in their prayers are resolute and manly, not a quibble among them.)

A related matter is the placing of pun sequences in the general dramatic structure. Samples 1 and 2 from our 'case' are from plays that begin in a rattle of street-wise punning, a bold overture to the heroic or high romantic themes that follow. An interior division of a play (an act or a scene) may similarly begin with a bout of puns – an example is *Twelfth Night* 3.1 (Viola and the Clown in verbal contest); or punning matches may occur as stage business, when it is necessary to suspend the action, to work a transition, or perhaps simply to furnish a bit-player with a few extra lines. Complaints about the distracting frivolity of the pun too often overlook the practical demands on a playwright writing for a company, a theatre, and a live audience with known tastes. Viewed in that light, Shakespeare's puns are not so much the seductions of a wayward poet as the props of a practical tradesman.

PARODY, STRAIGHT AND SHIFTY

His plays are textures of varied discourses, ways of talking in diverse styles on shifting topics. This willed diversity of style, with its teasing vocal echoes, tilts again and again towards parody – but of what kind? 'Straight' parody is a close imitation, usually of a mocking, even destructive tendency, of a known literary work or a recognized style. It is the Ministry of Silly Walks; 'Walk this way', says the innocent author, floorman in a well-stocked emporium, and the parodist, sneaking along behind, mimics the old joke, 'Chum, if I walked like that I'd look a right jessie, wouldn't I?' Straight parody is the jessification of the often undeserving.

In its dramatic context, however, the notion of parody may be extended to cover forms of mimesis other than the purely literary. The varieties of dramatic language imitate the varieties of 'natural' discourse, in their explorations of a continually changing social stance, the theme of 'Who do you think you are?' in all its reflexive positions ('Who do you think *I* am?', 'Who do *I* think I am?', 'Who do *they* think they are?', or eventually – with a questioning glance towards the only begetter of all these – 'Who does *he* think they are?'). There is a dramatic concept of *decorum*, of speech appropriate to persons in their allotted stations: an idea of how princes speak, or peasants, or policemen proceeding about their duties in a north-westerly direction ('Allo-allo-allo, what have we here?' – and to see what fun Shakespeare has with that ancient joke, see Dogberry and co. in *Much Ado About Nothing*, 3.3 and 4.2).

Decorum shades into *register*, the approved or conventional way of managing recurrent societal exchanges and procedures; there is a register of legal language, a register of commercial transactions, a register – frequently occurrent in Shakespeare – of disputation, demonstration, categorical argument, the apparatus of pedantry. Parody may lurk under all these things; see, for example, how Touchstone's parody of lawyerly bombast plays an intimidatory part in persuading poor William to surrender his connubial rights in Audrey (*AYL* 5.1).

In the plays, 'parody direct', literary parody, can co-exist with 'parody oblique', the questioning, through implied imitation, of a false stance, an affected decorum, a misman-aged register. There is one clear difference, however, in that 'direct' parody is objectively recognizable, whereas the 'oblique' is something subjectively perceived by a reader, as imagination works on the action of the play, and the intentions of the author come into question.

PARODY OBLIQUE: POSING IN ARDEN

Some lines in *As You Like It*, a play in which humorous questions of register are never far from the observer's mind, provide a fair example of 'parody oblique'. Inherent in the play is the theme of exile, its trials and discomforts, the godforsaken *longueurs* of camping out, the compensatory merits of which are not apparent to everyone. 'Aye, now I am in Arden, the more fool I,' says Touchstone; 'when I was at home I was in a better place' (2.4.14–15). It is Touchstone – as reported by Jacques – who proposes a succinct account of doing time in the forest:

> And thus from hour to hour we ripe and ripe
> And thus from hour to hour we rot and rot
> And thereby hangs a tale.

(2.7.28)

This is punning, and dirty punning, too, 'tale' being a homophone of 'tail', which is Old Low Elizabethan for 'prick'. As for 'hour' and 'ripe' and 'rot', they are perhaps not homophones, but certainly smirking echoes of 'whore', 'rape' and 'rut'.

The good Duke Senior, on the other hand, a nobleman of exemplary virtue and patience, takes a more gracious view of this silvan life:

DUKE SENIOR
> Sweet are the uses of adversity,
> Which like the toad, ugly and venomous,
> Wears yet a precious jewel in his head;
> And this our life, exempt from public haunt,
> Finds tongues in trees, books in the running brooks,
> Sermons in stones, and good in everything.
> I would not change it.

(2.1.12–18)

The rhetoric could hardly be more decorous; a decent way, indeed, for a Duke to speak about his troubles, as an attendant gentleman is prompt to assure him:

> Happy is your Grace,
> That can translate the stubbornness of fortune
> Into so quiet and so sweet a style.

(18–20)

All is as it should be, then? No suggestion that 'I would not change it' is not wholly sincere, or that this exiled Duke would happily prepare, at the drop of a revolution, to hasten back to pleasures, palaces and old scores, and never mind the toads? Well then, *decorum* is the right word; the appropriate *style*, as the gentleman calls it; a manner of speaking, a way of consoling yourself while the rain ruins your best ruff; which is all very well if you are a Duke ... And there it is, the suggestion muttering in the back of the reader's mind. How to imagine that gentleman's stance? Allow him the slightest sign of a shrug, a suppressed grimace, a false intonation – 'Happy is your Grace' – ('All right for some, isn't it?') – and the Duke's speech takes on a parodic colouring. The sentiment is implicitly parodied. The 'style', too, is one that admits a parodic turn; it has some of the marks of the literary fashion of Euphuism (of which more presently), in its image from 'unnatural-natural history' – the toad and his jewel – and the sequence of balanced, parallel constructions, marked by alliteration. Insidious parody or due decorum? reader, you may choose, then change your mind, then choose again.

PARODY DIRECT:
ACTING AT THE BOAR'S HEAD

But come we to Eastcheap, and Jack Falstaff, and Prince Hal, and we have no choice but to recognize parody direct, in one of the funniest sequences in all of Shakespeare. It comes after

Falstaff's ignominious rout at the Gadshill caper, when the veteran, with his sullen company of hacked swords and nosebleeds, comes back to the Boar's Head to face some merciless interrogatory teasing from the Prince and Poins. The old ruffian is cornered, but sees an opportunity to reassert himself when a messenger from court arrives, summoning the Prince to answer to his father, who has been hearing no good of him. What Falstaff proposes is a rehearsal of the event – and he will play the King, much to the amusement of the Hostess – 'O Jesu, this is excellent sport, i'faith' (*1H4* 2.4.385–6) – who in tears of mirth declares his impersonation 'as like one of these harlotry players as ever I see!' (391–2). Falstaff's notion of a speech of royal reproof to a wayward prince begins:

> Harry, I do not only marvel where thou spendest thy time, but also how thou art accompanied. For though the camomile, the more it is trodden on the faster it grows, yet youth, the more it is wasted the sooner it wears … If then thou be son to me, here lies the point – why, being son to me, art thou so pointed at? … for, Harry, now I do not speak to thee in drink, but in tears; not in pleasure, but in passion; not in words only, but in woes also.
>
> (394–8, 401–3, 410–12)

This is splendid parody, the more so for being William Shakespeare's parody of his creature Jack Falstaff's parody of a decorous speech from the throne, done as a parody of the style of John Lyly, called 'Euphuism', after the virtuous hero of Lyly's widely known conduct books, *Euphues* and *Euphues His England.* There is a hint of the Euphuistic manner in Duke Senior's praise of the outdoor life, mentioned above, but here is the genuine parodic article, the silly walk that mimes the mincing gait. Lyly is here, with his natural history (the camomile) and with the absurd, cumulative antitheses, in their alliterating ranks, that make the reading of *Euphues* at times a wearisome business. (Note how Shakespeare/Falstaff, in the manner of the adroit parodist, suggests an incongruous stumble in the style – instead of 'I do not speak to thee in teen [anger], but in tears', a plausibly Lylean phrase, the comic 'I do not speak to thee in drink, but in tears'. It would not go unremarked, even by the groundlings.

There would be at least a part of Shakespeare's audience, the gentlemen in the side galleries, who would recognize and relish the Lylean reference. Others, like the Hostess, might miss the literary model, but perceive the 'take-off' of courtly decorum, and further, of *courtroom* decorum, after the roles are reversed, and the Prince, accusing Falstaff, makes the speech for the prosecution:

> Wherein is he good, but to taste sack and drink it? wherein neat and cleanly, but to carve a capon and eat it? wherein cunning, but in craft? wherein crafty, but in villainy? wherein villainous, but in all things? wherein worthy, but in nothing?
>
> (449–53)

Falstaff matches this rhetoric with an equally florid plea for the defence:

> No, my good lord; banish Peto, banish Bardolph, banish Poins – but for sweet Jack Falstaff, kind Jack Falstaff, true Jack Falstaff, valiant Jack Falstaff, and therefore more valiant, being as he is old Jack Falstaff, banish not him thy Harry's company, banish plump Jack, and banish all the world.
>
> (467–74)

It is the moment of Falstaff's triumph. It is also the moment – then or shortly afterwards – when the sheriff's men hammer at the door; an event perhaps not so fateful as the knocking on the door in *Macbeth*, but a sign, considered in hindsight, that as between Jack and Hal, the good times are over.

THIS BROKEN MUSIC

Word-play and rhetorical imitation enter essentially into the texture of Shakespeare's dramatic writing. There may well be readers who do not care much for this, who groan at the puns and shrug off the parody as a clowning of outdated and forgotten styles, irrelevant to the real action of the play. Dr Johnson groaned at the puns; more, he found them trivial and distracting and could not understand Shakespeare's apparent obsession with them. 'A quibble was to him,' he complained, 'the fatal Cleopatra for which he lost the world, and was content to lose it.'[2] But the world of the play is not lost when Shakespeare chases a quibble or gives language its mimetic rein; these things are a part of the creative world of the play, no less than the fine sonorous verse, no less than striking metaphor and image, no less than costumes and settings. The language of a Shakespeare play is divided among voices, like part-song in which melody and counter-melody are layered among diverse registers, by and by to be resolved in a harmonic whole. A versatile, *knowing* cultivation of language at many levels is a hallmark of our master poet and his creative mind. Other plays there may be in which stylistic variation is more strictly and cautiously governed, but Will's are alive with the sound of his broken music, and the naff pun and the sly parody serve their turn as vehicles of a reverberant, ironic and ultimately compassionate laughter.

Notes

1 Thomas Morley, *A Plain and Easy Introduction to Practical Music* (1597), ed. R. Alec Harman (London: Dent, 1952), cited in *Early English Keyboard Music: An Anthology*, Vol. 1, edited and annotated by Howard Ferguson (London: Oxford University Press, 1971), 26.

2 Samuel Johnson, *Preface to Shakespeare* (1765), cited in *The Oxford Anthology of English Literature: Vol. 3, The Restoration and the Eighteenth Century*, ed. Martin Price (London and New York: Oxford University Press, 1973), 565.

FURTHER READING

Hussey, S.S., *The Literary Language of Shakespeare* (London and New York: Longman, 1992, 2nd edition)

Hussey offers a helpful introduction to the range of styles and registers that Shakespeare parodied and practised as his literary language evolved from early experimentation to mature and late styles.

Kökeritz, Helge, *Shakespeare's Pronunciation* (New Haven, Conn.: Yale University Press, 1953)

This book may not appeal immediately to students unprepared for technical analyses of sixteenth- to seventeenth-century phonology, but it provides nevertheless a splendid, lucid, non-technical display of information on homophonic puns and word-play.

Mahood, M. M., *Shakespeare's Wordplay* (London: Methuen, 1957)

Mahood's classic study remains the best guide to the dramatic and poetic functions of Shakespeare's 'serious' puns, especially their role in tragedy, as illustrated from *Romeo and Juliet, Hamlet* and *Macbeth.*

Nash, Walter, *The Language of Humour* (London and New York: Longman, 1985)

In this work, addressed to both general reader and students of stylistics, Nash provides a more detailed account of the linguistic foundations of pun and parody and examines relationships between the verbal patterns of humour and its stylistic and social function. The examples are mostly modern, but such characters as Dogberry, Shylock and Toby Belch make guest appearances, demonstrating how Nash's analyses can illuminate Shakespeare's comic discourse too.

Onions, C.T., *A Shakespeare Glossary*, enlarged and revised by Robert Eagleson (Oxford: Clarendon Press, 1986)

This venerable text, which has run through several reprints since its first publication in 1929, remains a valuable, indeed necessary, companion to the study of Shakespeare's vocabulary, not only for 'look it up' purposes but also as a resource for browsing among shades and shifts of meaning in Tudor–Stuart English. Entries are supported by citations from the plays, allowing the user to compare contexts, to gain an insight into the common usage of the time, and in due place to glimpse Shakespeare's innovative power.

6

DESCRIPTION

William C. Carroll

When Bottom and the other mechanicals in *A Midsummer Night's Dream* arrive in the forest outside Athens to rehearse their play, Quince approves of the location: 'here's a marvellous convenient place for our rehearsal. This green plot shall be our stage, this hawthorn-brake our tiring-house [i.e. attiring place, backstage]' (3.1.2–4). Even this brief description of the 'green plot' of grass and the sprawling thicket of 'hawthorn', as Quince gestures about him, evokes a perfect, sheltered spot in the forest. But there is no forest at all: the actor playing Quince is describing the actual stage he stands on as a forest which he will pretend to be – a stage; the real tiring-house as a bush which he will pretend to be – a tiring-house. The joke here depends on the audience already having granted the illusion that the 'green plot' was the forest, hence when the 'forest' is now called a 'stage', illusion and reality seem reversed. This moment of metadramatic confusion and play is energized by the power of simple description. For the Elizabethans, description was perhaps *the* most elemental building block of language and representation – a kind of rhetorical DNA – so omnipresent and so central that it could almost seem invisible, unless an author became self-conscious about it, as Shakespeare so frequently does, or a description seemed manifestly at odds with other kinds of evidence, usually visual.

Renaissance rhetoricians and poets defined description in the traditions of Aristotle and Cicero, and offered a number of subcategories for analysis. According to Henry Peacham,

> a description is when the Orator by a diligent gathering together of circumstances, and by a fit and natural application of them, doth express and set forth a thing so plainly and lively, that it seemeth rather painted in tables, than declared with words, and the mind of the bearer thereby so drawn to an earnest and steadfast contemplation of the thing described, that he rather thinketh he seeth it than heareth it. . . . hence it is, that by true proportion and due colour, cunning and curious images are made so like to the persons which they present, that they do not only make a likely show of life, but also by outward countenance of the inward spirit and affection.[1]

There are a number of key elements in this definition which will repay some attention. A description is meant, first of all, to produce an image of the thing described in the mind of the listener so convincing that 'he rather thinketh he seeth it than heareth it'. Like the painter, the orator makes the image 'so like to the persons which they present' – so 'realistic', in more modern terms – that they make 'a likely show of life'; hence, a good description is one which is 'so like' the person or thing described. But Peacham goes beyond any sense of description as simple reflection when he ends with the point that 'not only' should description be 'a likely show of life, but also *by outward countenance of the inward spirit and affection*' (emphasis added). Description is not merely an account of surfaces, then, but of using the 'outward' signs to signal or reflect the 'inward' spirit; description should not (and could not) be a merely neutral technique, then, but one that always implied penetration, analysis, and representation. The poet and dramatist George Chapman, following the traditional rhetorical categories, called this descriptive power '*Enargia*, or clearness of represen[ta]tion', and noted that the painter does not 'draw the figure of a face only to make known who it represents', but must also, as Peacham had also argued, 'limn, give luster, shadow, and heightening' to add 'motion, spirit and life'.[2]

These complications in the definition of description become immediately apparent when the poet or orator describes something or someone who is not present, or could not even exist in reality; we all know what a unicorn looks like, from many visual and verbal descriptions, for example, but no one has ever actually seen one. Another Renaissance rhetorician, George Puttenham, called this aspect of description '*Hypotiposis*, or the counterfeit representation', when we

> describe and set forth many things, in such sort as it should appear they were truly before our eyes though they were not present, which to do it requireth cunning: for nothing can be kindly [i.e. naturally, convincingly] counterfeit[ed] or represented in his absence, but by great discretion in the doer. And if the things we covet to describe be not natural or not veritable, then yet the same asketh more cunning to do it, because to feign a thing that never was nor is like to be, proceedeth of a greater wit and sharper invention than to describe things that be true.[3]

Whether the object described is present or absent, or real or illusory, then, a 'true' description is not merely a purely reflective one – as if the object 'were truly before our eyes' – but one that also calls up the object in our mind's eye as if it truly existed.

The Elizabethan analysts went on to describe multiple subcategories of description, depending on the object described: *prosopographia* (description of a person), *prosopopoeia* (description of an imaginary person, or attribution of human qualities to a senseless object or creature), *pragmatographia* (description of an action or event), *topographia* (description of a place), *topothesia* (description of an imaginary place), *cronographia* (description of time), and so on, until non-realistic modes of representation were reached, such as *icon* (resemblance by imagery) and *paradigma* (resemblance by example).

In Shakespeare's texts, the word 'description' is used in both the narrower and broader senses defined above. In the sense of exact reflection, for example, Oliver says to Celia, 'Then should I know you by description' given of her (*AYL* 4.3.84), Cloten recognizes where he is because 'This is the very description of their meeting place' (*Cym* 4.1.23–4), and the Soldier finds

Timon of Athens' tomb because 'By all description this should be the place' (*Tim* 5.3.1). In a more elaborate scene, the villainous Iachimo in *Cymbeline* convinces Posthumus that his wife Imogen has betrayed him by describing, in the greatest detail, the inside of Imogen's bedroom, including the artwork of the tapestries – all of which he has observed after secretly inspecting her room while she is asleep. 'The description / Of what is in her chamber' (2.4.93–4) does not necessarily mean she is unfaithful, Posthumus responds, but then Iachimo produces the most punishing detail of all: 'under her breast / (Worthy the pressing) lies a mole, right proud / Of that most delicate lodging. By my life, / I kiss'd it' (2.4.134–7). This mole was memorably described to the audience in the earlier scene: 'On her left breast / A mole cinque-spotted: like the crimson drops / I'th' bottom of a cowslip' (2.2.37–9). The vividness of this description leads the audience to believe in its existence – even though the audience could never actually see such a thing on the stage[4] – as much as Posthumus does. In these cases, the 'description' of a person or place is said to match up exactly with the object: image and reality are the same.[5]

At other times in Shakespeare, however, description could seem completely inadequate to the representation of the object. Here, Enobarbus reports on the impossibility of describing Cleopatra, then proceeds to do it indirectly:

> For her own person,
> It beggared all description: she did lie
> In her pavilion, cloth-of-gold of tissue,
> O'erpicturing that Venus where we see
> The fancy outwork nature. On each side her
> Stood pretty dimpled boys, like smiling cupids,
> With divers-coloured fans, whose wind did seem
> To glow the delicate cheeks which they did cool,
> And what they undid did.

(AC 2.2.207–15)

Enobarbus' account does not really tell us what Cleopatra physically looked like – there can be no ordinary description of her – but rather reveals her exotic, ethereal otherness through a description (which continues many more lines) of everything around her; the closest we get to her own body is her 'strange invisible perfume' (222). So, too, Cassio explains to Montano that the beauty and worth of Othello's Desdemona is beyond any verbal account:

> he hath achieved a maid
> That paragons description and wild fame;
> One that excels the quirks of blazoning pens
> And in th'essential vesture of creation
> Does tire the inginer.
>
> (*Oth* 2.1.61–5)

The object which cannot be described is nevertheless described, in a familiar rhetorical strategy. The extraordinary and miraculous are therefore implied, a mood or feeling of wonder and awe imparted to the listener. Shakespeare employs this strategy to greatest effect, perhaps, in one of the final scenes in *The Winter's Tale*, when the revelations and reunions offstage are reported, all of them so extraordinary that the Third Gentleman can only say, 'I never heard of such another encounter, which lames report to follow it, and undoes description to do it' (5.2.57–9); still, the stunning nature of what has happened is brilliantly conveyed through a series of descriptions.

Description must do more than simply 'make known who it represents', as Chapman said: it must also reveal the 'motion, spirit and life' of the object. Consider now how a vivid, poetically brilliant description can be completely accurate as to the surface, and completely false to the 'motion, spirit and life'. In *Henry V*, Lord Grandpré tries to rally the French troops to battle by offering this astonishing description of the sad-looking, desperate English troops:

Why do you stay so long, my lords of France?
Yon island carrions, desperate of their bones,
Ill-favouredly become the morning field.
Their ragged curtains poorly are let loose,
And our air shakes them passing scornfully.
Big Mars seems bankrupt in their beggared host
And faintly through a rusty beaver peeps.
The horsemen sit like fixed candlesticks
With torch-staves in their hand, and their poor jades
Lob down their heads, drooping the hides and hips,
The gum down-roping from their pale-dead eyes,
And in their palled dull mouths the gimmaled bit
Lies foul with chewed grass, still and motionless.
And their executors, the knavish crows,
Fly o'er them all, impatient for their hour.
Description cannot suit itself in words
To demonstrate the life of such a battle
In life so lifeless as it shows itself.

(4.2.37–54)

If one could ever read anything from a description, one could say with complete confidence that the English troops are not long for this world – virtually corpses already, the crows circling overhead, their horses about to drop, their armour rusted and nearly useless, their morale at absolute zero. But Grandpré's description of course turns out to be completely wrong about the hearts and souls of the English soldiers, who go on to victory over the French at Agincourt – one of the greatest victories in English history, in fact.

Some Shakespearean descriptions, on the other hand, seem totally at odds with the object described; the discrepancy may be one of tone or even surface physical detail. One of the most notorious such descriptions in all of Shakespeare appears in the early tragedy, *Titus Andronicus*, when Marcus discovers his niece Lavinia, who has been raped and mutilated, her hands cut off and her tongue cut out, but still alive:

> Speak, gentle niece, what stern ungentle hands
> Hath lopped and hewed and made thy body bare
> Of her two branches, those sweet ornaments
> Whose circling shadows kings have sought to sleep in
> And might not gain so great a happiness
> As half thy love. Why dost not speak to me?
> Alas, a crimson river of warm blood,
> Like to a bubbling fountain stirred with wind,
> Doth rise and fall between thy rosed lips,
> Coming and going with thy honey breath.
> But sure some Tereus hath deflowered thee
> And, lest thou shouldst detect him, cut thy tongue.
> Ah, now thou turn'st away thy face for shame,
> And notwithstanding all this loss of blood,
> As from a conduit with three issuing spouts,
> Yet do thy cheeks look red as Titan's face,
> Blushing to be encountered with a cloud. . . .
> A craftier Tereus, cousin, hast thou met,
> And he hath cut those pretty fingers off,
> That could have better sewed than Philomel.
> O, had the monster seen those lily hands
> Tremble like aspen leaves upon a lute
> And make the silken strings delight to kiss them,
> He would not then have touched them for his life.
>
> (2.3.16–32, 41–7)

This ornate, stylized description of a gruesome spectacle was for a long time taken as sadly representative of a play which was despised by many critics, from Samuel Johnson to T.S. Eliot – indeed, many early critics of the play denied that it could be by Shakespeare at all, given its apparent failures. In its overly wrought language, its apparent insensitivity to the physical suffering of the woman described, and its supposed falsity of tone, Marcus' speech was taken to be one of the play's greatest liabilities; even critics who otherwise defended the play considered the speech a failure. More recent approaches to the play, however, have taken the same discrepancy between descriptive language and object as the very point of the passage. Jonathan Bate, in his Introduction to the Arden 3 edition of the play, argues that

> Marcus needs a long speech because in it he has to learn slowly and painfully to confront suffering. He has to make himself *look* steadily at the mutilated woman, just as we, the offstage audience, have to look at her. The working through of bad dream into clear sight is formalized in Marcus' elaborate verbal patterns ... a lyrical speech is needed because it is only when an appropriately inappropriate language has been found that the sheer force of contrast between its beauty and Lavinia's degradation begins to express what she has undergone and lost.
>
> (62–3)

Some feminist readers, however, have rejected this type of analysis and seen Marcus' description as all too typical of how women are perceived in the play; Marcus' language, with Lavinia's 'rosed lips', 'honey breath', blushing cheeks, 'pretty fingers', 'lily hands' and so on, is that of the romantic *blason* – a rhetorical device often employed in Renaissance love poetry, in which the male lover catalogues the parts of his lover's body in descriptively erotic terms.[6] Thus Marcus, it is argued, can only 'see' Lavinia as an erotic object, as she is seen by all the male characters, with the only vocabulary available to him that of male courtship; the anatomization of the female body parts by the male lover is darkly ironic here as an account of Lavinia's mutilated and missing body parts. The spectacular gap between language and object is more precisely fixed, then, by recognizing the origins of the rhetoric and vocabulary of Marcus' description. Critics have moved from considering Marcus' description a great mistake by Shakespeare, to debating sophisticated critical positions concerning violence, gender and stylization.

Elizabethan schoolboys were taught, through imitation of Cicero, Ovid, and other Latin writers, to vary their descriptions by various rhetorical devices, especially by **synonymy** 'or the figure of store', as Peacham called it – 'when by a variation and change of words that be of like signification, we iterate one thing diverse times'.[7] This principle of variation was intended to produce a pleasing effect as well as further calibrate the description of an object; if one word was insufficient, many might be required. Shakespeare certainly employed the figure of synonymy in all seriousness, but he also recognized how its use could be abused, and description warped into something comic. In *Love's Labour's Lost*, the pedantic schoolmaster Holofernes is one of Shakespeare's greatest parodies of rhetorical 'learning'; his language is so completely artificial as to seem unreal. For him, a single word will never do. Thus, the element above is '*caelo*, the sky, the welkin, the heaven' (4.2.5), while the element below is '*terra*, the soil, the land, the earth' (4.2.6–7); the youthful Hercules was '*a babe, a child, a shrimp*' (5.2.584), and so on. His rival linguist, the fantastical Armado, is described in comic terms that reflect (badly) on the speaker as much as on the object described:

> His humour is lofty, his discourse peremptory, his tongue filed, his eye ambitious, his gait majestical and his general behaviour vain, ridiculous and thrasonical. He is too picked, too spruce, too affected, too odd, as it were, too peregrinate, as I may call it.
>
> (5.1.9–14)

One rhetorician used the figure of the schoolmaster as a stock example of the abuse of 'accumulation', the 'heaping up of many terms ... like a schoolmaster foaming out synonymies'.[8]

Comic descriptions in Shakespeare are directed not only at the unwitting speaker, such as Holofernes, but also at the object. Among the most fantastic in Shakespeare is that by

Biondello in *The Taming of the Shrew*, as he describes
Petruchio's appearance (he is still off-stage) as he comes to
his wedding with Kate:

> Why, Petruchio is coming in a new hat and an old jerkin; a
> pair of old breeches thrice turned; a pair of boots that have
> been candle-cases, one buckled, another laced; an old rusty
> sword ta'en out of the town armoury, with a broken hilt, and
> chapeless; with two broken points; his horse hipped – with
> an old mothy saddle and stirrups of no kindred – besides,
> possessed with the glanders and like to mose in the chine,
> troubled with the lampass, infected with the fashions, full of
> windgalls, sped with spavins, rayed with the yellows, past
> cure of the fives, stark spoiled with the staggers, begnawn
> with the bots, swayed in the back and shoulder-shotten, near-
> legged before, and with a half-cheeked bit and a headstall of
> sheep's leather, which, being restrained to keep him from
> stumbling, hath been often burst and new-repaired with
> knots; one girth six times pieced, and a woman's crupper of
> velure, which hath two letters for her name fairly set down in
> studs, and here and there pieced with pack-thread.

$$(3.2.41–62)$$

The very excessiveness of this description is part of its
humour, but note also how this description of Petruchio –
whose general seediness on his wedding day is part of his plan
to 'tame' Kate – moves, in mid-sentence and without a change
in pronoun, to a description of his horse. And the horse is
described almost entirely by the diseases it suffers from:
'glanders', 'lampass', 'windgalls', 'spavins', 'yellows', and so
forth. This description works partly by the mere sound of all
these names – like any kind of jargon, only a specialist could
know what they all mean – but also by the multiplying nature
of them, as if there is no end to them. In the end, the horse,
which is never seen by the audience, is described as
memorably as Petruchio, who enters a moment later.

To give a description of something requires the speaker or writer to summon a vocabulary which refers to the object but is not simply its name; the words chosen have an evocative power of their own, as we have seen in Lord Grandpré's description of the English troops, but the resulting description may or may not be accurate. In some cases, almost anything the speaker says will provide a satisfactory description, as we may see in a final example from *Antony and Cleopatra*. Here, in the scene on board Pompey's galley, a festive banquet is underway, and Lepidus – one of the triumvirate of Roman rulers, for a brief time, along with Antony and Caesar – is quite drunk. Antony is telling stories about the extraordinary things to be seen in Egypt – the pyramids, the flooding Nile – and, as Lepidus dimly recalls, 'You've strange serpents there?' (2.7.24). Lepidus notes that the crocodile, like the 'serpent of Egypt', is supposedly born out of the Nile's mud by the fertilizing power of the sun. He asks Antony to say 'What manner o' thing is your crocodile?' (41). The following dialogue then occurs:

ANTONY   It is shaped, sir, like itself, and it is as broad as it hath breadth. It is just so high as it is, and moves with it own organs. It lives by that which nourisheth it, and the elements once out of it, it transmigrates.
LEPIDUS   What colour is it of?
ANTONY   Of it own colour too.
LEPIDUS   'Tis a strange serpent.
ANTONY   'Tis so, and the tears of it are wet.
CAESAR   Will this description satisfy him?

(2.7.42–51)

For Caesar, and at first glance to any reader, this 'description' seems comically circular, or tautological: the creature is shaped 'like itself', 'as broad as it hath breadth', of its own colour, and so forth. How could it not be? Only a drunken sot like Lepidus (carried off the stage at the end of this scene and never seen again in the play) would accept such a worthless description.

But Shakespeare is also making the point, through this comic moment, that Egypt *cannot* be described in ordinary terms, and certainly not to a super-rational Roman like Caesar. Like Cleopatra, the other 'serpent of old Nile' (1.5.26), this creature of Egypt is so esoteric and mysterious that it can only be described in reference to itself; the tautological nature of the description is exactly its hallmark, which forever closes it off to Roman understanding. Description, as ever, is in the eye of the beholder.

NOTES

1 Henry Peacham, *The Garden of Eloquence* (London, 1577), T3^v (p. 134).

2 George Chapman, *Ovid's Banquet of Sense* (London, 1595), A2^r.

3 George Puttenham, *The Arte of English Poesie*, ed. G.D. Willcock and A. Walker (Cambridge: Cambridge University Press, 1936), 238.

4 And certainly not on 'her' breast, since Imogen was played by a boy actor.

5 Even such a direct use of the word can prove ironic, however, as when King Henry VI compliments the Earl of Suffolk, 'Your wondrous rare description, noble Earl / Of beauteous Margaret hath astonish'd me' (*1H6* 5.5.1-2), so much so that he agrees to marry her – this, however, is the Margaret of France who will soon be known as the 'she-wolf of France', a virago for whom Henry disastrously gives up English possessions in France.

6 Shakespeare elsewhere parodies this literary convention in Sonnet 130, 'My mistress' eyes are nothing like the sun'.

7 Peacham, op. cit., X3^r.

8 John Hoskins, *Directions for Speech and Style*, ed. H.H. Hudson (Princeton, N.J.: Princeton University Press, 1935), 24.

FURTHER READING

Donawerth, Jane, *Shakespeare and the Sixteenth-Century Study of Language* (Urbana, Ill.: University of Illinois Press, 1984)

> This book investigates how language was studied and analysed in the sixteenth century; it pays close attention to the language texts Shakespeare might have known, and to the general controversies over the nature of language. The book continually relates these issues to

Shakespeare, analysing in detail five plays: *Love's Labour's Lost, King John, The Merchant of Venice, All's Well That Ends Well* and *Hamlet.*

Robinson, Randal, *Unlocking Shakespeare's Language: Help for the Teacher and Student* (Urbana, Ill.: National Council of Teachers of English and the ERIC Clearinghouse on Reading and Communication Skills, 1989)

This book is specifically aimed at high-school and undergraduate college teachers and students. It addresses the typical problems which modern students have in reading Shakespeare's language. It includes worksheets, with examples from Shakespeare's plays, to provide concrete exercises in reading 'difficult' language.

Mahood, M.M., *Shakespeare's Wordplay* (London: Methuen, 1957)

This book is still a rich example of a critical engagement with the richness of Shakespeare's language, primarily through the pun; Mahood's imaginative readings of the nuances and implications of Shakespeare's language are extremely suggestive. Individual chapters focus on *Romeo and Juliet, Richard II, Hamlet, Macbeth, The Winter's Tale* and the sonnets.

7

NARRATIVE

David Scott Kastan

This might be thought an unnecessary (or, at very least, an unexpected) chapter in a book on Shakespeare's dramatic language, for whatever else drama is, it is seemingly not a narrative art. Among the various forms of human communication, narrative is distinguished by the presence not only of a story but of a storyteller. Drama, on the other hand, might be said to be precisely that form of storytelling that has no teller. It abandons narrative for enactment. No narrator relates the story of any of Shakespeare's plays; rather, the complex interaction of the characters on stage enables the story to emerge in dialogue and action.

Nonetheless, Shakespeare is clearly interested in narrative and reveals himself a skilled practitioner of it. Not only is there the evidence of the two long narrative poems he wrote, *Venus and Adonis* (1593) and *The Rape of Lucrece* (1594); but there is also the continuous presence of narrators and extended narration within the plays: the long speech of Egeon that opens *The Comedy of Errors*, the Choruses of *Henry V*, the Ghost's report of his unnatural murder to Hamlet, Enobarbus' description of Cleopatra for a rapt Roman audience, Gower's commentary in *Pericles*, Prospero's recounting for Miranda of the history that brought them to the island in *The Tempest*, and the messengers and ambassadors that in various plays bring news to which major characters must respond.

Narrative is obviously a crucial technique in the plays, a necessary device for imparting information to both characters and the audience; but it is also a central thematic focus of the plays. Shakespeare shows us characters recounting events, recalling experiences, spreading rumours, telling lies, reporting news, giving evidence, expressing feelings, relating dreams; that is, Shakespeare shows us characters engaged in various forms of what is arguably the single most characteristic human act – the act of storytelling – and his exploration of how and why stories are told and how these stories are understood is one of the plays' defining concerns. Narrative is an essential form of human apprehension, and the plays give evidence of how insistently we depend on stories to make sense of our lives.

Hamlet, for example, might well be thought of as a play fundamentally about narrative, which functions throughout as the spring of both character and action. The Ghost tells Hamlet a story of betrayal and murder, and Hamlet's response, oscillating between the desire instantly to 'sweep to [his] revenge' (1.5.31) and his recognition of the need to confirm the facts of the story before he acts on its assertions, structures the plot. At last Hamlet does act to kill his father's murderer and, mortally wounded in the process, demands yet another story to conclude the action, urging Horatio to 'Absent [himself] from felicity awhile, / And in this harsh world draw thy breath in pain / To tell my story' (5.2.354–6).

Othello is, similarly, a story largely about storytelling. Desdemona falls in love with Othello, as his tale of his eventful life stimulates her 'greedy ear' (1.3.150); and Othello comes to kill Desdemona, alienated from her love by the 'pestilence' of the stories that Iago pours into his credulous 'ear' (2.3.351). Charged by Brabantio with using witchcraft to win Desdemona's love, Othello offers the Duke and the senators in his defence 'a round unvarnished tale' (1.3.91) of the process by which he wooed her; but the play makes clear that no tales are ever 'unvarnished', no tales, that is, are ever innocent of the teller's craft or immune to their hearers' constructions. Even at the very end, the action focuses on stories and their unpredictable effects. Like Hamlet, the dying Othello finally demands that his story be told – 'Speak of me as I am ...' (5.2.340); and the play concludes with one final narrative gesture, Lodovico's promise 'to the state / This heavy act with heavy heart relate' (5.2.368–9), a promise of yet another story that, if wholly adequate, could only be a retelling of the play itself.

In all the plays, Shakespeare explores the ways in which human beings conduct their private and public lives through acts of storytelling. He focuses our attention on not only the content of a story, but its motive and method as well, reminding us that how and why a character tells a story is inevitably as important as what information is specifically conveyed.

As You Like It, for example, begins with what is obviously exposition. We learn the history that triggers the subsequent events of the play: Orlando's father has died, his oldest brother has been charged with his education, but Orlando has been denied the opportunities he desires and deserves as he has been kept 'rustically at home' (1.1.7). But the narrative does more than merely orient the audience. 'This is it, Adam, that grieves me' (20–1), Orlando concludes, addressing a long-time family servant; however, the purpose of the speech cannot be to inform Adam of what must be as well known, if not as heartfelt, to Adam as to Orlando himself. Clearly part of the dramatic point is just this superfluous telling, revealing, in what is obviously a familiar plaint (as well as in the expressive rhythms and repetitions of the speech itself), how deep are Orlando's frustrations, how fragile his apparent poise, and how needy he is of Adam's comfort.

Or, more complexly, in *The Tempest*, as Prospero relates to Miranda the history that brought them both to the island, the tangled motives of narrative are evident. Prospero's tale is an extraordinary account, a story of how his brother, Antonio, usurped Prospero's dukedom, entered into league with his 'inveterate' enemy (1.2.122), the King of Naples, and finally abandoned Prospero and the baby Miranda at sea in a 'rotten carcass of a butt' (146), in which they made their way to the island helped 'by Providence divine' (159) and the charity of one loyal friend. It does, of course, serve to provide necessary information, allowing both Miranda and the audience to know the prior events that motivate Prospero's actions; but his recapitulation of the treachery of his 'false brother' (92) is more than mere exposition. It is hardly an 'unvarnished' tale, but rather one provoking questions about the manner of its telling as much as about its matter. Why has Prospero waited so long to tell Miranda her own history? Why is it told in this particular way, so insistently marked by Prospero's reiterated (if hardly credible) concern that Miranda might not be alertly listening: 'Obey and be attentive' (38); 'I pray thee mark me' (67); 'Dost thou attend me?' (78); 'Thou attend'st not!' (87); 'I pray thee, mark me' (88); 'Dost thou hear?' (106)?

What emerges from the telling is a more complicated story than Prospero wants to tell. His anxiety no less than his anger is made apparent. His recurring focus on Miranda is less a plausible concern that she is not paying attention than an all-too plausible fear that she might not be responding as he hopes. The story Prospero would have his daughter hear is of his brother's betrayal, a story designed to secure her understanding and love for her father; but the story that he tells is one also of his own failure of responsibility, of his abdication of rule for the private pleasures of the books in his library.

> those being all my study,
> The government I cast upon my brother
> And to my state grew stranger, being transported
> And rapt in secret studies. Thy false uncle –
> Dost thou attend me?

(74–8)

His own failing is obvious, but still he wants his story to be a tale of the treachery of Miranda's 'false uncle'. No wonder it is at this exact moment that Prospero anxiously breaks off the narrative to see if Miranda is paying attention. Clearly she is not nodding off. What is less clear – and what Prospero worries about – is whether she hears the story as he intends it should be understood. Shakespeare's narrative art here is not identical with Prospero's. The embedded narrative of the history that brought Miranda and Prospero to the island not only provides information that the teller wants told but information about the teller that he does not realize himself.

Examples of storytelling used to reveal character could, of course, be multiplied. In *1 Henry IV*, for example, all of Hotspur's efforts at narrative get short-circuited by his energy and intemperance. Speeches lose their syntactic way, interrupted by the next new thought that rushes in. Style is personality, and this style finds its logical end in his dying speech. He acknowledges that time 'must have a stop' (5.4.82), but ironically he cannot finish even this story. The grammatical stop of his final line in which he realizes that he is 'dust / And food for –' (84–5) is denied him by death. Hal must supply the period: 'For worms, brave Percy' (86).

Narrative is thus unmistakably for Shakespeare a technique of characterization. How is something said? Under what circumstances? Narrative exists to convey information, but information not least importantly about its speaker. Narrative is an expository act, but Shakespeare understands it also as a psychological and a social gesture, whose complex motivations, often incompletely understood by the speaker, are part of the rich density of Shakespeare's dramatic art.

There is, however, another sense of Shakespeare's use of narrative that needs consideration: not the narratives within the plays but the plays themselves as forms of narrative. Shakespeare obviously is a pre-eminent storyteller. His stories are familiar, even to many who have never seen one of his plays. The lineaments of his plots are ineradicably a part of our cultural legacy, often reappearing in modern guise. *King Lear* is reborn in our time in Jane Smiley's *A Thousand Acres*; *Hamlet*, perhaps, as *The Lion King*. But even more significant than the evidence of modern rewritings of Shakespeare's plots is that the stories function as powerful metaphors for understanding our histories, whether it is the way in which our politicians' actions are measured against the behaviour of Shakespeare's kings, or how the O.J. Simpson trial seemingly demanded comparison with *Othello*, or, more generally, how *A Midsummer Night's Dream* is found to articulate the confusions of our own emotional lives.

Shakespeare's dramatic mode of storytelling, however, differs from the usual ways in which narrative functions in that no single voice controls the telling. His story emerges from the ensemble of voices that is the play. A clear narrative that can be extracted and retold emerges as Shakespeare shapes the plot of the drama, as Charles and Mary Lamb saw as they turned twenty of the plays into prose stories in their oft-reprinted *Tales from Shakespear. Designed for the Use of Young Persons* (1807).

This aspect of Shakespeare's narrative art can perhaps be seen most clearly by looking at the ways in which Shakespeare selects and organizes material from his sources. In *Henry V*, for example, Shakespeare inherits a well-known history, most immediately from the account in Holinshed's *Chronicles* (1587). In many ways, Shakespeare follows Holinshed's narrative quite closely: scenes and even speeches can be traced directly to the pages of the historical work. Nonetheless, Shakespeare does not merely dramatize the history he finds on the pages of the chronicle. The shape of Shakespeare's play differs significantly from the shape of the historical material he inherits.

Henry V ruled from 1413 to 1422. The nine and a half years of his rule were the shortest of the Lancastrian reigns but also the most successful. But Shakespeare turns the received story of the 'famous victories' of Henry V into an even more remarkable history, giving the reign almost mythic shape and significance. Shakespeare structures his history in part by omission. First, the anti-Lancastrian rebellions and the Lollard activity that dominated the first eighteen months of Henry's rule are completely ignored, replacing the reality of a tense and divided country with the dramatic illusion of a unified England enthusiastically committed to the will of its king. Second, the events of the French war are themselves selected and compressed so that the great victory at Agincourt leads directly to the peace at Troyes, omitting the chronicles' account of the intervening four years of intensive fighting before the peace was in fact achieved in 1420. Finally, the peace treaty in Shakespeare's play concludes the hostility, promising a time of 'Christian-like accord' (*H5* 5.2.347). In the chronicles, however, the Dauphin refused to accept the terms of the treaty, forcing Henry to return to France. This subsequent invasion met with greater resistance than the first, and Henry died in 1422 of an illness contracted during the long siege of Meaux in the winter of 1421–2, having failed to subdue the Dauphin's forces, and indeed having failed even to outlive the French King Charles and so never in truth becoming King of France.

Thus Shakespeare's dramatic version of the history, through omission and compression, gives the achievement of the reign a clarity and coherence it lacked in fact. Shakespeare's Harry leads a small band of valiant soldiers against a much larger force of arrogant Frenchmen. The astounding victory at Agincourt ends the French resistance, confirming England's moral and military superiority. The shape of this restructured history is a virtual cliché of propagandistic plotting, evidence of Shakespeare's deliberate transformation of the history into patriotic myth.

One sees this clearly in the treatment of the battle of Agincourt itself, where Shakespeare's English, outnumbered and exhausted, defeat a much larger army of French troops. The chronicles report that the improbable victory was gained in large part by superior military strategy but Shakespeare's Henry pointedly claims that victory came 'without stratagem, / But in plain shock and even play of battle' (4.8.109–10). The defeat of the French against the 'fearful odds' (4.3.5) that the English faced would be more explicable if mention were made of the sharpened stakes that Henry had ordered to be placed before his archers to prevent the French horsemen from overrunning his troops, but Shakespeare goes out of his way to emphasize the almost miraculous nature of the victory.

The casualty report from the battlefield reinforces this intent. The French, as in the chronicles, are said to have lost ten thousand men while the English lose merely

> Edward the Duke of York; the Earl of Suffolk;
> Sir Richard Keighley; Davy Gam, esquire;
> None else of name, and of all other men
> But five-and-twenty.

> (4.8.104–7)

This is almost an exact transcription of the account in Holinshed, but it omits the rest of the sentence, where Holinshed says that it is only 'as some do report'.[1] Edward Hall, whose chronicle Shakespeare also read, adds more sceptically: 'if you will give credit to such as write miracles'.[2] Both historians are well aware that 'other writers of greater credit affirm that there were slain above five or six hundred persons'.[3]

Even at the larger number, the victory is of astonishing proportions, and Shakespeare's acceptance of the report of least credit (along with his omission of the English forces' strategy of the sharpened pikes) suggests that probability is here being deliberately refused. The credible is rejected in favour of the miraculous; the historical logic of probable cause is abandoned in favour of the poetic logic of giant-killing. Shakespeare structures his history to give it a shape that history itself denies, but it is a shape that is central to Shakespeare's dramatic aims.

Even as he dramatizes history, Shakespeare feels free to invent his own story, shaping the inherited facts to his dramatic interests. In *Henry V*, Shakespeare seems clearly to want a history of Henry V to appear even more unmistakably heroic than it does in the chronicles. But if Shakespeare makes Henry's heroic energy unmistakable, he does not allow us to take it for the whole truth about the English King. Henry's political and military successes are obviously given great emphasis, but Shakespeare embeds their telling in a complex set of non-historical qualifying frames – the obviously idealizing choruses and the comic plot – that makes the restructured history seem manifestly partial, and leaves Henry's glory vulnerable to the contrasts and contradictions that are produced.

Certainly the truth of the reign is in part the heroic conception of the King that Shakespeare inherits and intensifies, but Shakespeare uses the other aspects of his plot to expose and explore the cost, both human and moral, of Henry's success. We see Henry V as hero, but the play as a whole makes us see more clearly than ever Henry does exactly what this means. Shakespeare's story, of course, is the story of Henry's success, but Shakespeare insists upon the heavy price he pays for it in both moral and psychological terms. In the multiple angles of vision that Shakespeare's play provides as history's authority is subordinated to dramatic design, we discover the fallible humanity of even this 'mirror of all Christian kings' (2.0.6).

Attention to Shakespeare's use of narrative surely must include his own extraordinary storytelling skills. Whatever else his plays are, they are themselves compelling stories, carefully organized plots in which character memorably reveals itself in represented action. Drama, however, is so obviously the literary form without a controlling narrative voice, an art of dialogue and movement, that this narrative aspect is often ignored. Indeed it is something of an embarrassment to some, seemingly ignoring the primary, theatrical life of the plays.

But not to see Shakespeare's plays as remarkable experiments in narrative is to miss something essential about them. The various, distinctive voices of his characters are not what should prevent the drama from being thought of as a narrative form; but rather, as those voices cohere in the service of a powerful ordering impulse on the part of the playwright, should be recognized as the very materials of Shakespeare's masterful narratives. Shakespeare orchestrates the multiple voices of his characters to produce stories that are almost uniquely memorable and meaningful, stories that have become part of what we know about the world and, indeed, part of what makes us fully and complexly human.

Notes

1 *Chronicles*, vol. 3, sig. 3G6[r].

2 *The Union of the Two Noble ... Families* (1548), sig. d2[r]; spelling modernized.

3 Holinshed, *Chronicles*, vol. 3, sig. 3G6[r]; Hall, *Union*, sig. d2[r]; spelling modernized.

Further reading

Hardy, Barbara, *Shakespeare's Storytellers: Dramatic Narration* (London: Peter Owen, 1997)

> Hardy sees narrative as central to Shakespeare's dramatic explorations of human behaviour. She focuses both on the stories that characters tell and the plays themselves as stories, with useful accounts both of the various functions of narratives in the plays and of the ways in which *Hamlet, King Lear* and *Macbeth*, especially, use narrative as one of their central themes.

Kastan, David Scott, *Shakespeare and the Shapes of Time* (London: Macmillan, 1982)

> Focusing on Shakespeare's history plays, tragedies, and romances, this book explores the relationship of the form of dramatic action and assumptions about historical time. In the ways in which the plays of each genre shape their stories, Kastan finds evidence of their distinct, though provisional, conceptions of time as the fundamental dimension of human experience.

Rees, Joan, *Shakespeare and the Story: Aspects of Creation* (London: Athlone Press, 1978)

> Rees explores the relationship of story to play, focusing on the ways in which Shakespeare organizes his plots as evidence of the operation of his creative imagination. For Rees, always the most interesting aspects of the plays are those which threaten the narrative framework, where the energy of a character, for example, disrupts the shape of the story and forces Shakespeare to discover the deepest logic of his material.

Wilson, Rawdon, *Shakespearean Narrative* (London: Associated University Presses, 1995)

> Wilson is interested in both Shakespeare's command of narrative conventions and his exploration of narrative functions. Applying the concepts of recent narrative theory to Shakespeare's plays, he analyses the narrative acts in the plays in terms of the conventions that structure them and the effects they produce.

8

PERSUASION

Lynette Hunter

People tend to think persuasion is about logic. This is a generalization, but many of us would recognize saying 'that's not logical' before dismissing someone's opinion. By 'logic' we usually imply a fairly formal structure, where an argument proceeds from point to point to a conclusion – this is rational logic. Sometimes the argument claims that 'if' this event and that event come together, 'then' such and such will result – this is syllogistic logic. At the same time we know logic isn't everything, otherwise how could we choose between two perfectly formed newspaper reports leading to different points of view? We are aware that logic can abuse the situation, and many would also recognize saying 'you can rationalize anything', when logic is misapplied.

With more experience we learn more about how to assess the ways we are persuaded, and course we become more sophisticated in our own skills for persuading other people. One of the things we quickly learn is that the character or projected image of the speaker is central to persuasion. It is far easier to believe a story we are told by someone we trust, than someone we do not know, who comes perhaps from a different background, different perspective, who may be a known liar. But it is perhaps less easy to put our finger on just what happens to us when we listen. For example, when people make a connection between the events of the Jewish Holocaust in World War Two and a contemporary event, whatever we have emotionally and intellectually invested in the Holocaust (or not) is called into play.

With literature we depend on genre, such as science fiction, realism or poetry, to alert us to both the position of the speaker/writer and our own position in response. We get clues from whether the writing is comic or documentary (*style*), and whether it sets out to teach, to pass an opinion or to entertain (*register*). From an early age we also learn an immense amount about language and other systems of communication such as fashion. Sarcasm is the root linguistic weapon of school-children, who learn how to mock others before moving on to the more subtle effects of irony. Advertising continually teaches us about all kinds of techniques and strategies: perhaps most centrally it focuses on how to trick the mind into making positive connections with the items it is promoting, frequently through pun and word or image association. These techniques of communication have structures that affect us in ways that are like, but not the same as, those of logic. While we do not often think self-consciously about how language structures our arguments, someone educated in the sixteenth century would.

Between 1510 and 1517 John Colet and Erasmus, a scholar from the Netherlands, established St Paul's School in London, which became a model for grammar schools throughout the country over the next hundred years. Central to the education offered was the system for the study of persuasion that they and their slightly earlier colleagues in other continental countries had rediscovered in the fifteenth century: classical rhetoric, mainly from the Roman writers Cicero and Quintilian but also from the Greek philosopher Aristotle. It is difficult to overestimate the importance of these writers for sixteenth-century England, Shakespeare and his contemporaries. Their contribution is analogous to, say, Newton's work on gravity, Euclid's on geometry, Einstein's on relativity. All male children who went to school learned the elements of rhetorical persuasion from the age of six to twelve, and sometimes fourteen, with a few continuing their work at university. There's considerable evidence that sixteenth-century education, with rote-learning on a massive scale, was highly successful.

Just as we do today, they learned about how the speakers present themselves (*ethos*), the effect on the audience (*pathos*), and register, style and genre. They learned a considerable amount about formal logic, but much more about the other devices and techniques, which were called the 'figures', and which for many, drove the entertainment industry of the time. What this chapter will attempt to do is look at scenes from three plays by Shakespeare and explore the methods of persuasion being used. I am particularly interested in looking at how the figures acquire persuasive force and become just as important as formal logic in structuring our ideas. But first I'll turn to more formal kinds of reasoning and look at *Measure for Measure*, before briefly exploring the persuasive power of figures in establishing ethos or character in *Antony and Cleopatra*, and finally examining the use of ethos and pathos in *Julius Caesar*.

Measure for Measure is a textbook study for formal reasoning. The Duke does it by the book, Isabella is more flexible, and Pompey makes fun of it. Other characters in the play also develop aspects of logic in different ways. When the Duke persuades Claudio, who is about to be put to death for getting his betrothed pregnant, he starts his speech with the proposition 'Be absolute for death' (3.1.5), proceeds with 'Reason thus ... ' (6) and continues:

> either death or life
> Shall thereby be the sweeter. Reason thus with life:
> If I do lose thee, I do lose a thing
> That none but fools would keep. A breath thou art,
> Servile to all the skyey influences
> That dost this habitation where thou keep'st
> Hourly afflict. Merely, thou art Death's fool;

For him thou labour'st by thy flight to shun,
And yet run'st toward him still... .
                              Thou'rt by no means valiant;
For thou dost fear the soft and tender fork
Of a poor worm... .
                              Thou are not thyself;
For thou exists on many a thousand grains
That issue out of dust. Happy thou art not;
For what thou hast not, still thou striv'st to get,
And what thou hast, forget'st. Thou art not certain;
For thy complexion shifts to strange effects
After the moon... .
                              What's yet in this
That bears the name of life? Yet in this life
Lie hid moe thousand deaths; yet death we fear
That makes these odds all even.

                                        (5–13, 15–17, 19–25, 38–41)

Why should Claudio embrace death? First, because to do so
makes both life and death sweeter, and second because if life is
lost, you lose only that which fools would keep. What then
follows is a series of syllogisms explaining why life is
something only fools would keep. In fact, these are a special
kind of syllogism, called an **enthymeme**. If a syllogism works
to a formula, 'If that and that, Then this', 'If A + B, Then C', an
enthymeme is the word given to an argument where one of the
terms is missing, 'If A and ?, Then C' is the most typical.
Because there is a missing term, the argument of each example
depends on the listener filling the gap. For example, 'Thou'rt
by no means valiant; / For thou dost fear the soft and tender
fork / Of a poor worm' (15–17): here the listener makes the
logical third term 'If you fear a worm, then you are not
valiant'. What is interesting about the process is that each
syllogism comes to depend on a figure to make sense.
Sometimes it's a metaphor, as with the first argument that

begins 'A breath thou art …' (8), sometimes a paradox, as in the second argument, 'Merely, thou art Death's fool; / For him thou labour'st by thy flight to shun, / And yet run'st toward him still' (11–13). Other figures used to complete the logic are *pun*, *allegory*, **simile**, *allusion* and **personification**.

A logical argument such as the Duke's, that strings argument after argument, is called a **sorites**. A sorites often repeats a word at the beginning or end of each clause, and here the phrase that keeps the list together is 'thou art'. We know that the argument is finished when the Duke generalizes out to 'we' (38–41). The arguments in themselves would be fairly simple to counter, but the length of the list makes it difficult to do so. It is not only the sorites but the display of argumentative breadth and persuasive skill of the speaker that is daunting, and remember, the Duke is disguised as a friar at this point, and carries with him all the respect due to spiritual guides. So as well as formal logic, he is playing upon his ethos as a trusted figure.

Claudio says of Isabella, his sister, 'She hath prosperous art / When she will play with reason and discourse, / And well she can persuade' (1.2.181–3). It falls to her to persuade Angelo, the Duke's literal-minded deputy, not to kill her brother for his crime, and this she attempts to do in two detailed scenes at 2.2 and 2.4. Her first argument begins plainly, indeed too simply, and when rebuffed, Lucio has to urge her to continue. The second plea she makes,

> I do think that you might pardon him,
> And neither heaven nor man grieve at the mercy
>
> (2.2.49–50)

establishes her key terms of 'mercy', 'heaven' and 'man', to which Angelo adds 'power'. She proceeds logically through these terms, demonstrating the way power and mercy should work:

> No ceremony that to great ones longs,
> Not the king's crown, nor the deputed sword,

The marshal's truncheon, nor the judge's robe,
Become them with one half so good a grace
As mercy does.

(59–63)

Then power and judgement:

I would to heaven I had your potency,
And you were Isabel! Should it then be thus?
No; I would tell what 'twere to be a judge,
And what a prisoner.

(67–70)

And concludes with the example of Christ who brings together judgement and mercy:

Why, all the souls that were, were forfeit once,
And He that might the vantage best have took
Found out the remedy. How would you be
If He, which is the top of judgement, should
But judge you as you are? O, think on that,
And mercy then will breathe within your lips,
Like man new made.

(73–9)

She doesn't explicitly comment on Christ's power, but implies that of course his power is far greater than Angelo's and yet he can show judgement and mercy while Angelo is 'tyrannous' (109). At this point her careful reasoning explodes into metaphors:

Could great men thunder
As Jove himself does, Jove would ne'er be quiet,
For every pelting petty officer
Would use his heaven for thunder; nothing but thunder.
Merciful Heaven,
Thou rather with thy sharp and sulphurous bolt

Splits the unwedgeable and gnarled oak,
Than the soft myrtle.

(111–18)

She continues by accusing Angelo of being the 'proud man, / Dress'd in a little brief authority, / Most ignorant of what he's most assur'd', the 'angry ape' who 'makes the angels weep' (118–23).

To understand the kind of persuasion Isabella uses we need to recognize that there are two main kinds of 'figure': devices that play with transferring semantic meaning from one word to another, and those that play with the conventions of grammar and sentence structure. These are often named as the *tropes* and *schemes*, respectively. One of the factors that makes Isabella seem so logical is that she rarely uses tropes. Only at crucial points where she is driven to extremes does she let go into an image like that of the 'angry ape'. Even at these points, she invests the **metaphor** with a literal intensity that implies that she might actually believe the connection between the image and the reality it describes. Yet throughout her speech, reasoning is informed by the schemes. The appearance of careful balance and thoughtful reason is sustained by the figure of **isocolon** that balances phrases of equal length, giving them an equal argumentative weight (see lines 60–1 above). At several points in her argument she mixes up pronouns, in an attempt to get Angelo to identify with Claudio's predicament, and to think through his new role as law enforcer. This technique, **enallage**, becomes central to the interaction of the two characters. One of her more telling strategies is to call upon authority outside her own argument, not only by referring to Christ, but also in her use of proverbs and adages (128–9, 131–2). The strategy is vital because her argument is based on getting Angelo to recognize that it is precisely because he depends on his own authority that he is making an error of judgement. He needs to recognize the limits to that authority.

In her second argument two scenes later, there is a difference in the way she deploys the key terms. Once more she sets these up at the start with 'I am come to know your pleasure' (2.4.31) and 'Heaven keep your honour' (34). While the key terms of the first argument had stable meanings, here they do not. Both 'pleasure' and 'honour', in the light of Angelo's threat, are terms both of respect and of sexual reference. The unintended pun, an **antanaclesis** where, in repetition, a word shifts from one meaning to another, is available to the audience but possibly not to Isabella. When she does suddenly understand that Angelo is proposing that sex with her will save her brother, her explosion into metaphor (again with that edge of literalism) 'Th'impression of keen whips I'd wear as rubies, / And strip myself to death as to a bed / That longing have been sick for, ere I'd yield / My body up to shame' (101–4), is the more forceful if the audience has taken her ethos to be 'the innocent'.

After her metaphoric outburst (101–4) she generalizes from Angelo's platitude that all women are frail (123), finally saying that she is but herself, 'I have no tongue but one' (138). This odd statement implies not only that she is certain of herself, that she speaks only the truth, but that there is no double meaning in her words. This extraordinary unselfconsciousness gives the audience an idea of Isabella's own limitations. At the same time, it demonstrates that in asking Angelo to imagine himself as another person, central to her previous argument, she has released in him something he cannot control. Indeed she says, 'Let me entreat you speak the former language' (139). Their remaining exchanges are carefully logical, but note how the key terms reappear: Angelo confesses his 'love' and asserts his sincerity with 'on mine honour' (146), while Isabella, left on her own at the end of the scene, speaks of her brother's 'prompture of the blood' or sexual passion, as well as his 'mind of honour' (177–8).

Isabella's two arguments locate some of the central issues of the play: human and divine power, mercy, judgement, passion, conduct, honour – and their limits and extents. Yet her method of persuasion, her rhetoric, also makes an unselfconscious argument about her character, for she does not include herself in the criticism she makes of others. At the end of the first argument she says her prayers will save Angelo, thus assuming a divinity or perfection of her own that is unintentionally parallel to his own self-regard. And she doesn't notice the slippage in the words 'honour' and 'pleasure' used with their sexual meaning by Angelo, when she reapplies them to Claudio, someone she loves. Her belief that she speaks only the truth blinds her to her own inconstancy.

Immediately preceding these scenes, in 2.1, the audience is treated to Pompey's great parody of legal logic. It's a warning of what is to come. The scene starts with Elbow, who accuses Froth of harassing his wife. Elbow is important to the parody of persuasion that follows because he speaks in malapropisms, referring to the two accused as 'notorious benefactors', meaning 'malefactors'. Pompey's key device, to take literally anything that is said, is the opposite of malapropism, but he also displays a keen command of a range of strategies. He uses the technique of repeating a word to link sentences together into a sorites: even though they are the weak phrases 'being then', 'telling you then', 'very well then', they carry him from establishing the ground, to cross-examining Froth, to establishing Froth's character, to his summing up. The repetition of 'I beseech you' in his culminating argument, which he takes over from Elbow himself, makes it seem as though he is agreeing with him:

ELBOW   I beseech you, sir, ask him what this man did to my wife.
POMPEY   I beseech your honour, ask me.
ESCALUS   Well, sir, what did this gentleman to her?
POMPEY   I beseech you, sir, look in this gentleman's face. Good Master Froth, look upon his honour; 'tis for a good purpose. – Doth your honour mark his face?

ESCALUS   Ay, sir, very well.
POMPEY   Nay, I beseech you, mark it well.

(140–8)

Another strategy Pompey uses is to repeat the same word again and again, **ploce**, a common device in argument for achieving a sense of common ground with the audience. Here it's overused, as in the insistent repetition of 'dish' (90–8), and can be recognized as a deliberate way of laying false trails.

Whenever Escalus intervenes, Pompey manipulates the language by taking it literally. Frustrated with the wandering argument, Escalus says, 'Come me to what was done to her' (116), and Pompey replies, 'your honour cannot come to that yet' (117), punning on 'honour' and 'come' in a way that prefigures Isabella's use of words in 2.4. The next time Escalus intervenes, with 'What was done to Elbow's wife, once more?' (137), Pompey again takes him literally, 'Once, sir? There was nothing done to her once' (139). In his summing up, he leads Escalus to the desired conclusion using the sophistical logic of specious reasoning, to get him to admit that Froth's face is 'the worst thing about him' (152–3), hence he could not possibly have harmed Elbow's wife. And he clinches his argument by taking Elbow's 'respected', a malapropism for 'suspected', for the word it is, which for a Renaissance audience would be a surreal perversion of the *elench* – gathering a conclusion contrary to the assertion – but here the assertion is clearly a mistake:

ELBOW   First, and it like you, the house is a respected house [meaning 'suspected']; next, this is a respected fellow; and his mistress is a respected woman.
POMPEY   By this hand, sir, his wife is a more respected person than any of us all.

(158–62)

(with an ambivalent meaning: is Pompey correctly using the word *respected*? or is he taking on Elbow's malapropism and insulting his wife? or is he self-consciously confusing the case by using a word that Escalus will hear one way and Elbow another so that they will not be able to agree?)

Whether we choose to read Pompey's word-play as self-conscious or not, his skill with formal logic, which depends on definition, syllogism and rational argument, offers a salutary counterpoint to the other displays of persuasion in the play.

In *Measure for Measure*, what we think of the characters does affect how we respond to their rhetoric. Is the Duke a wise, careful and thoughtful man – or a manipulator? In a completely different manner *Antony and Cleopatra* presents two central characters neither of whom has a straightforward ethos; in fact none of the characters in this play do. The play is marked from the start by a figure. It realizes a **hyperbole** that is introduced as a contradiction or **antithesis** in the opening lines: is Antony a 'strumpet's fool' or the 'triple pillar of the world' (1.1.13, 12)? Until 5.2.81–2, when Cleopatra claims 'His legs bestrid the ocean; his reared arm / Crested the world . . . ', and makes him into a colossus, we have no reason to believe one or the other. Nor can the audience be sure of Cleopatra.

Throughout the text we find not rational and syllogistic logic, but persuasive figures that indicate tension, friction and explosion.[1] The repetition of a word from the end of one sentence, to the beginning of another, **anadiplosis**, underlines the way people are pulled in different directions when the two sentences are contraries. For example, Octavia's 'Husband win, win brother' (3.4.18), or the exchange '[Charmian] Madam / She was a widow – [Cleopatra] Widow? Charmian, hark!' (3.3.26–7). Repeated words following immediately on each other (**epizeuxis**), such as 'why, why, why?' (3.7.2) or 'Well is it, is it?' (3.7.4), release rhythm and emotion. **Catachresis**, or the device that wrenches words away from their proper meaning, as in 'We have *kissed* away / Kingdoms and princes' (3.10.7–8), or 'he will *fill* thy wishes *to the brim* / With principalities' (3.13.18–19), or 'Whose *eye becked* forth my wars and *called* them home' (4.12.26) (italics added), has the effect of suddenly intensifying significance as the listener attempts to make sense of the new location for the image. The play is filled with exclamations of vehemence and hyperbole, made more emphatic by the undercurrent of the colloquial. For example the iteration of *thou* at 4.2.11, the device ploce, works to construct conversational ease; at the same time the repetition of words with one or more in between, or **diacope**, although similar to ploce, has a very different insistent and desperate effect, as in Cleopatra's 'help' at 4.15.13–14. Here it is not formal logic that is effecting the persuasion, nor is it strictly ethos and pathos being constructed in a direct manner. As with most of the plays, and a great deal of everyday language, the logical persuasion is effected through the figures, both tropes and schemes.

Shakespeare's work offers many examples of persuasion that focus on the character of ethos above all else: for example, Iago persuading Othello of his wife's infidelity, by seeming reluctant to do so. Yet one of the best examples of the persuasive force of character is not by a villain, but a politician, Mark Antony in *Julius Caesar*.

The famous speech Antony makes over the dead body of Julius Caesar in 3.2 is preceded by a speech from Caesar's assassin, Brutus. Brutus' words are marked by assertion, command, circular argument and tautology: all being weak logical devices for persuasion because they are self-justifying. With the naïvety that comes with such self-regard, when Brutus introduces Antony he identifies him with the crowd, immediately giving him an advantage. The persuasive force of this scene is largely to do with the way the speaker is presented, his ethos, and the response drawn out of the audience, or pathos. Mark Antony begins by reversing Brutus' address from 'Romans, countrymen and lovers' (3.2.13) to 'Friends, Romans, countrymen' (74), calling on them to identify first as 'friends'. Note how the list expands from one syllable to two to three, like a widening arc embracing the audience. He uses proverbs, common knowledge the listeners will accept and therefore begin to find common ground with the speaker:

> The evil that men do lives after them:
> The good is oft interred with their bones.
>
> (76–7)

Using Brutus' exact vocabulary of ambition, honour and friendship, Antony sets up the refrain of 'Brutus is an honourable man' (83) that will hold the entire argument of the next 170 lines together as he plays with constructing a positive ethos for himself and Caesar, and a negative ethos for Brutus.

When Antony pauses the momentum for development passes to the crowd, and in their responses we recognize their appreciation of his logic:

> Mark ye his words? He would not take the crown;
> Therefore 'tis certain he was not ambitious.
>
> (113–14)

But we also recognize their appreciation of his pathos, 'Poor soul, his eyes are red as fire with weeping' (116), and of ethos, 'There's not a nobler man in Rome than Antony' (117). His second major development starts off by introducing the words 'rage' and 'mutiny', only to deny that he wants to do this (126), and proceeds by skilfully bringing the crowd together with himself and Caesar as 'friends' (141) implicitly against Brutus. As he walks into the crowd, they call him 'noble' Antony.

Having constructed his own ethos, Antony builds Caesar's. He develops the visual spectacle of Caesar being killed. He shows them the tears in Caesar's gown, saying

Look, in this place ran Cassius' dagger through:
See what a rent the envious Caska made:
Through this, the well-beloved Brutus stabbed,
And as he plucked his cursed steel away,
Mark how the blood of Caesar followed it …
This was the most unkindest cut of all:
For when the noble Caesar saw him stab,
Ingratitude, more strong than traitor's arms,
Quite vanquished him: then burst his mighty heart …

(172–6, 181–4)

to conclude that as Caesar fell, 'you, and all of us fell down' (189), with that 'us' fully including the crowd with himself and Caesar. Any treason of Brutus and friends against Caesar becomes treason against the crowd. Note how the refrain of 'honourable' moves here (205) from a praising epithet to **irony**. Irony always implies a silent background of agreed knowledge: when someone from England looks out at the rain and says 'What a lovely day', people who are used to the inexorability of the rain recognize the humour; strangers may simply wonder if the speaker is feeling all right. At this point in Antony's argument the crowd accepts that the word 'honourable' is twisted when applied to Brutus, for he is now a traitor.

In his final development, Antony has to instigate the crowd to rebellion without openly condemning Brutus, because he has promised not to and has to maintain his own trustworthy ethos. Here he moves into a breathtaking piece of persuasion with 'I am no orator, as Brutus is', but 'a plain blunt man' who loved Caesar (210–1). He continues this humility topos, that constructs his ethos as honest and direct, with:

For I have neither wit, nor words, nor worth,
Action, nor utterance, nor the power of speech
To stir men's blood. I only speak right on:

> I tell you that which you yourselves do know,
> Show you sweet Caesar's wounds, poor poor dumb mouths,
> And bid them speak for me
>
> (214–19)

which in the vocabulary of 'wit', 'words', 'worth', and later 'action', 'utterance' and 'power', precisely delineate the rhetorical skill he denies he has. At the same time, Antony uses obvious conceits that he could expect them to notice,[2] especially the device of vivid representation necessary to an illusion of reality, or *enargia*, to present a gross vision of Brutus with his tongue in every wound of Caesar's body. The argument peaks as he links his name with Brutus' and moves them to rebellion in Brutus' name. Antony succeeds because he understands pathos and ethos, while Brutus relies on logic. Manipulating the grounds on which the crowd believes things, Antony begins by identifying with Brutus, gradually distances himself from him while reducing him to a traitor, and then in a daring reversal claims that Brutus speaks through him urging them to rebellion:

> But were I Brutus,
> And Brutus Antony, there were an Antony
> Would ruffle up your spirits and put a tongue
> In every wound of Caesar that should move
> The stones of Rome to rise and mutiny.
>
> (219–23)

It is a curious fulfilment of Brutus' final words, 'I have the same dagger for myself, when it shall please my country to need my death' (45–7). At the same time Antony starts off distanced from Caesar, gradually reclaiming him from Brutus' accusations, making the crowd identify first with himself, as noble, and then through him with Caesar.

Note that both identifications occur by means of Caesar's physical body, a visual spectacle or *hypotyposis* that is used as a prop by Antony to claim proof and authenticity for his persuasion: the Renaissance as now could argue that 'seeing is believing'. But more than this, note the figures he uses to construct this spectacle, which develop tropes in an un-embarrassed way in order to persuade: the metaphor of Caesar's wounds as 'poor poor dumb mouths' (218), the excessive vulnerability and complete disempowerment that renders Caesar not only a presence that can no longer speak, but to the position of a baby or an aged, toothless human being, that needs protection. And the final figure that invites the crowd to put 'a tongue / In every wound of Caesar', to become Brutus, to become killers, to 'rise and mutiny'.

Formal logic never works on its own, and this is something the sixteenth century knew better than today. The Duke, Angelo and Isabella all to some extent get trapped in it, while Pompey has the sense to make fun of it. But logic as the structuring of argument and persuasion, what Erasmus called *dispositio*, is far more subtle than formal rationalism. It goes a long way to define what we think of today as character or ethos, the position of the speaker, and can help us also to recognize our own positions when we read a text. To understand the complexity of persuasion in Shakespeare's dramatic language we need to understand the persuasive system, rhetoric, that he is using: not only logos, but ethos, pathos and especially the ordering structures of the figures that pervade our use of language.

Notes

1 For other figures in *Antony and Cleopatra*, and other writing of the period, see Joseph, listed below.

2 See David Daniell's notes to this speech in the Arden 3 edition of *Julius Caesar*, p. 265.

FURTHER READING

Joseph, Sister Miriam, *Shakespeare's Use of the Arts of Language* (New York: Hafner, 1966)

> Although written many years ago, this work is still a mine of information about the different elements of language in the Renaissance, and what commentators at the time had to say about them. Mainly concerned with Shakespeare's plays, but providing some material written by his contemporaries, Joseph works through the persuasive effects of grammar, argument, logic, pathos and ethos. Every device is illustrated with examples from the plays, and her index allows us to locate devices used by particular plays.

Murphy, James J. (ed.), *Renaissance Eloquence: Studies in the Theory and Practice of Renaissance Rhetoric* (Berkeley: University of California Press, 1983)

> The essays collected in this volume bring together some of the most thought-provoking writers on persuasion in the Renaissance. They range from education in schools and universities, to cultural contexts in Europe, to the issue of deceitful versus morally persuasive rhetoric, to specific work on style in sixteenth and early seventeenth-century writing. Many of these essays have subsequently been developed by the writers themselves and others, especially in the journal *Rhetorica*. Nevertheless they provide a good starting point, and represent probably the most comprehensive approach to argument and persuasion in the Renaissance.

Vickers, Brian, *In Defence of Rhetoric* (Oxford: Clarendon Press, 1988)

> This book offers a historical context for literature and rhetoric and a summary of the main parts of rhetoric, as well as one detailed chapter on the Renaissance and another surveying a range of the figures, with useful examples found in an appendix. Vickers argues that the Renaissance brought together rhetoric, logic and philosophy, after fragmentation during the medieval period. This theory is highly contentious, but his argument is an effective demonstration of some of the issues. A later chapter on rhetoric in the modern novel offers a platform for those concerned with relevance to the present day.

9

DIALOGUE

Lynne Magnusson

Perhaps the most fundamental quality of dramatic language is
that it is interactive. A character's utterance is never an isolated
speech or poem. In dramatic dialogue, a character's words
must be oriented towards the answering words of others. An
effective dramatic utterance looks backward in response to
another's word and also forward in anticipation of a 'future
answer-word'.[1] Shakespeare's stylistic excellence consists in
large part of making us feel how his characters' speeches
function as answer-words in an ongoing dialogue. Consider,
for example, King Lear's agitated words as he re-enters the
stage with the Duke of Gloucester after seeking out his
daughter and son-in-law, Regan and Cornwall:

> Deny to speak with me? They are sick, they are weary,
> They have travelled all the night? – mere fetches ay,
> The images of revolt and flying off.
> Fetch me a better answer.

(2.2.277–80)

Though Lear's words contain no literal repetition of any
speech we have previously heard on-stage, we nonetheless hear
his words as picking up and repeating what has just been said
to him. Lear's words clearly come across as responses. At the
same time, however, the words themselves are creating the
illusion of the conversation they apparently refer back to.
Regan or Cornwall, it seems, must have answered Gloucester's
message from Lear that they should come to him with words

like 'Tell him we cannot speak now. Regan is sick, and we are both too weary to meet with him now – we've been travelling all through the night.' Gloucester must have reiterated their words to Lear in the form of an indirect quotation. Simply by repeating the hypothetical words as questions, Lear registers them as inappropriate answers, as an affront to his dignity. Furthermore, Lear's concluding words – 'Fetch me a better answer' – project forward a 'future answer-word' – and not just by naming explicitly the 'better answer' he expects from Regan and Cornwall. By using the imperative form of command, 'Fetch me', rather than a gentler request, Lear expresses implicitly his expectation of Gloucester's 'answer' – that is, that his subordinate will make a compliant answer and take immediate action upon his commandment.

If this engagement with the words of others is so central to dramatic language, it seems odd that we have so few shared terms or concepts to help us, as theatre-goers, readers or actors, to understand and talk about dialogue as opposed to single-voiced poems or speeches. This chapter will bring together tools from the art of rhetoric and from everyday practices of conversation to help us analyse interaction in dramatic dialogue. Let us start by considering how we can adapt figures of speech previously encountered in this book from the art of rhetoric to describe the dynamics of such vivid encounters as the following one between King Lear and his retainer, the Earl of Kent:

KENT
                              Royal Lear,
  Whom I have ever honoured as my king,
  Loved as my father, as my master followed,
  As my great patron thought on in my prayers –
LEAR
  The bow is bent and drawn; make from the shaft.
KENT
  Let it fall rather, though the fork invade [shared **metaphor**]

> *The region of my heart*: be Kent unmannerly
> When Lear is mad. What wouldst thou do, old man?
> Think'st thou that duty shall have dread to speak,
> When power to flattery bows? To plainness honour's bound
> When majesty falls to folly.... .

LEAR

> Kent, *on thy life*, no more.

KENT

> *My life* I never held but as a pawn
> [**diacope**, repetition with intervening words]
> To wage against thine enemies, ne'er fear to lose it,
> Thy safety being the motive.

LEAR

> Out of my *sight!*

KENT

> *See* better, Lear, and let me still remain
> The true blank of thine eye.
> [shared metaphor with **polyptoton**, repeating a word in a
> different form]

LEAR

> *Now by Apollo* –

KENT

> *Now by Apollo*, King, [**ploce**, speedy repetition]
> Thou swear'st thy gods in vain.

> (1.1.140–62; emphasis added)

Here, focusing on the figures of repetition and shared
metaphors brings out a significant pattern in the dialogic
encounter. When Kent confronts Lear with his bad judgement
in casting off his youngest daughter Cordelia, Lear strongly
resists hearing his criticisms. Despite Lear's evasions, Kent
persists with his dogged efforts to confront and counsel his
master, even to the point of interrupting and speaking over
Lear's words, as Lear has done to him but with a significant
difference. The difference is that Kent picks up, repeats and

transforms Lear's own words and metaphors, in a sense aligning himself *with* his master even while taking on the serious risk of speaking out in public *against* Lear. Thus through rhetorical patterning Kent's answer-words express at once a sympathetic engagement and a confrontation with Lear's language, strategically negotiating the difficult duty of the servant-counsellor. In the patterns of repetition and transformation played out here, Shakespeare is developing a living rhetoric for dialogic exchange that is a considerable advance upon the formulaic **stichomythia** of Greek drama, with its rigid line-by-line speech alternation.

Recognizing how rhetorical figures can work across utterances helps to illuminate the dynamic of the Kent–Lear encounter. However, we would be missing a lot here if we did not also depend – perhaps without even being conscious of it – on our tacit knowledge of the rules and resources governing conversation. Dramatic dialogue, strictly speaking, is not the same as everyday conversation: its language is often heightened and organized beyond that of everyday speech, and it must communicate plot, setting and other information to an overhearing audience in a way not applicable to ordinary talk. Nonetheless, our knowledge of ordinary talk makes us aware that Kent and Lear are interrupting each other. It also makes us aware that it is a much riskier business for Kent, the subordinate, to interrupt his master than for Lear to interrupt Kent. We depend on our knowledge of how one speaker normally gives way to another in conversation, or 'speaker change', and of how power relations affect what can be said, when, and to whom. With developments since the 1960s in speech-act theory and conversation analysis, there has been a new awareness of the complexity and richness of everyday talk and other forms of oral interaction – a subject previously neglected when linguists and philosophers of language focused on written language.[2] As researchers in these emergent fields try to codify interactive speech behaviour, they are attempting to make explicit the implicit knowledge of competent speakers and social agents. For example, they have drawn up specific terms for describing the regular patterning of the 'turn-taking system' and the ongoing social maintenance work of 'politeness' as these operate in everyday conversation. But we do not need many new technical terms to make us see how attention to the practices of everyday talk can help us to analyse dramatic dialogue. It is just as important to see how Shakespearean plays like *King Lear* themselves reveal their author's deep knowledge and interest in the complexities of ordinary talk.

To appreciate the dramatic language of *King Lear* is to discover how it dislocates ordinary talk while at the same time drawing our attention to the dislocation. Some of the dislocations are both obvious and recognized artistic devices, as when Lear addresses his words not to people around him but to the gods, the thunder, or a joint stool mistaken for a daughter. Rhetoricians call this artful deviation from normal speech address **apostrophe**. But when the retired King Lear asks the surrounding company who put his messenger in the stocks – asks not once or twice, but three and then four times, before Cornwall answers 'I set him there, sir' (2.2.388) – the device may have no poetic or rhetorical name and yet we immediately recognize a violation of turn-taking in the disruption of the basic question/answer sequence. We know what it feels like when someone repeatedly ignores what we ourselves ask, and can see the power game that Cornwall and Regan are playing out simply by failing to respond. Similarly, when Kent in the passage quoted above shifts his form of address from 'Royal Lear' to 'old man', no matter how simple and descriptive the latter phrase may be, we recognize that he is deliberately flouting the usual forms of politeness and transgressing social hierarchy. In this case, Kent's own words cue us to the violation, underlining, in case we miss it, that 'old man' used as a form of address to King Lear is 'unmannerly'. Moreover, Kent's words offer a rationale for the violation, linking Kent's impolite form of address to Lear's unkingly behaviour ('be Kent unmannerly / When Lear is mad'). Both these examples suggest that talk and its dislocation are not trivial matters: instead, they are integral to the unfolding dramatic action and the characters' identities in one of Shakespeare's most profound tragedies.

Speech utterances in real life do more than just represent thoughts or communicate ideas. People *do* things to one another with words, whether they command, request, criticize, apologize, insult, vow, promise, or simply fail to respond. Language in everyday social use is *action* and *interaction*. These perceptions about actual conversation can help to broaden our understanding of dialogue in drama. This is not to say that ideas are unimportant in drama. Indeed, it is crucial to understand how dialogue contributes to the interplay of ideas in Shakespearean drama. Whether it is honour that is being debated, as in *1 Henry IV*, or time and political necessity, as in *2 Henry IV*, Shakespearean drama thrives on the provision of alternative points of view. Shakespearean dialogue as an encounter of ideas has certainly contributed to the long life and popularity of the plays, whether we imagine it as promoting complexity of thought and toleration of differences in an audience or as offering everyone a point of agreement. Nonetheless, the examples we have been discussing from *Lear* make it apparent that dialogue is not simply the medium in which the play's jostling ideas are communicated. Engaging in dialogue, the characters are acting forcefully (or impotently) upon each other and upon the world around them.

As the study of conversation also suggests, the identity construction of the characters may be caught up in the reciprocal exchange of answer-words. I posit an identity for myself and for you in how I speak to or act upon you in words, and your answer acquiesces to, challenges or adjusts the relational identities posited by my words. This negotiation of identity is evident in the *Lear* examples. Before his staged retirement as king, Lear has been used to hearing predictably compliant responses from daughters, sons-in-law, servants and noblemen to his questions and commands. These answer-words have confirmed and acknowledged his authority and his sense of who he is. The dislocations we have begun to notice in the answer-words also dislocate his identity, that sense of self which in each of us is vulnerable to the recognition and acknowledgement of the other. Asking four times without an answer tells Lear that he is unimportant, and is far from retaining 'The name, and all th'addition to a king' (1.1.137) as he had expected.

Or consider the dislocation of politeness in Goneril's request to Lear: 'Be then desired, / By her that else will take the thing she begs, / A little to disquantity your train' (1.4.238–40). 'Politeness theory', as developed out of speech-act theory by Penelope Brown and Stephen C. Levinson,[3] clarifies what is happening in this example. The theory suggests that most speech acts, such as commands or requests, threaten or place at risk the 'face' of one or more of the speakers involved. To compensate, speakers (usually quite automatically) mitigate or offset the risk with complex politeness strategies ('if you would be so good as to . . .'). The strategy chosen is closely connected with the relative power of the speakers and the closeness of their acquaintance. Hence, you may well 'command' your younger brother to 'shut up' but are more likely to 'request' that a noisy professor in the library 'might consider, if it would not be too much of an intrusion, speaking more quietly or, perhaps, continuing his (or her) conversation elsewhere'. If we edit Goneril's request by omitting the second line – 'Be then desired a little to disquantity your train' – it fits this second pattern: it is indirect and deferential and alerts us to the power of the person addressed – partly, of course, by suggesting that Goneril has no power or intention to coerce Lear. But add back in 'By her that else will take the thing she begs' and we recognize the bizarre contradiction between the non-coercive politeness formula and the interrupting, coercive threat.

Here again, Shakespeare dislocates a normal pattern of conversation, specifically a deferential politeness pattern, to dramatize a transformed power relationship and to challenge, in a subtle but terrifying way, Lear's sense of who he is. When we think of characters in *Lear* acting so forcefully on others as to impair their identities we may think first of such violent actions as Cornwall's blinding of Gloucester. But *Lear* is such a potent play because it makes us recognize how secure identities and our sense of the safe normality of daily life are equally caught up in how people talk together, in the most taken-for-granted conditions of speech exchange. It is as if Lear's daughters can make and unmake Lear with their words.

The force of dialogic action in Shakespearean drama is only occasionally as intense and personally threatening as it is in *Lear*, and we need to be attentive to the many different effects that Shakespeare achieves in verbal interchanges. In a comedy, a war of words between characters is more likely to bring into prominence the cleverness and wit of the exchange. Transformative effects upon the characters are sometimes also evident, as for example in the moments of self-criticism triggered by the wit-play of Beatrice and Benedick in *Much Ado About Nothing*. Nonetheless, the qualities of dramatic dialogue can be brought out effectively by attending to the two kinds of devices we have been exploring – on the one hand, poetic or rhetorical devices being played out across speech exchanges and, on the other hand, conversational rules and norms being applied or disrupted. Some basic questions prompted by stylistic rhetoric include: Does the dialogue set up relations between alternating speeches by picking up, repeating or transforming words or phrases? Do these repetitions take the form of figures of speech such as diacope or polyptoton? Is shared metaphor or punning involved? Does one utterance mirror or transform the other in some way? (See **isocolon** and

parison for relevant rhetorical terms in the A–Z.) Some basic questions prompted by conversational rules might include: What can be said about the pattern and length of the characters' speech 'turns'? Are there explicit question/answer sequences played out, or does one utterance implicitly 'answer' another in other ways? What speech acts – such as commanding, criticizing, or requesting – are being performed? What politeness strategies do characters use, and what do these reveal about power relationships? What forms of address are used between the speakers (e.g. 'thou', 'Royal Lear', 'masters')? What conversational or social norms are being disrupted?

It is also important to realize that questions about rhetorical art and everyday talk are not always at odds with one another. From either category, for example, might come the question of whether the characters interacting speak in similar or contrasting styles. In ordinary conversation, contrasting styles will often mark class, gender or occupational differences, and Shakespeare's ability to emulate and set in dialogue a multiplicity of real-world voices is unmatched. Yet in the plays, such differences often merge seamlessly with artistic contrasts, as with shifts from prose to verse or contrasts between highly ornamented and plain speech. And the contrasts may function, as in *Love's Labour's Lost* where the wordy displays of Armado would be tedious without such alternations as Costard's simple interjections, both to produce aesthetic effects and to mark social differences.

With the tools of rhetorical art and everyday conversation in hand for our analysis, we need finally to attend to the multiple functions of dramatic dialogue. Language in the theatre speaks in many directions: it is not just the answer-word of character to character, or of social group to social group. It is addressed, in some of its more practical functions, to the actor or theatre practitioner; it is addressed, moreover, in a multitude of ways, both direct and indirect, to a theatre audience. And it also positions the reader as another potential overhearer. To illustrate the multiple forms of address and some of the functions they correspond to, let's consider a simple illustration from *A Midsummer Night's Dream*, in which the Athenian craftsmen are planning rehearsals of a play to be performed at a royal wedding:

BOTTOM   I will discharge it [i.e. the role of Pyramus] in either your straw-colour beard, your orange-tawny beard, your purple-in-grain beard, or your French-crown-colour beard, your perfect yellow.

QUINCE   Some of your French crowns have no hair at all, and then you will play bare-faced. But, masters, here are your parts; and I am to entreat you, request you, and desire you, to con them by tomorrow night; and meet me in the palace wood, a mile without the town, by moonlight; there will we rehearse, for if we meet in the city, we shall be dogged with company, and our devices known. In the meantime I will draw a bill of properties, such as our play wants. I pray you fail me not.

BOTTOM   We will meet, and there we may rehearse most obscenely and courageously. Take pains, be perfect: adieu!

(1.2.87–103)

Quince's first remark sets up the character-to-character interaction by repeating and punning on Bottom's words: whereas Bottom is fantasizing about a beard coloured like a yellow-gold coin, the 'French crown', Quince uses the phrase to joke about bald heads ('crowns'), denuded of hair by the 'French disease', syphilis. The interpersonal dynamics are further illuminated by the patterning of conversational turn-taking among the six craftsmen on-stage in this scene. It is not surprising that Quince as play director takes the lead in the conversation, but Bottom's tendency to 'self-select' as respondent ('We will meet, and …'), to hold the floor at length to elaborate on many different possible colours for his beard, and to give directions to his companions ('Take pains, be perfect') tells us about his self-important character. At the same time that the dialogue does differentiate in these ways between the two speakers, it also works to signal a social-group likeness between them. The solidarity of down-to-earth working men is suggested by sentence structures working by simple accumulation ('and … and') and by forms of address like 'masters'. Nonetheless, as is often the case when Shakespeare represents lower-class characters, the dialogue injects a certain element of pomp into their speeches as well, as with Quince's triplet or **synonymia** – 'I am to entreat you, request you, and desire you' – and with Bottom's slightly inflated (and mistaken) word use – 'most obscenely and courageously'. Although the conversation occurs among social equals, this verbal emulation of their social betters situates the activity of the craftsmen within a class society, as if what they do is always being measured in relation to the doings of 'the better sort'.

As I have already suggested, these elements of dialogue representing interpersonal and social relationships among the characters are only part of the story. Quince's simple words, 'here are your parts', speak not just to the characters on-stage but also to theatre practitioners. They signal that stage props will be needed here, the 'parts' or scripts for Quince's players, and so provide information for a director's own 'bill [i.e. list] of properties'. They also cue the actors to the stage business of distributing these parts, just as Bottom's 'adieu' cues their exit. In fact, we might regard all the details about meeting 'in the palace wood, a mile without the town, by moonlight' as spoken to assist directors and players in planning possible property requirements for the upcoming woodland scenes. But that would be to underestimate the continuous address that dramatic dialogue is making to the audience. Given the natural lighting and relative bareness of the Elizabethan stage, the dialogue is here soliciting the audience to imagine, when the craftsmen reappear, woods, moonlight, tomorrow night. Indeed, when Quince and his mates do reappear, the double address of Quince's words to his mates and to the audience is even richer, as William Carroll has suggested in Chapter 6. 'Pat, pat,' Quince begins, 'and here's a marvellous convenient place for our rehearsal. This green plot shall be our stage, this hawthorn-brake our tiring-house' (3.1.2–3). What the audience, of course, 'sees' in concrete terms is a 'stage' and 'tiring-house': what the dialogue asks of the audience is to imagine that the craftsmen see 'a green plot' and then to double the imaginative transformation by seeing with them, again, a stage.

Crucial though it is to include the play's communication with its audience in our understanding of dramatic language, it is nonetheless harder to conceptualize the play's 'dialogue' with its audience than the dialogue between its characters. Part of the difficulty is that conversation cannot really serve as an effective model. An actor's words may well seem to solicit a sort of 'answer-word' from the audience and to anticipate its response. But theatrical performance sets a condition that is contrary to the conditions of everyday conversation: it suspends for a time the right of the audience to speak, to be heard, and then to be answered again. By the logic of conversational turn-taking, this might seem to indicate a position of powerlessness or unimportance for the audience, but *A Midsummer Night's Dream* suggests otherwise. It suggests otherwise partly by setting up analogous situations to tell us that the audience position is a place of empowerment. The powerful fairies Oberon and Puck, for example, oversee the young lovers' mix-ups as if they watch a stage comedy, while the royal Theseus and his court (though not entirely silent) are audience to the craftsmen's *Pyramus and Thisby*. Moreover, when Puck makes a final direct address to the audience, his deferential style of apology positions audience members not as his inferiors but as 'gentles', persons worthy of high esteem. Thus is the audience's silent hearing and judging of the play's complex manner of address situated as a speech posture not of unimportance but rather of privilege.

In sum, the resources of rhetoric and the resources of conversation, taken together, can serve as useful tools for the analysis of dialogue and its multiple functions within Shakespearean drama.

NOTES

1 M.M. Bakhtin, *The Dialogic Imagination: Four Essays by M.M. Bakhtin*, ed. Michael Holquist, trans. Caryl Emerson and Michael Holquist (Austin: University of Texas Press, 1981), 280.

2 For a basic introduction, see Malcolm Coulthard, *An Introduction to Discourse Analysis* (London and New York: Longman, 1985, 2nd edition).

3 *Politeness: Some Universals in Language Usage* (1978) (Cambridge: Cambridge University Press, 1987).

FURTHER READING

Elam, Keir, *Shakespeare's Universe of Discourse: Language-Games in the Comedies* (Cambridge: Cambridge University Press, 1984)

Elam makes use of modern theories taken from linguistics and semiotics alongside Renaissance approaches to language in an analysis of the dialogue of Shakespearean comedy (with particular attention to *Love's Labour's Lost*). He demonstrates that the apparently highly stylized exchanges between characters on Shakespeare's stage are to a large extent governed by the same rules and conventions as everyday conversation.

Herman, Vimala, *Dramatic Discourse: Dialogue as Interaction in Plays* (London and New York: Routledge, 1995)

Herman offers a comprehensive review of a variety of approaches developed in recent years to the study of conversation, including ethnography, which attends to the overall situation of communication;

conversation analysis, which attends to turn-taking and sequencing; linguistic pragmatics, which attends to speech acts, logical progressions and politeness; and gender studies, which examines sex-differentiated models of speech. The book suggests applications of each approach to the analysis of dramatic dialogue, with illustrations drawn both from Shakespeare and from such modern dramatists as Osborne, Pinter, Chekhov and Beckett. It also articulates some important differences between conversation and dialogue.

Kennedy, Andrew K., *Dramatic Dialogue: The Duologue of Personal Encounter* (Cambridge: Cambridge University Press, 1983)

This book focuses on the interpersonal features of dramatic duologue (encounters with only two persons), offering a 'strong' concept of dialogue as transformative to character, effecting an exchange of values and 'worlds'. Kennedy argues usefully that dramatic dialogue differs from conversation in (1) developing a 'cumulative dialogue' within the totality of the play, (2) including 'counter-speech', or the counterpointing of verbal styles, and (3) providing acting and reading signals. He introduces such paired terms as balance and domination, modes and moods, sympathy and alienation, and sincerity and dissembling for the analysis of dialogue. The book draws its examples from Greek tragedy, Shakespeare, Restoration comedy and modern drama.

Magnusson, Lynne, *Shakespeare and Social Dialogue: Dramatic Language and Elizabethan Letters* (Cambridge: Cambridge University Press, 1999)

This book opens up an interactive approach to Shakespeare's language and the rhetoric of Elizabethan letters. Moving beyond claims about the language of individual Shakespearean characters, Magnusson develops a rhetoric of social exchange to analyse dialogue, conversation, sonnets and letters as the verbal negotiation of historically specific social relationships. The book relates concepts from discourse analysis and linguistic pragmatics, especially 'politeness theory', to key ideas in epistolary handbooks of the period, including those by Erasmus and Angel Day. Arguing that Shakespeare's language is rooted in the everyday language of Elizabethan culture, it creates a way of reading both literary texts and historical documents which bridges the gap between new historicism and linguistic criticism.

10

CHARACTERS IN ORDER OF APPEARANCE

Pamela Mason

In Shakespeare's theatre members of an audience primarily fulfilled their titular function. They went to hear a play. Nowadays we may give undue importance to scenic splendour and our picture-frame stages may make us remote from characters and situation especially in the opening moments of a play. This is when Shakespeare establishes a contract between his actors and an audience. Though the nature of that contract will vary as each play sets out its own terms and conditions, there is inevitably an emphasis upon the immediacy of the experience. A thrust stage works particularly powerfully to create the moment-by-moment nature of performance. Characters establish relationships not only with each other but with the theatre audience through what they say, what they don't say and how they do or do not say it. Shakespeare demands that his audience pay careful attention to subtle differences in register and tones of discourse. Verse may be used to reveal tensions within a character or between those speaking. Alternatively, the greater informality of prose can create the impression of a more relaxed mood within which the conflicts may only gradually emerge.

Once upon a time theatre programmes would generally seek to help an audience by listing 'characters in order of appearance'. The programmes which applied that principle to Shakespeare produced some very odd results, for the order in which characters appear often defies any notion of rank or precedence. More significantly, the opening moments of

Shakespeare's plays establish a method and lay out ground rules. More often than not the playwright chooses to disconcert or unsettle his audience in the opening moments.

In *King Lear* we have to wait for our central protagonist to appear. However, we meet first a man who has much in common with him, and the play begins with an all too-human piece of crass insensitivity. After some brief reflection upon matters of state, Gloucester, anxious to prove his credentials as a man of the world, crudely alludes to the bastardy of his younger son:

> there was good sport at his making ...

> (1.1.21–2)

His tone expresses a would-be philosophic shrug of the shoulders, and Kent's restraint, even embarrassment, could well be prompted by Edmund's presence. One of the first decisions a director of *King Lear* has to make is whether Edmund should stand apart, whether he should hear, not hear or not appear to hear his father mocking his unmarried mother:

> whereupon she grew round-wombed, and had, indeed, sir, a son for her cradle, ere she had a husband for her bed. Do you smell a fault?

> (13–15)

Kent's reply is commendably diplomatic. He had taken the initiative to include Edmund in the conversation:

> Is not this your son, my lord?

> (7)

and now he says what he can to spare the young man's feelings. In a few moments he will go further than he need to show kindness and consideration:

> I must love you, and sue to know you better.

> (29)

By refusing to join in Gloucester's ribaldry, Kent's character and moral stance are established. His sensitivity to what Edmund must be feeling prepares us for his readiness to support Cordelia, though his diplomacy here is in sharp contrast to his outspokenness later. Perhaps the textual evidence would seem to suggest that Edmund should overhear what Gloucester says. This can be important in establishing Edmund's motivation. Although Gloucester may have 'so often blushed to acknowledge him' that now he is 'brazed to't' (9–10), there is no reason to suppose Edmund equally inured.

But the opening moments of *King Lear* provide an audience with additional evidence of an old man's insensitive bungling. Gloucester is not the only character for whom such an accusation is apt. The first few lines of the play prompt an audience to wonder about the political wisdom of a king with favourites. Decisions about the division of the kingdom have been taken. Two shares are precisely equal and Gloucester, Kent, Albany and Cornwall are all well aware of the precise arrangements Lear has made. The King will restate that 'we have divided ... our kingdom' (36–7) before he proposes to reward his daughters for their expressions of affection. The scene conceived by Lear is a public charade and the last few lines of Lear's opening speech are nonsensical:

> Tell me, my daughters ...
> Which of you shall we say doth love us most,
> That we our largest bounty may extend
> Where nature doth with merit challenge.

(48, 51–4)

The decision has already been taken and Goneril will be given her share before the others have their turn to speak. It is an old man's whim, a self-indulgent absurdity that may be excused privately. However, in the full panoply of the court and in the presence of two husbands it is impossible to take the words of Goneril and Regan at face value.

Kent provides a reassuring presence throughout the play's opening moments. We respect his sensitivity, and his response to Edmund has already guided an audience to an appropriate judgement of Gloucester's adultery and subsequent boasting. In a very short time Kent will define Lear's actions as 'hideous rashness' (152) and he will seek to provoke Lear to see more clearly:

What wouldst thou do, old man?

(147)

At the beginning of *King Lear* we are introduced to two plots headed by fathers who are inept in their relationships with their children. Both men are heading towards chaos and confusion. We rely upon Kent as a still point in this madly spinning world.

Othello begins with two characters on stage. But there is no equivalent figure to Kent here. The play begins with an exchange between two characters which prompts us to make the same mistaken assessment of Iago that Othello, Desdemona, Cassio and everyone else in the play, including Iago's wife Emilia, make. This is where our sophisticated knowledge, the false idea that you should read a play before you see it, can get in the way. The vehemence of Iago's ''Sblood' (1.1.4) is in exasperated response to the mealy mouthed 'Tush' (1) of a man who evidently has more money than sense. When we contrast the open invitation to judgement of 'Despise me / If I do not' (6-7) with the playground whinging of 'Thou told'st me …' (5) we are far more likely to align ourselves with Iago than with Roderigo. We are not given time to wonder who Iago's referees are, but the pressure of performance prompts us to accept at face value that he has been refused promotion by a man who 'loving his own pride and purposes' (11) ignored the endorsement of 'three great ones of the city' (7). The word Iago uses to describe his general's action is 'evades' (12) and we may be struck by the contrast between the plain-speaking

Iago and the evasive, possibly cowardly superior officer who
uses bombastic language 'horribly stuffed with epithets of war'
(13). By his own clipped utterance Iago seems to be offering us
a factual report, yet in fact he is dramatizing the event. After a
melodramatic pause signalled by an incomplete line of verse:

And in conclusion

(14)

Iago conveys his sense of rejection with 'Nonsuits my
mediators' (15), words which signal a sense of legalistic,
summary dismissal. He then quotes the man's own words:

'Certes,' says he,
'I have already chose my officer.'

(15–16).

There is a remarkable sense of this other character being
animated for us here. Othello's first words in the play are
spoken by Iago and effectively distance us from the man whose
play we have come to hear. We are manipulated by Iago to
regard Michael Cassio and the man who appointed him with
some scepticism. At this moment our sympathies are most
likely to be with the experienced soldier who has demon-
strated his loyalty and commitment but who has been passed
over for promotion. The job has been given to someone with
the paper qualifications, and the way in which Iago seems to
shrug it off (''tis the curse of service', 34) can only earn him
credit, particularly contrasted as it is with Roderigo's absurd
emotionalism.

Iago's invitation to 'be judge yourself' (37) includes the
audience, and in this opening sequence he draws by far the
greater share of our admiration and respect. He seems strong,
sensible and down to earth, whereas Roderigo seems merely
weak and foolish. The title of the play signalled an intensely
personal focus, prompting us to identify the unnamed 'he'.
Although elsewhere Shakespeare may guide us away from

focusing upon individuals, character, motive and action dominate here. We will be forced to reassess our opinion of major players as events unfold, but quite crucially we will sympathize with the way Othello is duped by Iago because we have also been deceived.

The Winter's Tale offers in its title a likelihood of suffering and a promise of regeneration. The suffering will be intensely felt and is essentially a shared experience, but we are secure in our knowledge that it will not be long before daffodils begin to peer. The title also explicitly guides us to the centrality in this play of the notion of a story. We are well aware that the appeal of such stories, of all such fairy tales, comes not from any novelty but indeed from the familiarity with which we hear them.

Once again we begin with two characters on stage. Only one of them is named and he is the one who will, like Kent in *King Lear,* provide us with a golden mean or standard by which we can judge the behaviour of others later in the play. However, neither character nor individuality is immediately important. The fact that Archidamus is only named in the speech prefixes merely serves to give a private satisfaction to the actor. As a theatre audience we simply see him as an alien figure. Camillo is introduced by name, which may make us marginally more likely to identify with him. Nevertheless, hearing and absorbing the ebb and flow of the prose rhythms in this first scene will more probably prompt us to interpret it not as naturalistic conversation but as a duet for two voices.

The opening lines are formal and measured and encapsulate the pattern of the play's narrative. There is 'great difference' between Bohemia and Sicilia (3–4), and our first introduction to Leontes and Polixenes is in terms of their roles as Kings. There is a sense not only of narrative pattern but also of cyclic change, since Camillo is anticipating a return visit 'this coming summer' (5).

Emotional intensity goes beyond verbal expression. In striving for a definition of the hospitality of Sicilia,

Archidamus finds it 'so rare', so far beyond the ordinary and everyday that he can only admit a human inadequacy:

> I know not what to say
>
> (13)

In Bohemia they would have to resort to dulling with 'sleepy drinks' the senses of any visitor (13–14), so creating a suspension of disbelief or a trance-like state which would allow no praise but permit no blame.

The mutual love between Leontes and Polixenes is established in this first scene initially through natural imagery. Their affection was 'rooted' and consequently enforced separation merely caused it to 'branch' (23–4), so that they 'seemed to be together, though absent' (29). The moment expands beyond the confines of a theatre building. They 'shook hands, as over a vast' and 'embraced, as it were, from the ends of opposed winds' (30–1). These images are of potential power and yet there is also a significant element of precipitous danger. Mamillius is the focus of hope and optimism for the future, 'a gentleman of the greatest promise' (35–6). He provides 'unspeakable' comfort to the court (34), a worth that goes beyond words. He embodies the regenerative force of the young for he 'physics the subject' and 'makes old hearts fresh' (39–40).

The ingredients of the story are assembled. We have been alerted to the centrality of the natural cycle and discouraged from investigating character or motivation. An audience has been directed to listen to the story and focus upon the pattern of events rather than worry about matters of motivation and psychology. It is insistently and emphatically 'like an old tale still' (5.2.62). Polixenes' later attempt to explore Leontes' motive and reason for action will be stifled by Camillo's guidance:

> 'tis safer to
> Avoid what's grown than question how 'tis born.
>
> (1.2.432–3)

Archidamus has something in common with Philo and Demetrius, who open *Antony and Cleopatra.* Any list of characters in order of appearance would give them a prominence which would be very misleading. Essentially they too merely are voices. The grandeur of their names again serves only for the actors' private satisfaction. To the audience they remain anonymous, but that is not to say that they are unimportant in terms of their theatrical function. We are likely to approach *Antony and Cleopatra* with certain expectations, but any preconceptions we may have had about characters and events are immediately challenged by the forceful 'Nay' reinforced by 'but' (1.1.1). We are being given a contrary point of view. It is a masculine, military and essentially Roman perspective which is angered and disturbed by the uncharacteristic behaviour of 'our general'. The possessive makes the partisan nature of the criticism explicit.

What an audience receives from the anonymous soldier is a series of descriptions which contrast the past with the present. Military precision and order was maintained by Antony's 'goodly eyes' which 'glowed like plated Mars' (2, 4). He is now deviating from the clarity and directness of purpose expected of a Roman officer, for his eyes 'now bend, now turn' (4). From the speaker's perspective it can only be a superficial attraction or 'view' which has distracted Antony. The play's first mention of Cleopatra is as 'a tawny front' (6), where the military pun does not hide the contempt for what is perceived as superficial. There is also perhaps an unpleasant, racial slur. As Antony's eyes have been distracted, so has his heart. The man who was wont to 'burst / The buckles on his breast' in great fights (7–8) is now reduced to servicing the physical requirements as 'the bellows and the fan' of this 'gipsy' (9–10). The sense of extreme polarization is apparent in 'reneges all temper' (8). There is no middle way. Not only does the imagery imply that any emotion is transient, it also firmly counters any assumptions an audience may have about the world's greatest love story. What is described to us is labelled 'lust' (10).

As Antony and Cleopatra and their attendants enter, the Roman soldier directs his stage and theatre audience to 'Look where they come', to 'Take but good note' and to 'Behold and see' (10–11, 13). The series of imperatives will guide his stage companion to share his certainty of judgement, but an audience might not take so kindly to such repeated instruction. It is doubtful whether in the theatre any more than anywhere else we like being told what to think. Shakespeare's craft encourages members of an audience to think for themselves, to judge characters and to assess the situation. We are being subtly dissuaded from simply indulging in an emotional response. Our first view of the central characters is framed, therefore, by a Roman, military perspective and throughout Antony and Cleopatra's opening dialogue we will be aware of the onstage audience provided not only by Philo and Demetrius but also by the Egyptian attendants. It is an unremittingly public scene, and that awareness complicates our attitude towards the words and actions of the central characters.

Cleopatra's opening line immediately takes us to the heart of the matter:

If it be love indeed, tell me how much.

(14)

In questioning the truth of Antony's love for her, she sounds the keynote of debate in the play. The line can be taunting, teasing, flirtatious, beguiling, cheeky or wayward, but essentially it serves to articulate Cleopatra's uncertainty and her need for reassurance. Later, when questioning Antony's reaction to Fulvia's death, Cleopatra returns again to her anxiety:

Now I see, I see,
In Fulvia's death how mine received shall be.

(1.3.65–6)

Her words anticipate how she will feign death to test Antony's reaction and see 'If it be love indeed'.

Antony's opening words are at once expansive and evasive:

> There's beggary in the love that can be reckoned
>
> (1.1.15)

but the lovers' patterned, rhetorical exchange is curtailed by the announcement of news from Rome. Antony's verbal reaction is a minimal 'Grates me! The sum' (19), but whether he actually finds it so easy to dismiss the news is arguable. His physical performance may well signal his inner tensions, subject as he is to the pull of opposing forces. Cleopatra may appear to be perverse in her insistence that he should hear the messengers, but she displays simultaneously her political astuteness and her personal insecurity. She taunts Antony about his subservience to Rome, establishing an opposition in terms of virility between him and Caesar. Even in her mocking impersonation of Caesar's likely message is the play's concern with balance and antithesis evident:

> 'Do this, or this;
> Take in that kingdom, and enfranchise that.
> Perform't, or else we damn thee.'
>
> (23–5)

She is the other woman in the eternal triangle, true to type in being obsessed about her lover's relationship with his wife, but she can also be regally imperious as with 'As I am Egypt's Queen' (30). She diminishes Antony to the status of Caesar's lackey and henpecked husband to 'shrill-tongued' Fulvia (33).

Cleopatra succeeds in provoking Antony into making a public reaffirmation of his commitment. The solidity of Rome and all it stands for can dissolve, for 'Here is my space' (35). Antony dedicates himself to the immediacy and importance of their passion by asserting that 'The nobleness of life / Is to do thus' (37–8). He also sets up what will prove to be a crucial

antithesis between the ethereal relationship to which they aspire and the dungy earthbound reality of mundane existence. But by responding with 'Excellent falsehood' (41) Cleopatra contributes to the litany of contradictions within this first scene. She is acutely aware of her onstage audience and she plays to them:

Why did he marry Fulvia and not love her?

(42)

Antony sweeps aside her riddling questioning as 'conference harsh' (46). For 'the love of Love' (45) he urges the abandonment of all restraint in favour of 'sport' or hedonistic indulgence. His urgency excludes the outside world:

There's not a minute of our lives should stretch
Without some pleasure now.

(47–8)

Just as we may have hesitated to endorse the soldiers' faith in the rigid, disciplined codes of Roman responsibility, we may now be reluctant to embrace an attitude at the opposite extreme that is so intemperately expressed.

Antony commits himself to Cleopatra as 'no messenger but thine' (53), and he expresses a yearning for an intimacy away from the pressure of the public, political worlds they both inhabit. In his desire for the two of them to 'wander through the streets' (54) Antony expresses precisely that which the play will deny them. They cannot escape the 'world's great snare' (4.8.18), and the fiercely public nature of this first scene establishes that fact. They can only exit from the stage, brushing aside those who seek to intervene with 'Speak not to us' (1.1.56). Shakespeare makes it very clear that there is no privacy for them, no space in which they can be alone in 'this vile world' (5.2.313).

As Antony and Cleopatra leave the stage towards the end of the first scene, an audience's reflection upon what has been witnessed is complicated by the discussion between the two Roman soldiers. The result of the earlier injunction to look, observe carefully and judge is that Demetrius confirms his solidarity with the Roman perspective. That is hardly surprising, but there is no danger of mistaking the soldier's attitude for objectivity. The awkwardness of his syntax indicates how his allegiance to Rome takes priority:

Is Caesar with Antonius prized so slight?

(1.1.57)

Any sympathetic understanding of Antony's predicament and of his inner debate in which he struggles to reconcile private concerns with public responsibilities can only originate from the audience. Both observer-soldiers are confident that what they have seen 'approves the common liar' (61) – in itself an intriguing paradox – in relation to how Antony's actions are reported in Rome. In this first scene Shakespeare sets up the matter of the play with its intertwining of personal and political debate. However, he is also establishing very firmly a method of enquiry which will disconcert our preconceptions and repeatedly challenge an audience's enthusiasm for escapist experience. The play's technique has events and meetings framed by commentary. Character and actions are continually subjected to analysis and judgement. The play abounds in 'report' which provides a basis for analysis, and Antony is well aware of this and will plead with Octavia to 'read not my blemishes in the world's report' (2.3.5). The anonymous soldiers in the first scene function as a framing device which essentially works to complicate our response.

There is a received and facile assumption that the first few lines of a play are there for bottom-shuffling or shoulder-jostling as an audience, dragged from bar or tavern by bell or trumpet, settles to watch a play. That simply does not match the sense of expectation and excitement that is so characteristic of theatrical experience throughout the ages. We need to be wary of somewhat quaint notions of a chattering, walnut-cracking, orange-sucking Elizabethan audience. People went to 'hear' a play. In the Prologue to *Romeo and Juliet* an audience is urged to pay attention with 'patient ears' (13), and the opening Chorus of *Henry V* defines our participatory role as 'Gently to hear, kindly to judge our play' (34). Again and again Shakespeare's plays establish at the outset that they require an alert, attentive audience.

FURTHER READING

Barton, John, *Playing Shakespeare* (London: Methuen, 1984)

> Deriving from a remarkable series of televised workshops Barton's book offers analysis of Shakespeare's language from the firmly pragmatic perspective of how an actor seeks to *play* the text. Discussions between leading members of the Royal Shakespeare Company (RSC) are the basis for the first half of the book, which explores how Shakespeare's text works by examining the use of verse and prose, set speeches and soliloquies, language and character. The second half concentrates on more subjective areas such as irony and ambiguity, passion and coolness. Barton, with the RSC since its beginning, is central to the way we think of speaking Shakespeare today.

Brown, John Russell, *William Shakespeare: Writing for Performance* (Basingstoke: Macmillan, 1996)

> Brown engages with Shakespeare's plays as the raw material for performance rather than as texts to be confined to the study. The importance of the historical context in which Shakespeare worked is acknowledged, but the dramatist's method is also examined within the context of how modern dramatists approach the business of crafting a play. Analysis consistently seeks to promote the need to study the plays with a heightened theatrical consciousness.

Parsons, Keith and Pamela Mason (eds), *Shakespeare in Performance* (London: Salamander, 1995)

> The sixteen contributors share a commitment to the continuing life of Shakespeare's plays. After introductory chapters establishing the

context in which Shakespeare worked and outlining how theatrical tastes have changed, individual essays 'say what the plays treats on' with abundant reference to recent productions. The book is recommended particularly for its lavish use of illustrations, which can encourage readers to engage with the range of interpretative possibilities that have been explored in performance.

11

SHAKESPEARE'S LANGUAGE
IN THE THEATRE

Peter Lichtenfels

Actors and directors approach a play and use its language in similar but significantly different ways than readers do, because their needs are different. But anyone who has ever been in a play or gone to see a play will know how much the theatre can tell us about dramatic language. This chapter will explore some of the basic strategies that theatre people bring to Shakespeare's dramatic writing, and will also look at what those plays give us when we think of them from the point of view of producing them on the stage. We'll start with some of the practicalities of props and staging, and then move on to look in detail at a few ways that actors can approach the language: by 'choosing' silence or choosing words, and by exploring words' physicality in body, rhythm and sound.

DIALOGUE, PROPS AND STAGE EFFECTS: WHAT DO THEY TELL US ABOUT ACTION/ACTING?

It is often said that Shakespeare is his own best director because he tells the actor or reader what he wants them to do within the text. The first task of the actor is to carry out a close reading of the text, to find out what the text literally says as opposed to how or why it says it. Let's look at a short passage from *Richard III*, 1.2, and see what acting instructions Shakespeare's language gives us within the dialogue:

RICHARD

    Stay, you that bear the corse, and set it down.

ANNE

    What black magician conjures up this fiend

    To stop devoted charitable deeds?

RICHARD

    Villains! set down the corse or by Saint Paul

    I'll make a corse of him that disobeys!

HALBERDIER

    My lord, stand back and let the coffin pass.

RICHARD

    Unmanner'd dog, stand thou when I command!

    Advance thy halberd higher than my breast,

    Or by Saint Paul I'll strike thee to my foot,

    And spurn upon thee, beggar, for thy boldness.

ANNE

    What, do you tremble? Are you all afraid?

(33–43)

In the first line Richard gives an instruction to the pallbearers. His first word is 'Stay'; the implication must be that they are moving. He tells us that he is speaking to the pallbearers, 'you that bear the corse'. He orders them to 'set' the body 'down', therefore the pallbearers must be carrying the corpse. Richard ignores Anne's intervention because his next line still focuses on the pallbearers. He doesn't repeat the word 'stay' but does repeat 'set down'. This suggests that the pallbearers have stopped moving, though they are still carrying the body. Why have they stopped? The halberdier's line asks Richard to 'stand back and let the coffin pass' so he must be blocking the procession's path. We learn from Richard's next speech that the halberdier is standing near him and pointing his weapon below his chest: 'stand thou when I command!', and 'Advance thy halberd higher than my breast'. Anne's second speech tells us that the pallbearers and the halberdier are frightened of Richard: 'do you tremble? Are you all afraid?'

An actor would go through the whole play in this way, understanding the actions being asked for from word to phrase to line. We should not confuse this with interpretation, which is very important, but comes later in the process. Here's an example from our passage of what I mean by interpretation. We already know that the dialogue asks Richard to have blocked the procession's path by the time the halberdier speaks. The actor still needs to decide or interpret when Richard does this: is it during his first speech, or in Anne's lines, or at some point in his second speech? Looking at the text literally anchors the language in specifics for the actor and it can do the same for the reader.

Actors look for other clues in the language – stage effects, the use of props – to further their understanding of the action or acting. An example is Shakespeare's use of light – are we in day or night – which gives context to a scene, and necessitates the use of stage effects and props. I am going to use two examples from *Romeo and Juliet* to explore what I mean. During the following discussion it is worth remembering that the original performances took place in natural light, and that a character seeing or not seeing each other would have been played as a convention.

The first part of 5.3 is set in front of Juliet's tomb, in a darkened graveyard. When the scene begins, Paris is looking for Juliet's tomb. He says to his page 'Give me thy torch, boy. Hence and stand aloof. / Yet put it out, for I would not be seen' (1–2). He is interrupted in his grieving by Romeo's entrance, and hides himself. Romeo enters searching for Juliet's tomb and asks his manservant to give him his torch: 'Give me the light' (25). After a few lines the manservant leaves and Romeo is left alone. He begins to pry open the tomb. Paris says to himself 'This is that banish'd haughty Montague' (49). He is intent on arresting Romeo and calls out 'Stop thy unhallow'd toil, vile Montague' (54). In Romeo's next two speeches he addresses Paris as 'good … youth', 'youth', 'boy' – but not by his name. They fight and Paris dies. It is then that Romeo says, 'Let me peruse this face. / Mercutio's kinsman, noble County Paris!' (74–5). The question for the actor becomes, how does Paris know it is Romeo, whereas Romeo only recognizes Paris after he has killed him? The answer is that Romeo's torch is still burning, serving as his working light by which to open the tomb. Therefore Paris is looking from darkness into light and recognizes Romeo; whereas Romeo looks into the darkness and cannot recognize him, since Paris has put out his light. The graveyard is so dark that even while they fight Romeo does not know who he is. This information has a direct bearing on the way the actors will play their parts: Paris can see Romeo, but Romeo can't see Paris. Even the difference in the way the actors will move is the difference in confidence with which we move in a well-lit space and a dark space.

Light plays just as central a role in our second example. In the earlier 'balcony scene' (2.2) we are in night time. Romeo clearly sees Juliet since he is looking towards the lit window or balcony where Juliet is standing, 'It is my lady, O it is my love!' (10). However Juliet talks into the darkness to a figure she can't see: 'What man art thou that thus bescreen'd in night / So stumblest on my counsel?' (52–3). She is afraid and this gives the actor playing Juliet clues: her 'ears' will have to serve as her eyes, 'My ears have yet not drunk in a hundred words / Of thy tongue's uttering, yet I know the sound' (58–9). The problems at the beginning of this scene are the same as those faced by actors in the first example. But in this scene the light changes several times as daylight approaches, and so the actors have to be continually aware and ask how this changes the relationship.

MAKING THE TEXT YOUR OWN

It can be relatively easy for readers to understand the importance of looking at the text for information about action or props or stage effects. What is perhaps less familiar is understanding that when characters are in a scene or actors are on-stage, it is because they wish to change something. They change things through actions/acting, including words and silences. Characters always use their most effective strategy for change, and therefore actors always have to take active responsibility for the words and silences within the text to realise or 'play' the characters' actions. In other words, Shakespeare writes the words and silences but an actor has to choose them.

Choosing silence

Let's look at the citizens in *Richard III*. We know they are vocal and have strong opinions because we hear them in 2.3. At the beginning of 3.7 there is a scene between Richard and Buckingham, his right-hand man. Richard has asked Buckingham to find out whether the citizens will agree to his becoming king. Buckingham replies that they were 'mum' (3), 'spake not a word' (24), were 'dumb statues or breathing stones' (25). The two men raise the stakes and try to manipulate the crowd of citizens by stage-managing a rally at Baynard's Castle: Richard will play a contemplative holy man unwilling to become king, Buckingham and the Lord Mayor of London will press him to accept, and the citizens, in the middle, will be coerced. The citizens enter and the scene then goes through a series of persuasive ploys, yet at the end of each ploy the citizens say nothing – they choose to remain silent. The scene becomes ever more desperate for Richard, so his front men begin to put words in the mouths of the citizens until the fiction that they wish him to become king is agreed. The citizens continue to say nothing and their silence is deafening. They are not strong enough to take on Richard militarily, and after 184 lines of being on stage they simply and finally say 'Amen'. The scene is a contest of wills where

Richard and his acolytes use words, and the citizens use silence to get what they want. Choosing silence makes it into a hollow victory for Richard.

Silence is also the strategy of important yet elusive characters such as Jessica in *The Merchant of Venice* who says very little yet is on stage for a substantial part of the play. In 2.5 Shylock comes on with Launcelot, his former servant who now works for Bassanio. Shylock calls out for Jessica three times to no effect, yet Launcelot shouts once and she enters. We already know she is planning to run away with Lorenzo, and that Launcelot is their go-between. Does she not answer Shylock as an act of resistance, but answer Launcelot because she is eager for news? Once on-stage, except for a final couplet when she is alone, Jessica speaks only two lines. Why? Shylock is invited out to supper by Bassanio, and for the next 32 lines he hovers between going and staying, finally deciding that he will go. During these speeches Jessica remains quiet for a number of reasons: she needs to make contact with Launcelot and hear whether Lorenzo will run away with her this evening, but it must be unspoken since they are in Shylock's presence. She also needs to listen to Shylock's plans because it will affect the ease with which she can run away. Also if she remains silent then she remains in the guise of the dutiful daughter, and will not raise any suspicions in her father. Launcelot manages to give her the good news in a roundabout manner and leaves. Jessica then replies to Shylock's suspicious question in the briefest way possible, and again falls silent until he leaves the stage. Does the nature of her silence change? Is she silent because she needs all her energy not to betray the joy inside her? Is Jessica's silence also shame, because this is the last time she sees her father to whom she doesn't say goodbye? She does all this while continuing her deception. In this short scene we have found five good reasons why it is to Jessica's advantage to speak only two lines and remain silent for the rest. Jessica is central to a number of scenes in the play yet for the most part says little. In all of these she does so for strong reasons the actor has to choose how to play.

Choosing words

Actors and readers have to try to understand why characters choose silence, and they also have to understand why characters choose words. When we looked at silence we thought about issues that actors would be concerned with, that could also help readers. If we now turn to 'choosing words', let's also look at approaches actors can take to open out readings. In day-to-day life we often don't think about the individual words we use, but actors have to learn to actively choose the precise words of their dialogue. Among the many areas that have been developed by actors when they deal with the text are: finding the rhythm of the speech in the action, or the action in the words; inhabiting the language; and body memory.

Choosing the words through rhythm

Let's take another look at *Romeo and Juliet* 5.3, a scene we have already examined for darkness and light. Romeo sends his servant Balthazar away in order to be alone to open Juliet's tomb. From line 45 to 80, during which Paris enters, recognizes Romeo, challenges him, fights him and is killed by him, Romeo also opens the tomb. An actor or reader might conjecture that this action begins with line 45, because Romeo addresses the tomb directly:

> Thou destestable maw, thou womb of death
> Gorg'd with the dearest morsel of the earth,
> Thus I enforce thy rotten jaws to open
> And in despite I'll cram thee with more food.

(45–8)

Try reading these lines aloud to yourself. We know that the tomb is still closed at line 73, because Paris' dying words ask Romeo to open it. And Romeo has opened it by line 81, because he takes up Paris' body to lay it inside. Once the actor has mapped out this sequence, he has to work out how to open the tomb: is it a difficult job, taking all the lines available? Does he work at it intermittently? Will it open quickly? The actor has to work with a mattock or hammer, and a crow or wrenching iron, so he needs to learn how to use these tools to help him open the door. We know it will take effort to open. The action of using the mattock and wrenching iron will inform the rhythm of the verse.

If the actor does the actions of hammering, levering and prying open the tomb, and the actor invests the energy that it takes in real life, then it begins to make sense how and why he says the above lines. Try saying the lines while using the effort to prise open a tomb door. They are an expression of the physical effort. For example, if we take our four lines, the actor can bring together the actions of hitting the iron with the mattock or of levering the door, with explosive stress on the words 'maw', 'death', 'Gorg'd', 'morsel', 'earth', and so on. The stressed words could be more random than this, but the coincidence of an important word with the physical action is more helpful to the action while allowing the audience to hear the important words or 'keywords' in order to follow the story. Rather than saying the line to inform the physical effort, here the physical effort releases the line.

There are many work scenes in Shakespeare's plays. Another example you might like to look at is in *Hamlet* 5.1, where the rhythm of the language of the gravediggers (clowns[1]) is informed by the digging of Ophelia's grave. The opening dialogue is a combination of digging ('make her grave straight', 3–4), and telling stories to each other to pass time and help with the task; debating whether Ophelia should be given a Christian burial if she committed suicide; and telling jokes and singing songs. Like all workmen who do hard labour, the actors playing the parts need to establish a rhythm of activity and rest. Let's go to the point when Hamlet speaks to one of the gravediggers between lines 117 and 128:

HAMLET   Whose grave's this, sirrah?
GRAVEDIGGER   Mine, sir.
  [*Sings.*] O a pit of clay for to be made –
HAMLET   I think it be thine indeed, for thou liest in't.
GRAVEDIGGER   You lie out on't, sir, and therefore 'tis not
  yours. For my part, I do not lie in't, yet it is mine.
HAMLET   Thou dost lie in't, to be in't and say 'tis thine. 'Tis
  for the dead, not for the quick: therefore thou liest.
GRAVEDIGGER   'Tis a quick lie, sir, 'twill away again from me
  to you.

Find a classmate or friend and read the lines out loud, you taking the role of the gravedigger. Read it through standing in the grave, yet do nothing but answer Hamlet. Then begin to dig – put yourself through the same effort as if you were an actual digger; use the energy it takes to push the spade into the earth, the concentration of strength to lift the earth out, the best way to throw it away so that there is strength for the whole task; use your body in such a way as not to get backache, etc. – and say the lines once more. Now when you go through it, remember to keep digging while Hamlet says his lines. You will quickly understand how Shakespeare's language helps you. Notice that the gravedigger uses short phrases of varying lengths which helps inform the rhythm of his digging. All his words are one syllable long, except for three which are two syllables – clearly he needs his breath for the primary task of completing the grave. Through the action of digging, the language and the scene begin to come alive.

Choosing the words through body and sound

The way we speak in our daily lives is different from the density, weight, colour or scale needed to make Shakespeare's language come alive. Actors train so they can fill the space demanded by the language. Remember that Shakespeare wrote for an audience of two thousand; the words were spoken in the open air, and in a noisy environment. The text uses rhetorical skills and conventions to build the scale of the language which Shakespeare's audience would have recognized, the way we recognize conventions in film today.

However well actors play convention to build the scale needed, they also have to take responsibility for the text, choose the words, play 'intention' (a theatre term which asks the actor to play a character's task on-stage, e.g. stop a funeral procession, open a tomb, dig a grave), and become a character. It is a matter of finding the balance between the way the body moves and breathes, and how that affects speech. The actor can do so through rhythm, as we explored above, but can also do so through body and sound. For example Romeo: when he first enters in 1.1 he presents the physical characteristics of the lover from *commedia dell'arte*, a popular mode of sixteenth-century Italian theatre,[2] and he speaks through Petrarchan love clichés. Petrarch wrote love sonnets that were already considered old fashioned in Shakespeare's day. So the actor's work is to get the audience to understand that an artificial and possibly outdated convention is operating, to engage the audience in the character inhabiting that convention and to give the character intention.

The actor could draw on *commedia* where lovers' characteristics are totally self-centred. His physical self-presentation is self-consciously on display. Hence when he moves across the stage he does not turn sideways to face the direction he is going in, but keeps his torso full-frontal, usually leading with his chest, often with the chin tilted partly upward, calling attention to the face and semi-profile. The lover walks as if on a cat-walk, displaying his beauty and his obsession with 'love'. Although there is a convention operating, the character is part of it because he is afraid of not being noticed, so the actor has to find elements in the display of the body that can be played to problematise the apparent ease of the cliché.

In *commedia*, lovers are in love with themselves. Romeo's opening dialogue ensures that whatever the topic of conversation, it is always refocused on himself. In the first scene, Romeo notices that there has been a brawl between Montagues and Capulets and says 'Here's much to do with hate', but in the second half of the line immediately turns the attention back on himself: 'but more with love' (175). Once you understand the convention about his entrance, you get a context for playing the scene: not naturalistic or realistic as everyday street life, but on a larger scale as a character totally obsessed with being a lover – his suffering is greater than anyone else's. But an understanding of the convention alone is not enough. To build scale actors need to choose the words and in this example they do so through the physical presentation of the body demanded by convention, but they can also do so through sound.

There are many strategies actors use to create size or scale through sound. One example is breaking down each word into its basic consonant and vowel sounds. Take a few lines from part of a speech and speak them aloud. Then go back and with each word, while you think about how it sounds out loud, say the consonants with the sounds that they have when that word is spoken, leaving a silent space where vowels are. You will quickly feel how much energy and perhaps lightheadedness and certainly how much longer it takes to say the words this way rather than in our everyday speech. And then do the opposite. Think about how the word is sounded and pronounce the vowels in their clusters aloud, leaving a silent space where the consonants are. Keeping the sense of the word alive is more difficult with this second exercise, but it should be easier on the breath. Now go back and read your chosen passage aloud again and note the difference. Many things become apparent: repetition of sounds; favouring of consonantal words; the shifts between consonants and vowels; and the question, where do the sounds come from in the body and what emotional effect might they have on the character? You begin to realize the effort that it takes to say words and how much we often glide over. The work is as physical as opening a tomb door, or digging a grave. In theatre, when actors work like this, it is part of what we call 'owning the language'.

If a character in the text is wrapped up in sounds, they can also have an effect on the way the actor carries the body. An audience can recognize the repeating of sounds on a subliminal if not on a conscious level. For example, in the first scene, Romeo's 'Ay me' (161) is repeated as 'O me' (171), and then he goes into a series of exclamations or **apostrophes**:

> O brawling love, O loving hate,
> O anything of nothing first create!
> O heavy lightness, serious vanity …

(176–8)

Romeo's dialogue, and his name gives a clue to this, is filled with the sound 'o'. It's a difficult sound to make as an actor because it falls flat if not filled with breath and energy, which here could be yearning, or sighing, or pain, or groaning. It's an unformed word. In this scene it becomes a self-conscious display of a lover's suffering. The over-the-top repetitiveness of the sound could tell the audience that this is *commedia*, yet that is not interesting in itself. The actor needs to recognize the scale of the verse and to embrace it. Only if the actor fills the sound with excessive energy will the audience recognize that the character is overplaying his hand. The 'intention' of the actor's character, the lover in love with himself, then becomes ridiculous only to the audience.

The exercises with sound also allow us to find the physical equivalent of rhythm shifts in the verse. For example, let's have the actor work on the line

Maintains such falsehood, then turn tears to fire

(*RJ* 1.2.91)

The first half of the line, 'Maintains such falsehood', has three stresses. There is one main stress within each of the polysyllabic words (*Maintains, falsehood*), and one secondary stress on *such*. By contrast, the second part of the line, 'then turn tears to fire', is made up of five monosyllabic words, three of which (*turn, tears, fire*) carry a main stress, and one (*then*) a secondary stress.

The consonants in the first half of the line are dominated by nasal sounds (for example *m, n*, – that is, sounds where part of the air escapes through the nose as well as the mouth), and fricative sounds (for example *s, ch, f*, – that is, sounds where a small closure in the mouth allows the air to escape noisily and gradually). Notice that the words in this part of the line are linked by their fricative sounds. Thus the end of *Maintains* merges with the start of *such*, and the *ch* of *such* slides into the *f* of *falsehood*. All this gives a slower feel to the first part of the line. By contrast, plosive consonants dominate the latter half of the line (for example the letter *t* – that is, sounds which are more explosive because the air escapes suddenly), and since they begin three separate words, 'turn tears to' (two with main stresses), the rhythm appears to speed up. However artificial the words, with their elaborate antithesis of fire and tears, the sudden shift in pace of the sounds provides a rhythmic clue to Romeo's tension.

Actors can't continuously play the complexity and density that comes from breaking down the words in this way, but it is remarkable how the body remembers the experience. Actors who are familiar with the dialogue to this extent will come to the words they say at every performance with a vast body memory for the sounds which will inform the choices they make about those words. Once more, the actors are not doing something to the word, but the word is releasing energy for them.

The strategies explored in this chapter are all to do with close readings of a particular kind: they search for what the text asks for, rather than how or why it says it. Interpretation comes later. These exercises or strategies locate the words in physical activity for the actors. The words are not just marks on a page to be glided past, but take time, energy and commitment to explore. Readers may well find these strategies strange, but they are faced with a similar challenge when they take up the text and try to understand it. These explorations, used by actors, are doors that can open up to readers different ways of understanding Shakespeare's plays.

NOTES

1 See Harold Jenkins, Arden 2 edition, p. 376.

2 See John Rudlin, *Commedia dell'Arte: An Actor's Handbook* (London: Routledge, 1994), 106–9.

FURTHER READING

Barton, John, *Playing Shakespeare* (London: Methuen, 1984)

The book springs from a 1984 television series for Channel 4, where Barton and well-known actors investigate Shakespeare's text in front of the camera. The first half of the book explores how Shakespeare's text works by examining the use of verse and prose, set speeches and soliloquies, language and character. The second half concentrates on more subjective areas such as irony and ambiguity, passion and coolness.

Barton, with the Royal Shakespeare Company since its beginning, is central to the way we think of speaking Shakespeare today. Get hold of the video, and use the book and the video together. It is very good in letting you into the world of theatre, and how actors access Shakespeare's language.

Berry, Cicely, *The Actor and His Text* (London: Harrap, 1987); later
retitled *The Actor and the Text*

Berry was Head of Voice at the Royal Shakespeare Company for many
years, and, with John Barton, a central influence on the way we think
of speaking Shakespeare today. The book is especially good on text,
ways of infusing life and meaning into words that are first
encountered on the printed page. It is full of useful exercises, and
practical strategies to making the language your own. Berry's book is
widely used within the theatre profession.

Linklater, Kristin, *Freeing Shakespeare's Voice: The Actor's Guide to Talking
the Text* (New York: Theatre Communications Group, 1992)

Linklater is the most celebrated of American voice teachers. The book
begins by accessing language from vowels and consonants, then
building into words, then into phrases. Linklater goes on to look at
form: the verse and prose of Shakespeare's language. The book has
many useful exercises for the reader to access Shakespeare's language;
and is written in a lively and passionate style. Linklater's book is much
used within the theatre profession.

12

LANGUAGE AND THE BODY

Keir Elam

MEAN MEANING[1]

The 'meaning' of the body on stage is one of the most problematic areas of current criticism, partly because so few people have paid attention to it until quite recently. Yet the body has now become a focus for discussions about the continuing power of theatre that try to explore why audiences respond strongly to watching the actual bodies of human beings interacting within a three-dimensional space (conventionally a stage) immediately present to them, rather than on a screen as with television and film. Much of this chapter will try to develop an understanding of how this happens by looking first at the dumb-show in *Hamlet*, which raises many of these questions, and then looking at four 'types' of body that appear simultaneously on the stage: the dramatic, the historical, the discursive and the performative.

At the end of the players' dumb-show in *Hamlet*, Ophelia asks:

OPHELIA What means this, my lord?
HAMLET   Marry, this is miching malicho. It means mischief.

(3.2.138–40)

Ophelia's difficulty in reading the dumb-show is one of the many moments in *Hamlet* in which the problem of the meaning of the body is foregrounded.[2] Her bemused question to Hamlet, in his capacity as 'director' of the play, seems to imply that the actor's body can only 'mean' or signify something to the extent that it can be translated into words – which in the case of the dumb-show are of course lacking. On the other hand, Hamlet's reply is unhelpful: 'miching malicho'[3] is a phrase that is left deliberately untranslated, so any audience or reader will have to work out what it means. In other words they will have to translate it into words, to interpret it. This is clear most notably in modern editions of the play which suggest, for example, that it means 'stealthy iniquity' or 'sneaking wrongdoing' or the like.[4] It is as if Hamlet is saying to Ophelia: find your own meaning; and saying to the audience, in the words of the modern dramatist Samuel Beckett: 'make sense who may'.[5]

Hamlet underlines his point by going on to pun on the verb 'mean', in its two most familiar senses of 'signify' and 'intend' (namely, to intend to do something, as in 'I meant to write to you'). On the one hand, the dumb-show 'means' mischief because it signifies mischief by representing assassination on stage. But on the other hand, and for Hamlet this is the primary meaning, it means mischief because it is intended to bring mischief about. In this latter sense, the players' gestures on stage mean something if they are translated not into words but into action, specifically the killing of King Claudius. Not only does the body 'mean' what is said about it as we verbally interpret or translate it, but above all the body 'means' what the body does.

In practice, Ophelia is less ingenuous than she might appear in expecting the mime-show to deliver a paraphrasable meaning. 'Belike this show', she goes on politely to suggest, 'imports the argument of the play' (3.2.141–2). And in effect she is right: the full version of the inner play, *The Mousetrap*, goes on to add dialogue that tells the story of the dumb-show, making it apparently redundant. Indeed Hamlet himself jumps up from the audience to offer an interpretation designed to remove all danger of ambiguity: 'This play is the image of a murder done in Vienna' (239–4), etc. But although the play is an 'image', or a translation/interpretation, Hamlet's earlier reply to Ophelia, 'miching malicho', which implied that the play was untranslatable into words, is also right. The actors' bodies may convey images of other events when we interpret them, but in both the dumb-show and the spoken version of *The Mousetrap*, they also focus attention on a real body of the actor/player – even if that actor is embodying another character, another 'body'. In this case the player's body means, or stands for, the fictional King's body and not for some interpretative verbal tag.

These two levels on which the actor's body 'means' something, both the direct physical embodiment and the fictional interpretation of a story, are complicated when Hamlet introduces into his interpretation the issue of historical reference: his explanation regarding 'a murder done in Vienna', complete with names ('Gonzago is the Duke's name, his wife Baptista', 241). The fictional King's body, represented by the Player, thus stands in turn for the 'historical' Duke Gonzago's body. The audience, Ophelia included, eventually gets this point. But only two of the spectators are supposed to catch a further level of meaning or reference, which offers another puzzle: namely the allusion to actual persons present in the audience. In one reading of *The Mousetrap*, Gonzago is Hamlet's father and Lucianus is Claudius. In another reading, Gonzago refers to or 'means' Claudius (being threatened by Hamlet), and thus Gonzago's fictional victim 'means' Hamlet's father and the nephew Lucianus 'means' Hamlet himself.

The actors embody not only a fictional King and his court, nor only the historical Duke Gonzago and his nephew Luciano, but also, in terms of the play, the real bodies of King Claudius and Hamlet. The real bodies of the actors gain performative power insofar as they incarnate the bodies of the 'real' people in the world of the play. This is the mischief-making meaning that impinges directly on events in Denmark; this is Hamlet's mousetrap, his allusive mirror up to nature, his 'thing' to catch the conscience of King Claudius. And Claudius, both one of the referents in the play and the main audience for all four meanings, does in the end get the point, although he takes a while to reach it, and then acts or at least reacts, by leaving the room.

The problems with bodies and their significance do not end here for either Hamlet or Ophelia. Her puzzled question regarding the reading of the body becomes for herself and for others a refrain throughout the tragedy. In the same scene she obstinately insists 'Will a tell us what this show meant?' (3.2.145), and again Hamlet replies enigmatically, by punning on 'show' ('Ay, or any show that you will show him', 146) in its theatrical sense and in its sexual sense (as a variant of 'shoe', slang for 'vagina'). The reply echoes the preoccupation with bodily meaning[6] in his earlier question 'Do you think I meant country matters?' (118). Just so, in the previous scene, Ophelia's sexuality had been the ground for more questioning:

HAMLET   Ha, ha! Are you honest? … Are you fair?
OPHELIA   What means your lordship?

(3.1.103–6)

It is again Ophelia's body and its sexuality ('[Hamlet] … but as your daughter may conceive …', 2.2.185) that induces Polonius to a triumphantly mistaken interpretation: 'How say you by that?' (187). Later on, Polonius' own (dead) body becomes the source of further troubles about meaning and significance. Hamlet makes a riddling reference to the worms eating it (4.3.19–28) that provokes the King into the same kind of bemused question asked earlier by Ophelia. In response, he receives yet another enigma when Hamlet plays again on the word *show* and its meaning of 'perform' or 'demonstrate':

CLAUDIUS   What dost thou mean by this?
HAMLET   Nothing but to show you how a king may go a
   progress through the guts of a beggar

(4.3.29–31)

And so it goes on. The semantics, or meaning-structure, of the
body in the play is not so much a mousetrap as a maze.

It is, in any event, precisely this issue of the troubled, but in
all senses, meaningful relations between language and the
body in Shakespeare's plays that is the primary concern of this
chapter. In particular, I wish to address the ways in which the
text can inscribe the body – not only the character's but also
the actor's – as an indispensable part of its meaning-making.

THE (PLAYER) KING'S FOUR BODIES

In another of Hamlet's riddles about the body, during
Rosencrantz and Guildenstern's farcical attempt to interrogate
him on the whereabouts of Polonius' corpse, he toys
sardonically with the medieval legal notion of the 'King's two
bodies'[7] – 'The body is with the King, but the King is not with
the body. The King is a thing – ' (4.2.26–7) – and duly succeeds
in producing further incomprehension ('[Guildenstern] A
thing, my lord?', 28). But in *Hamlet*, and on the stage in
general, the King's body is not one 'thing' or even two, but, as
the discussion that follows will endeavour to show, at least four,
including and extending the levels of bodily meaning that
Hamlet indicates in his reading of *The Mousetrap*.

THE BODY DRAMATIC

The figure of Hamlet's fictional Duke is what we might term
the body dramatic, which is the product of a trained dramatic
actor coming together with the language of the play, the 'part'
written for them that unites the stage with the dramatic world

of Elsinore. The ability of the conventions of dramatic representation to enact imaginary *personae* both impresses and depresses Hamlet in his 'Hecuba' monologue (2.2), in which he reflects on the capacity of the 'player here, / But in a fiction, in a dream of passion' (551–2) to give body to a dramatic figment through his words and his passionate movements ('Tears in his eyes, distraction in his aspect', 555).

The body historical

In Hamlet's exegesis the body dramatic, as we have seen, is distinguished from the body historical, which purportedly alludes to an actual Duke of Vienna. Just so, Hamlet, and Shakespeare's play *Hamlet*, refer back in some degree to the 'historical' Amleth of Saxo Grammaticus's *Historiae Danae*. But the 'historicity' of the body goes beyond such direct allusion in bringing together the historical codes of behaviour and ideology – namely, early modern customs and beliefs – that the fictional character (or body dramatic described above) expresses. The most clearly 'historicized' body in *Hamlet* is that of the ghost. Its very existence speaks of a specific system of religious or superstitious belief, or better – and crucially for Hamlet – conflicting systems of belief that make the 'reading' of the apparition highly problematic: is it spirit or devil?

Other bodies in the play are equally, if less obviously, determined by early modern culture. The language, behaviour and physical appearance of the courtier Osric are entirely dictated by the modes of Renaissance courtesy. Particularly emblematic is the episode of Osric's hat. During his exchange with Hamlet (5.2), he shows off a range of the verbal and bodily rituals of courtly politeness, but he fails to replace his hat on his head. He is upbraided by Hamlet: 'Your bonnet to his right use: 'tis for the head' (94), which, as Andrew Gurr notes, 'makes a mockery of [Osric's] body language with his hat' (1993, 15). But Osric's hatless state has precise historical implications: 'Only when courtiers were addressing royalty did they keep their hats in their hands' (1993, 16). Osric is politely pretending to treat Hamlet as that which he will never become, the rightful king.

THE BODY DISCURSIVE

Osric's dress and behaviour become the objects of others' mocking discourse, a fact that introduces a third, and here all-important, dimension of the body (and one that, as we have seen, is missing from Hamlet's dumb-show) namely the body discursive. It is primarily through the words of the play that the character or *dramatis persona* is established as a 'physical' presence in the fictional world on the stage. Characters become embodied in the drama sometimes through what they say about themselves ('[Francisco] 'Tis bitter cold, / And I am sick at heart', 1.1.8–9), or through what they say about others ('[Barnardo] How now, Horatio? You tremble and look pale', 56). The body in question may be present, as it is in this incipit to *Hamlet*, or may be invoked *in absentia*. A good example of the latter is the case of Polonius, whose body becomes a major point of reference only when dead and offstage. Indeed, the most vivid examples of the body being realized through words, or discourse, normally take place at a spatial or temporal distance, in a rhetorical strategy called *hypotosis*, or 'counterfait representation' (Puttenham 1589). Notably, there is Ophelia's description of Hamlet *déshabillé* (hatless like Osric, but for quite different reasons: 'Lord Hamlet, with his doublet all unbrac'd, / No hat upon his head … ', 2.1.78ff.); or, more famously, Gertrude's portrait of the drowned Ophelia herself (an offstage scene much visualized or 'embodied' in nineteenth-century painting: 'Her clothes spread wide, / And mermaid-like awhile they bore her up … ', 4.7.175ff.).

However, the more characteristic way that the body enters discourse involves modes of reference that are less semantically complete than such full-blown descriptions. What creates the main linguistic bridge between the speaking actor and the world of the dramatic fiction are words in the text that allude to what the body of the actor must do in performing the character. Such allusion often calls on the actor to complete the sense of the words by gesture or by other means. It is deixis – *I, here, now*, and demonstratives such as *this* and *that* – that creates the illusion of unity between the character's utterances and the actor's speech and movements on stage (see Serpieri 1985, Elam 1980). In drama, everything revolves around the body of the actor; action is oriented towards and away from the position defined by the words and gestures (linguistic and spatial co-ordinates) of the speaking and moving 'I' of the character in the 'here' and 'now'.[8] Dramatic representation is literally egocentric: it is the body of the speaker ('I') that determines the nature and position of 'this' and 'that', of the people and objects that furnish stage and dramatic scene alike.

Hamlet has what is probably the most celebrated deictic moment in drama, an exchange of *this*es and *that*s irresistibly inviting the actors to position the physical object of the conversation by putting it on show:

GRAVEDIGGER   This same skull, sir, was Yorick's skull, the
      King's jester.
HAMLET   This?
GRAVEDIGGER   E'en that.

(5.1.178–81)

As the Arden 2 editor Harold Jenkins observes, 'The demonstratives [this/that] make clear that the skull changes hands and at this point', whether what the performers hoist up be a real skull, some stylized equivalent or a merely imaginary object.

The tragedy also contains what is unquestionably the most spectacular, not to say grotesque, instance of 'incomplete' pronominal reference in the history of the theatre, that obliges the actor to indicate specific parts of his own body in order to give something resembling sense to the allusion. The line in question involves once again the maltreated body of Polonius, still alive, although the reference unwittingly anticipates and indeed invites his own death:

POLONIUS
Take this from this if this be otherwise.

(2.2.156)

Polonius' tragicomic outbreak of *this*es, confidently yet wrongly affirms the cause of Hamlet's madness to be his love for Ophelia: take this (your head, your reason?) from this (your neck, your voice?) if this (love for Ophelia) be otherwise. The utterance as it stands is nonsensical, since it is impossibly ambiguous if pronounced on stage with no bodily accompaniment. The question becomes, what kind of accompaniment? which parts of the body are implicated? This question may seem redundant but many audiences and scholars have debated it. Most readers and actors assume, in the absence of stage directions in the early texts, that the first two *this*es refer respectively to the speaker's head and neck/shoulders, but not so the editors of the play. Where the eighteenth-century editor Theobald did add the obvious stage direction 'Points to his head and shoulder', the first Arden editor, Edward Dowden (1899), argued that Polonius is referring to his staff of office and the hand that bears it. The history of Shakespearean performance argues otherwise.

What this example suggests is that the apparent embodiment given to the character by the three superimposed planes of bodiliness – dramatic, historical and discursive – is illusory. Dramatic convention, historical reference and the language of the text multiply bodily levels, but are still contained within the fiction of *Hamlet*, and as such remain virtual until they come together with another body that is altogether of a different order, the performative body of the actor. Ironically, the bodies at these three levels are only apparent or virtual – they are without material substance, still disembodied. The irony is especially powerful in the case of an actor playing an actor, or in *Hamlet*, the Player who is himself caught up in the dream of passion Hamlet speaks of in the 'Hecuba' speech, 'in a fiction' (2.2.552). The only material body around is not the Player's but the player's, the real actor's.

THE BODY PERFORMATIVE

This materiality brings us to the fourth body level, the body performative, which lies quite beyond the realm of the dramatic world and of Hamlet's metadramatic meditations. It is the actor on stage – no longer 'in a fiction' but working physically in front of us – who, by lending the materiality of his person to the character he represents, brings the bodies dramatic, historical and discursive together in a multi-dimensional illusion of presence. The player, for example Richard Burbage as the first Hamlet, allows his body to be usurped, one might say snatched, in order to represent a character. The physical and behavioural characteristics of the actor's body performative are traditionally read as traits belonging to the body dramatic, to dramatic convention. But convention cannot account for the power of an actor's embodiment of the *dramatis persona*. Thus at the beginning of the eighteenth century Richard Steel charitably discovers improbable signs of youthfulness in the seventy-year-old body of Thomas Betterton (as Hamlet), a quality that he then obligingly attributes to the Prince himself and his world: 'by prevalent power of proper manner, gesture and voice, appeared through the whole drama a youth of great expectation, vivacity and enterprise' (*Tatler*, 20 September 1709). A hundred years later William Hazlitt devotes emphatic praise – recalling the Prince's own eulogy to the Player – to the passionate stage movement of the great actor Edmund Kean, read as absolute embodiments of Hamlet's own psychological state, such as his way, in the exchange with Ophelia in 3.1, of 'coming back after he had gone to the extremity of the stage, from a pang of parting tenderness to press his lips to Ophelia's hand. It had an electrical effect on the house. It was the finest commentary that was ever made on Shakespeare' (1814, quoted in Rosenberg (1992), 539).

THE BODY IN THE TEXT:
A CAUTIONARY TAIL

And yet. And yet the supposed identity of the bodies in play – of Hamlet's with Kean's, of Ophelia's with, say, Ellen Terry's – is in the end the biggest fiction of them all. Between their respective worlds. the fictional and the real, the divide is absolute. The actor may donate his or her organs to the part, but remains irreducibly other, a human being not a *dramatis personae*. However vividly the Prince may describe Claudius' and Gertrude's perspiring bodies in the act of making love ('in the rank sweat of an enseamed bed', 3.4.92) – and Gertrude in turn may portray Hamlet's sweaty effort in the duel ('He's fat and scant of breath', 5.2.292), the perspiration of, say, Kenneth Branagh under the lights is quite a different matter.

The illusion of bodily identity is one of the more frequent sources of **irony** in Shakespeare's plays. *Twelfth Night*, a comedy more or less contemporary with *Hamlet* and in many ways complementary to it – it holds, as it were, a mirror up to the tragedy – plays in various ways with the body-to-body relationship. This is part of its overriding concern with the usually erroneous reading of corporeal signs within a complex plot of disguise, identical twins and other kinds of interpretative trap.[9] A particularly acute moment of such body-exposing irony occurs in 1.5, during the first meeting between Olivia and the cross-dressed Viola/Cesario, where the latter has the arduous task of representing Orsino's supposed love for Olivia by proxy. Viola interrupts her set speech, designed to figure forth Orsino's suffering mind and body by means of trite Petrarchan compliments, as soon as she begins, pretending to be uncertain as to who is the legitimate addressee:

> VIOLA   Most radiant, exquisite, and unmatchable beauty – I pray you tell me if this be the lady of the house, for I never saw her. I would be loath to cast away my speech: for besides that it is excellently well penned, I have taken great pains to con it.

> (165–9)

Viola/Cesario's reluctance to waste her/his speech on the wrong face or ear makes fun of Olivia by confusing her unflatteringly with her chambermaid. More to the point the interruption exposes the conventional, premeditated and delegated character of her performance. It is not by chance that she uses acting parlance *con*, which prompts Olivia to ask 'Are you a comedian [i.e. actor]?' (177). 'I am not that I play' (179) confesses Viola, referring at once to her own cross-dressed state and to her current business of representing (in all senses) the absent Orsino. She is drawing attention to the dramatic qualities of her speech, and undercutting any performative power.

The main object of discourse in the exchange is supposed to be the all-conquering body of Countess Olivia, but it turns out instead to be the self-enamoured body of the narcissistic Duke, which Viola/Cesario and Olivia ironically turn into a text:

> OLIVIA   Where lies your text?
> VIOLA   In Orsino's bosom.
> OLIVIA   In his bosom? In what chapter of his bosom?

> (217–19)

Orsino's bosom is legible as text partly because Viola's 'excellently well penned' acting is designed to figure it rhetorically, to describe it from a distance in the body discursive. But it is also a text because Olivia rightly suspects that the sublime love the bosom is supposed to enclose is another fiction, another 'dream of passion' worthy only of the conventional histrionic efforts of a 'comedian'. What it is not is a body performative. Between Viola's disguised body performative and Orsino's 'fictional' body dramatic, there is an unbridgeable gulf, gender apart. Orsino's bosom is in the text only insofar as his body is inscribed in Viola's performance, and to the extent that she shows his sentiments to be tritely literary, his bosom is exposed in turn as a conventional rhetorical construct.

'Where lies your text?', Olivia's facetious question, complements Rosecrantz's anxious plea, 'you must tell us where the body is' (4.2.24–5). In both cases the answer is: elsewhere.

Notes

1 Cf. 'A very mean meaning', Katherina in *The Taming of the Shrew*, 5.2.31.

2 *Hamlet* is the Shakespearean play with the highest number of occurrences of the word 'body' and its derivatives ('bodies', etc.): seventeen, followed by *Measure for Measure* with fourteen.

3 This is the Folio reading; the Second Quarto has 'munching Mallico'.

4 Respectively the Arden and Norton edition glosses (Arden 2, p. 296; The Norton Shakespeare, General editor Stephen Greenblatt, New York: Norton, 1997, p. 1711).

5 Samuel Beckett, *What Where*, in *Complete Dramatic Works* (London: Faber, 1986), 476.

6 On this line and its 'bodily' stage history, see the essay by Neil Taylor and Ann Thompson (1996), editors of the forthcoming Arden 3 *Hamlet.*

7 Namely, the king's 'natural' or physical body as distinct from his abstract 'political' body (in his role as sovereign): see the celebrated study by Ernst Kantorowicz (1957).

8 As Vimala Herman puts it, 'The body of the speaker in the deictic context is also the primary point of reference for spatial dimensions – like left, right, front, back, since these are projected from the deictic centre' (1995, 27).

9   On the body in *Twelfth Night*, see Belsey (1985), Callaghan (1993), Elam (1996a and 1996b), Greenblatt (1988).

References

Belsey, Catherine (1985) 'Disrupting sexual difference: meaning and gender in the comedies', in John Drakakis (ed.), *Alternative Shakespeares* (London: Methuen/Routledge), 166–90

Callaghan, Dympna (1993) '"And all is semblative a woman's part": body politics and *Twelfth Night*', *Textual Practice*, 7, 428–52

Elam, Keir (1980) *The Semiotics of Theatre and Drama* (London: Methuen/Routledge)

Elam, Keir (1996a) 'The fertile eunuch: *Twelfth Night,* early modern intercourse and the fruits of castration', *Shakespeare Quarterly*, 47.1, 1–36

Elam, Keir (1996b) '"In what chapter of his bosom?": reading Shakespeare's bodies', in Terence Hawkes (ed.), *Alternative Shakespeares 2* (London: Routledge), 140–63

Greenblatt, Stephen (1988) 'Fiction and friction', in *Shakespearean Negotiations: The Circulation of Social Energy in Renaissance England* (Oxford: Clarendon Press), 66–91

Gurr, Andrew (1993) *Shakespeare's Hats* (Rome: Bulzoni)

Herman, Vimala (1995) *Dramatic Discourse: Dialogue as Interaction in Plays* (London and New York: Routledge)

Kantorowicz, Ernst (1957) *The King's Two Bodies: A Study in Medieval Political Theology* (Princeton, N.J.: Princeton University Press)

George Puttenham, *The Art of English Poesy*, ed. G.D. Willcock and A. Walker (Cambridge: Cambridge University Press, 1936)

Rosenberg, Martin (1992) *The Masks of Hamlet* (Newark: University of Delaware Press)

Serpieri, Alessandro (1985) 'Reading the signs: towards a semiotics of Shakespearean drama', in John Drakakis (ed.), *Alternative Shakespeares* (London: Methuen/Routledge), 119–43

Taylor, Neil and Thompson, Ann (1996) 'Obscenity in *Hamlet* III. ii: "Country matters"', *Textus* 9.2 (monographic issue on 'Shakespeare's Text[s]', ed. Ann Thompson and Keir Elam), 485–500

FURTHER READING

Drakakis, John (ed.) *Alternative Shakespeares* (London: Methuen/ Routledge, 1985)

> This collection offers several approaches to the study of Shakespeare's plays. Of particular interest to students and teachers of language and poetics are A. Serpieri's 'Reading the Signs', which offers a semiotic study of *Julius Caesar* and *Othello*, and C. Belsey's 'Disrupting Sexual Difference', which carries out a clear and helpful close reading of several texts in the context of meaning and gender.

Thompson, Ann and John O. Thompson, *Shakespeare, Meaning and Metaphor* (Brighton: Harvester Press, 1987)

> This book applies non-literary research on metaphor to a number of Shakespearean texts – *Troilus and Cressida*, *King Lear*, *Hamlet*, Sonnet 63 – and more generally to Shakespeare's use of metaphors from the domain of printing. The approaches used are drawn from philosophy, psychology, linguistics and anthropology, and the authors argue that they can illuminate Shakespearean usage even though they do not address it directly but focus on everyday language. In turn the approaches themselves are tested and illuminated by the range and complexity of Shakespearean examples.

Part II

READING
SHAKESPEARE'S
ENGLISH

INTRODUCTION

A proper appreciation of any great writer must begin with his language...

Samuel Hussey

The chapters in the first part of this book have displayed and discussed various aspects of Shakespeare's rhetorical and theatrical craftsmanship. In this second part we look more closely at the basic linguistic materials with which Shakespeare was working, as a writer living at the end of the sixteenth and in the early seventeenth century. It is essential that, in reading literature of any period, we engage with the language of the time as far as we can, even if it is impossible for us to reconstruct exactly how it was spoken or interpreted. In the case of Shakespeare, we might want to ask (for instance) what usages he and his audience would have regarded as fashionable or stigmatised, formal or intimate, commonplace or innovative. Attempting to answer such questions is as important as attempting to understand the social, historical or cultural contexts within which his plays were written. Indeed, we may arrive at a fuller understanding of Shakespeare's society and its attitudes and assumptions precisely by probing the nuances of Elizabethan English and the ways in which it differs from our own. In the following chapters, however, the authors do not attempt to describe four hundred years of language change, but concentrate in particular on potentially unfamiliar features that may cause problems in comprehension and interpretation; and more importantly on features which they think will heighten students' enjoyment and appreciation of the plays they are studying.

13

VARIETIES AND VARIATION

Katie Wales

'STANDARD' ENGLISH

Although very little is known about Shakespeare's early life, at least we know that he was born in Warwickshire; but there is very little significant linguistic evidence of this in his plays. Unusual words like *quat* ('pimple') in *Othello* (5.1.11) and *fap* ('drunk') in *The Merry Wives of Windsor* (1.1.164) are cited as possibly from this area. To a twentieth-century reader or listener a marked absence of dialectal features might seem a fact unworthy of comment: after all, in all kinds of writing, literary or not, a 'standard English' is used, the same for everyone wherever they live in the British Isles (and even beyond), and a standard taught to everyone at school, particularly in spelling and grammar. So it is difficult to tell in print where writers come from. In Shakespeare's time, however, the idea of a written standard was not universally acknowledged, although it was certainly a predominant feature of government legislation and bureaucracy (so-called 'Chancery English'), and this since the end of the fifteenth century. Before then, in the Middle Ages, people wrote in the dialect of their own area for all kinds of writing. Spellings were certainly variable, however, even at the end of the sixteenth century, and there were no English grammar books or comprehensive English dictionaries where playwrights like Shakespeare could check on words or constructions. (At school they learnt about English through Latin, as will be noted again later.) But because the seat of government was in London, the capital, and because it was a city of prestige, prosperity and culture, the dialect of London was definitely a literary standard by Shakespeare's time, used in printing books following William Caxton's example a hundred years before. London was also the heart of theatre culture, and so the language of Shakespeare's plays, like those of Christopher Marlowe, Ben Jonson and John Webster, for example, reflect this London-based standard, particularly in the grammar, but also in the fashionable vocabulary.

Nowadays also we tend to think of there being not only a standard written English, but a standard spoken English as well: an accent of some social prestige associated with royalty and the upper classes ('The Queen's English'), the BBC ('BBC English'), and people educated at public schools and Oxbridge ('Received Pronunciation' (RP)). Unlike the written standard, it is only used by a minority of British English speakers, yet it is highly regarded, even by the majority who speak a (modified) regional accent. There is strong evidence to suggest that by Shakespeare's time the monarch and the court were indeed providing a model for imitation in speech, judging by comments made in print by schoolmasters and commentators. Indeed one of the earliest references to the monarch's English as a model comes from Shakespeare himself, from *The Merry Wives of Windsor*. Mistress Quickly warns that with Dr Caius, a Frenchman, 'here will be an old abusing of God's patience and the King's English' (1.4.4–5). The most famous comment on this emerging 'spoken standard' comes from the rhetorician George Puttenham's *Art of English Poesy* (1589), a guidebook for aspiring poets. Although he is concerned with their writing practices, poets at that time would be expected to read their poetry aloud. Puttenham advises his readers to avoid the speech of Northerners because

> it is not so courtly or so current as our Southern English is ... Ye shall therefore take the usual speech of the court, and that of London and the shires lying about London, within 60 miles, and not much above.

Not surprisingly, the growing class of the *nouveau riche*, the wealthy middle-class London merchants and their wives, so tellingly depicted by Shakespeare's contemporaries such as Thomas Middleton, John Marston and Thomas Dekker, wanted to sound as fashionable as they dressed. And it is highly probable that these same playwrights and Shakespeare himself, if seeking the patronage of the court for their plays, would wish to sound 'trendy' in their own speech. For Shakespeare especially, since so many of his plays are set in royal courts, however 'foreign', it is also highly likely that the discourse of his kings, queens and princes reflects the kind of language used in London courtly circles.

REGIONAL DIALECT

As a result of both the development of a written standard by Shakespeare's time, and signs of a growing socially acceptable London-based accent, the situation was emerging with which we are still familiar today: namely, that dialects and accents far away from the capital were likely to be denigrated or laughed at, and their users seen as uneducated or socially inferior. So regional dialect is equated with social variation. Shakespeare's contemporaries, like Jonson, for instance, were quick to make dramatic capital out of this, adding dialect to the stock of comic features to be exploited, and so giving rise to the long tradition of 'stage dialects' from the north-east to the south-west. Shakespeare's own plays (especially the Histories), when not ostensibly set in exotic locations such as Athens, Venice, Bohemia and Egypt, for instance, most readily evoke the streets of London, so the representation of regional dialect is sparse. Even though there are several references in the two parts of *Henry IV* to the bluntness of the 'northern youth' Hotspur, whose influence lies north of the Trent, Shakespeare does not indicate northern features in the text. It was left to the actor playing Hotspur to bring out his character in this way. Similarly, one can certainly imagine that the 'Clowns' of the Comedies in particular were likely to be played by actors adopting a 'rural'-sounding accent in their roles as simpletons as part of their 'comic business' on stage.

One rare textual indication of dialect, however, is that in *King Lear* (4.6) when Edgar, freshly dressed as a 'peasant' after assuming the disguise and rambling speech of a mad beggar, leads his blinded father as requested to the Dover cliffs. To Gloucester Edgar's speech now appears different from before ('Methinks you're better spoken', 10); but as soon as Goneril's steward Oswald enters, intent on killing him, Edgar resumes his peasant speech, intervening to protect him:

> Ch'ill not let go, zir, without vurther 'cagion [occasion] ... Good gentleman, go your gait [way] and let poor volk pass. And 'ch'ud ha' been zwaggered [bullied] out of my life, 'twould not ha' been zo long as 'tis by a vortnight. Nay, come not near th'old man; keep out, che vor [warn] ye, or I'se [shall] try whether your costard or my baton be the harder. Ch'ill be plain with you ... Ch'ill pick your teeth, zir. Come, no matter vor your foins [thrusts].
>
> (231–41)

Here, that the dialect is intended to suggest southern/south-western speech can be seen from the *ch-* forms for 'I' (archaic *ich*), as in *ch'ill* (I will), *ch'ud* (I would), and the voicing of the initial consonants /f/ and /s/ as /v/ and /z/, as in *zir* and *volk*, for example. Now, given that Edgar slays Oswald, Shakespeare is hardly using the dialect here to poke fun at West Country peasants. Along with his disguise as Tom the Bedlam beggar, the dialect serves to prevent Edgar's discovery, both to his father and to Oswald himself, and keeps him on the margins, as it were. In *King Lear* as a whole, changing identities are frequently signalled by the doffing and donning of garments, and variations of language: think of Lear himself on the heath in Act 3.

SOCIAL VARIATION: SOCIOLECTS

Shakespeare's plays do reveal another kind of dialect variation, which we can specifically see as social rather than rural, and which does seem to be the butt of gentle fun and even ridicule. Pedantic unimportant officials like Dogberry in *Much Ado About Nothing*, and Elbow in *Measure for Measure*; a craftsman like Bully Bottom the weaver in *A Midsummer Night's Dream*; and a London tavern hostess like Mistress Quickly in the so-called 'Falstaff' plays are prone to muddle long or difficult words: what we now term *malapropisms*. Particularly amusing are the words which actually mean the opposite of the word intended: such as Dogberry's 'condemned to everlasting *redemption* (for 'damnation') (4.2.56).

For women a difficulty with long words was certainly understandable (and listen also to the Nurse in *Romeo and Juliet*), since they never had the same schooling opportunities as men in the Middle Ages and Renaissance, and so never learnt the difficult words directly that inevitably came from Latin or Greek roots. (But probably only 30–50 per cent of men in Shakespeare's time were minimally literate.) Yet there is a sense in which we must see Mistress Quickly's and the Nurse's malapropisms in the general context also of a 'women's language' which the audience is meant to laugh at: part of a literary stereotype that goes back at least as far as Chaucer's Wife of Bath, and on to Dickens's Mrs Nickleby and Flora Finching. Mistress Quickly and Juliet's Nurse are similarly prone to a familiar, chattering kind of style, full of repetition and digressions, one in prose, the other in verse as well as prose. For example:

MISTRESS QUICKLY   But I have another messenger to your worship. Mistress Page hath her hearty commendations to you too; and let me tell you in your ear she's as fartuous [*sic*] a civil modest wife, and one – I tell you – that will not miss you morning nor evening prayer, as any is in Windsor, whoe'er be the other; and she bade me tell your worship that her husband is seldom from home, but she hopes there will come a time. I never knew a woman so dote upon a man – surely, I think you have charms, la; yes, in truth.

(*MW* 2.2.89–98)

NURSE

> But, as I said,
> On Lammas Eve at night shall she be fourteen.
> That shall she, marry, I remember it well.
> 'Tis since the earthquake now eleven years,
> And she was wean'd – I never shall forget it –
> Of all the days of the year upon that day.
> For I had then laid wormwood to my dug,
> Sitting in the sun under the dovehouse wall.
> My lord and you were then at Mantua –
> Nay I do bear a brain.

(*RJ* 1.3.20–9)

This kind of language to a modern audience, sensitive to feminist criticism, raises uneasy questions about an inferred relationship of garrulity with scatter-brainedness or empty-headedness as women's particular characteristics; but then we must remember Polonius in *Hamlet*, for example.

The better educated and the upper classes had their own kind of problems with difficult or Latinate words, since they often paraded their knowledge of them unnecessarily, and overused them: dubbed 'inkhornisms', since they seemed to flow too easily from the inkwell or inkhorn. Shakespeare seems to have disliked this sort of verbose affectation (the word *inkhorn* itself is twice used disparagingly, in the first two parts of *Henry VI*) and made the users of it objects of ridicule: witness the 'braggart' knight Don Adriano de Armado in *Love's Labour's Lost*. His very first appearance with Moth his page is marked by utterances like:

I spoke it, tender juvenal, as a congruent epitheton
appertaining to thy young days, which we may nominate
tender.

(1.2.13–15)

As the notes to the Arden 3 edition indicate, *epitheton*
('description') is used only here by Shakespeare, and generally
Armado seems particularly fond of words ending in *-ate*, as in
nominate. For Shakespeare, like Jonson, social follies and excesses
are mirrored in language, so that many supposedly well-bred
characters the audience would dislike are given irritating or
'over-the-top' linguistic habits. Jonson succinctly summarizes
this view in his notebook *Discoveries*, published after his death:
'Wheresoever manners and fashions are corrupted, language is'.

The other end of the social scale is particularly revealed in
Shakespeare's 'Falstaff plays'. The low-life scenes in an
Eastcheap tavern provide not only comedy in action and
language but also what we must suppose is realistic colour,
portraying the city of London of Shakespeare's period. At first
glance, it might appear that he is simply adopting the time-
honoured rhetorical principle of decorum, making the
language in a 'low' style appropriate to the setting and low-
status citizens; just as a more elevated style ('high') would be
appropriate to depictions of court life and aristocrats. (See
further Chapters 2 and 3.) To this tradition was added by
Elizabethan and Jacobean dramatists the convention of prose
for comedy and 'low' characters and scenes, and verse for the
higher-status characters and serious discourse. But it is
actually more complex than that for Shakespeare in these
particular plays (as indeed in others). For one thing, in the two
parts of *Henry IV* these low-life scenes actually have a
significant role to play in Prince Hal's developing maturity.
Secondly, Falstaff himself, around whom the action revolves in
these scenes, is a knight ('Sir John'), but his language is as
coarse and as vivid as his lower-class hangers-on, full of oaths

and terms of amiable abuse. Just as Doll Tearsheet uses terms like '*lack-linen* mate ... *cutpurse* rascal ... *bottle-ale* rascal ... *basket-hilt* stale juggler' (*2H4* 2.4.122–3, 126, 129),[1] so too we can note the descriptive compounds of Falstaff's terms of address: *eel-skin, neat's-tongue, bull's pizzle, stock-fish, tailor's-yard, pint-pot, tickle-brain*, etc. (*1H4* 2.4.241–4, 393–4). The young prince has learnt this language too; and he proudly notes how the lads of Eastcheap have their own 'cant', i.e. 'underworld' terms: they

> call drinking deep 'dyeing scarlet', and when you breathe in your watering they cry 'Hem!' and bid you 'Play it off!' ... I can drink with any tinker in his own language ...
>
> <div align="right">(<i>IH4</i> 2.4.15–17, 18–19)</div>

The language of thieves and rogues if not tinkers, what in modern terms would be described as an 'anti-language', had begun to attract quite a lot of academic interest by Shakespeare's time. Some terms actually passed into wider circulation, like *filch* for 'steal', which is still used today. Hal's own set of colourful terms of abuse for Falstaff include 'thou *clay-brained* guts, thou *knotty-pated* fool, thou whoreson obscene greasy *tallow-catch* ... this *bed-presser*, this *horse-back-breaker*, this huge hill of flesh' (*1H4* 2.4.222–4, 239–40). Of course, in the company of his father and fellow noblemen Hal can 'code-switch', change his dialect to the more formal language of the court, with its syntactic complexity and a more 'elevated' kind of diction. Look, for example, at his response to his father's rebuke in 3.2: it is very difficult to know exactly what he means, from the syntax:

> So please your Majesty, I would I could
> Quit all offences with as clear excuse
> As well as I am doubtless I can purge
> Myself of many I am charged withal

(18–21)

Moreover, as the Earl of Warwick rightly notes in *2H4*, Hal 'but studies his companions'

> Like a strange tongue, wherein, to gain the language,
> 'Tis needful that the most immodest word
> Be look'd upon and learnt

(4.4.69–71)

He correctly predicts that, in due course, the prince will reject both his followers and their language, while using his broad experiences as a yardstick in the judgement and evaluation of others: a true people's king. Indeed, there can also be anticipated here the scene in *Henry V* (4.1) where Hal, now king, mingles easily and unrecognized amongst his soldiers on the eve of the battle of Agincourt.

ENGLISH AND NATIONHOOD

In *Henry V* there are also important signs of Shakespeare's awareness of another kind of dialectal variation on a larger, national scale. Remember that in Shakespeare's time the idea of English as a major international language, a world language or *lingua franca*, would be unknown and largely undreamed of. Yet Samuel Daniel is uncannily prophetic in his poem *Musophilus* (1599):

> And who in time knows whither we may vent
> The treasure of our tongue, to what strange shores
> The gain of our best glory shall be sent,
> T'enrich unknowing nations with our stores?

The colonial expansion into the New World that is implicated in Shakespeare's last solo play, *The Tempest*, was just beginning, so American English, Canadian English, Australian English, etc., were part of the future. English was thus confined to the British Isles; but, unlike the Middle Ages, no longer simply to England. English was more and more being spoken in areas that had hitherto been Gaelic-speaking: Scotland and Wales. (But note how Glendower and his daughter are supposed to speak in Welsh, according to the stage directions in *1 Henry IV* 3.1.) Ireland actually preceded the New World as England's first colony across the seas, many of Elizabeth's favourites acquiring estates there. The poet Edmund Spenser (1552–99), for example, had an estate in County Cork, was secretary to the lord deputy, and wrote a treatise called *View of the Present State of Ireland*, in which he advocated the forcible anglicization of the Irish Celts. The spread of English went hand in hand with the increasing sense of the political power of England, and a pride in the English language. Not surprisingly then, London English, the prestigious variety, was increasingly being seen as a sign of the whole language, as a 'national' standard, and a symbol of unity.

Henry V is not only about England's relations with France, but also about England's relations with its own 'colonies' that preceded the Act of Union in the eighteenth century, and also more particularly that preceded the accession of James VI of Scotland to the throne of England in 1603 as James I. In the speeches in the First Folio of the three 'representative' captains, symbolically loyal to the English king, Fluellen, Macmorris and Jamy, from Wales, Ireland and Scotland (there is also Gower an English captain), there can be seen stock features that yet clearly indicate the emergence of Anglo-Welsh, Hiberno-English and Scots as distinct varieties of English. (Scots, in fact, was quite ancient: descended from Old English, but the political border had cut it off from northern English during the Middle Ages.) So, for example, there is Fluellen's greeting *Godden* (good day); the devoicing of /v/ and /b/ in words like *falorous* and *porn* (born); the discourse tag *look you* and oath *by Cheshu* (Jesu). Jamy has the northern *bath* for 'both', *ligge* (lie) and *sal* for 'shall'; and Macmorris has distinctive fricative consonants: *Chrish*; *tish* ('tis); *ish* (is).

Their speeches together are so rambling and repetitive that it is very clear that Shakespeare's English audiences would be meant to smile somewhat patronizingly at their discourses: a literary tradition that has continued until the twentieth century. Despite their loyalty to Henry V and the English, there is a kind of verbal warfare between the captains that perhaps mirrors the uneasy relations that have always existed between England and the rest of the British Isles, and their continuing differences, even linguistic, despite their unity.

ENGLISH AND LATIN

The image of the English language dominating the British Isles seems a modern one; but what about the idea of the educated Englishman being characteristically bilingual? This is certainly not true today. In Shakespeare's time, as right through the Middle Ages, the most influential language in Britain and Europe was Latin, the *lingua franca* of education, scholarship, science and religion. It was not only a written language as we know it today, but a well-used spoken language, at least in the universities of Cambridge and Oxford and the Inns of Court. Its pre-eminence was only heightened by the Renaissance discovery of classical Latin and Greek manuscripts. It is only as the prestige of Latin gradually declined after Shakespeare's lifetime that the prestige of English could finally be asserted. In his grammar school as a boy Shakespeare would have learnt his grammar largely through Latin and read, analysed and imitated Latin literary models, while choosing elements· in keeping with English rhythm and syntax. Latin culture and literature were the prime sources of allusions and the Latin language a fruitful resource for interlingual puns. So in *Love's Labour's Lost*, for example, Holofernes puns on *Quis, quis*, Latin 'who', and its pronunciation the same as 'kiss' (5.1.49). No wonder that many words from Latin appear in Shakespeare's plays apparently for the first time, usually with connotations of formality, erudition or abstraction: for example *castigate* (*Timon of Athens*); *abstemious* (*The Tempest*); *deracinate* (*Henry V*); *invulnerable* (*Hamlet*); as well as words like *oppugnacity* and *abruption* which haven't survived – smacking too much of 'inkhornisms'? Like all schoolchildren, however, Shakespeare must have sometimes found his lessons irksome. In the figure of the schoolmaster Holofernes in *Love's Labour's Lost* he gains some revenge: here is an overzealous pedant who talks in an anglicized Latin grammar: 'A soul feminine saluteth us' (4.2); and who even uses English and Latin in the same sentence: a 'macaronic' structure it is technically called. It is just as if he is, appropriately enough, imitating a school textbook:

> Yet a kind of insinuation, as it were, *in via*, in way, of explication, *facere*, as it were, replication, or rather *ostentare*, to show, as it were, his inclination …

(4.2.13–16; original italics)

OCCUPATIONAL DIALECTS

In a very obvious way, Holofernes' use of Latin also signals his profession, and this kind of linguistic variation is a stock device of dramatists of the period, and later novelists, namely to distinguish characters by their occupational dialects. A special vocabulary or 'jargon' is the commonest marker. The mercantile world of Antonio and Shylock in *The Merchant of Venice* is colourfully evoked in their first encounter (1.3) by the repetition of words between them like *ducats, bound/bond, usance, interest, forfeit/forfeiture*. (For possible differences of nuance, however, see Chapter 2.) The two gardeners in *Richard II* speak knowledgeably of binding up the 'dangling apricocks', and rooting away the 'noisome weeds' (3.4.29, 38); although this is also very obviously an allegory for the kingdom as a neglected garden. Kate, Lady Percy, in *1Henry IV*, throws back at her husband Hotspur in a rhetorical 'list' his soldier's jargon, uttered in his sleep:

> And thou hast talk'd
> Of sallies and retires, of trenches, tents,
> Of palisadoes, frontiers, parapets,
> Of basilisks, of cannon, culverin . . .
>
> (2.3.30–3)

Hotspur's response is that this is the only language he knows; anticipating ironically his enemy Henry's defence to another Kate in *Henry V*, in their wooing scene: 'I speak to thee plain soldier. If thou canst love me for this, take me . . .' (5.2.149–51). Henry is also a king, of course, and this occupation is conventionally and economically signalled by a grammatical rather than lexical feature, the so-called 'royal *we*' for 'I' or, on occasion, for 'I and my advisers', etc. So Henry's very first appearance on stage in the play is marked by this very formal marker, even speaking to an earl, who is also a relative:

> Not yet my cousin, *we* would be resolved,
> Before *we* hear him, of some things of weight
>
> (1.2.4–5)

So too, for the very first speech on stage of his father, King Henry IV. The *we* seems a little incongruous with the personal rather than public references, but indicates the extent of Henry's sense of duty:

> So shaken as *we* are, so wan with care,
> Find *we* a time for frighted peace to pant
>
> (*1H4* 1.1.1–2)

REGISTER AND SITUATIONAL VARIATION

The rich diversity of 'voices' evoked by the social and occupational dialects reflects the dynamic and complex linguistic diversity in any society that has been much stressed in the writings of the twentieth-century philosopher–linguist Mikhail Bakhtin. The world of the stage for a dramatist like Shakespeare is equally the staging of the world as he saw it. As Lynne Magnusson says in Chapter 2: 'The dramatist must give voices to a world and all its varied businesses.' But the linguistic stratification in society goes further: there is variation from situation to situation, sometimes called 'register' or 'discourse genre'. (See also Chapter 5.) As in real life, characters on stage manipulate appropriate forms and conventions of language according to whether they are proposing marriage, or presiding over a legal case; or (more unusually) making an oration after a leader's murder. In all cases there will be an appropriate tone, degree of formality, choice of lexis, and so on. In Shakespeare's time, a training in rhetoric would have made a dramatist sensitive to this kind of linguistic variation, since it would have been a regular exercise to enact situations in which different types of speech would be found, for example debates and legal arguments. But what drama, which is about action, can also show to particular advantage are the hundreds of speech 'acts' that make up any speech event or genre in everyday life: the promising, quarrelling, cajoling, threatening, ordering, flattering, lamenting, in our interactions with others. Many of these are clearly emotive acts, so that there will be variation according to mood, giving rise to jesting, boasting, swearing, etc. The opening scene of *Romeo and Juliet* is memorable for its mundane quarrel between two servants, which is yet clearly symbolic of the deep rift between the Capulets and Montagues. The language of provocation is reinforced by the body language, the taunting gesture:

SAMPSON   [servant to Capulet] I will bite my thumb at them, which is disgrace to them if they bear it.

ABRAHAM   [servant to Montague] Do you bite your thumb at us, sir?

SAMPSON   I do bite my thumb, sir.
ABRAHAM   Do you bite your thumb at us, sir?
SAMPSON   Is the law of our side if I say ay?
GREGORY   [servant to Capulet] No.
SAMPSON   No, sir. I do not bite my thumb at you, sir, but I
   bite my thumb, sir.
GREGORY   Do you quarrel, sir?
ABRAHAM   Quarrel, sir? No, sir.

(1.1.42–52)

THOU AND *YOU*: SOCIAL, EMOTIONAL AND RHETORICAL VARIATION

This particular linguistic battle (which ends in a sword fight) is striking for its superficial politeness: notice the studied repetition of *sir*, along with the pronoun *you*. In many quarrel scenes in Shakespeare's plays and those of his contemporaries the change of temperature or shift in emotion would conventionally be marked by the use of the pronoun *thou/thee*. Nowadays we tend to associate *thou* with religious discourse or with dialectal usage; it has unfortunately been lost from common-core standard English since the seventeenth century, overshadowed by *you* as a universal singular (as well as plural). But this pronoun, which derives from Old English, was a valuable device for Shakespeare and his contemporaries as a kind of linguistic 'barometer', to signal a rise in emotional intensity, however momentary, whether towards anger, hatred, contempt on the one hand, or strong passion and affection on the other hand. The alternation of *you* (or *ye*) and *thou* as singular pronouns appeared in English during the Middle Ages, under French influence, and originally had a social rather than emotional function, to indicate variations of rank and status: *you* to 'superiors', *thou* to 'inferiors', and *you* the generally 'polite' form. This social function had rather declined by Shakespeare's day. (See further Chapter 14.)

It is important to stress *thou*'s 'literariness', because you will also find it used in particular speech acts and genres which are not really imitating those of everyday life, but which reflect drama's status as literary art: for example, in rhetorical invocations or **apostrophes** to the heavens, gods, ghosts, dead comrades, swords, etc.; and in self-address in dramatic asides and soliloquies. (It also survives as a feature of 'poetic diction' until the middle of the twentieth century.) Hamlet's soliloquies provide a rich source of *thou*'s, often with multiple resonances. So, after the ghost of his father has urged him to 'remember me' and vanished, Hamlet, alone, echoes his words:

> Remember *thee*?
> Ay *thou* poor ghost whiles memory holds a seat
> In this distracted globe. Remember *thee*?

(1.5.96–7)

Hamlet's terrified *thou* of his first encounter with the supernatural ('Be *thou* a spirit of health, or goblin damn'd', 1.4.40), spurning 'it' in disgust, is now inextricably mixed with the emotive *thou* of pity and reawakened filial affection.

INDIVIDUAL VARIATION OR IDIOLECTS

The realistic variation of language from situation to situation, moment to moment, mood to mood, gives dramatic characters their dynamism as well as their plausibility. And it is from this variation that characterization is developed, and even individual 'idiolects', unique sets of stylistic features that distinguish one character from another, and that help the audience to evaluate or assess them. Think of any characters that stand out in Shakespeare's plays: why do they stand out? For what they do; or say; or how they say it? Think of

Polonius' long-winded sentences in *Hamlet*, for example, and his fondness for generalized statements or aphorisms in balanced phrases (**isocolon**):

> [to Laertes:] Give every man thy ear, | but few thy voice;
> Take each man's censure, | but reserve thy judgment
>
> (1.3.68–9)

Think of the very first time we encounter Leontes in *The Winter's Tale*: the impression we gain of his emotional and mental instability from the repeated use of questions, exclamations and **parentheses**; for example:

>   Is whispering nothing?
> Is leaning cheek to cheek? is meeting noses?
> Kissing with inside lip? stopping the career
> Of laughter with a sigh (a note infallible
> Of breaking honesty)?
>
> (1.2.284–8)

How do such characters differ linguistically from their opponents, foils or counterparts? Moreover, idiolects are not necessarily static, the same throughout the play. The balance of power, for instance, can shift from one character to another: think of Othello and Iago together, for instance; or Macbeth and his wife.

In conclusion: Shakespeare's artistry, of course, is to construct idiolects, sociolects, dialects, etc., in the medium not of real speech but of written verse, all constrained by the overriding genre of poetry, and the rhythms of iambic pentameter. But these same rhythms secure their memorability, unlike those of ordinary speech, and their resonance through time.

Note

1 Italics are added in these and subsequent examples unless otherwise stated.

FURTHER READING

Adamson, S.M., 'The literary language', in R. Lass (ed.), *The Cambridge History of the English Language, Vol. 3, 1476–1776* (Cambridge: Cambridge University Press, 1999), 539–653

> The first half of this chapter (pp. 541–95) offers an introduction to the Renaissance theory and practice of rhetorical richness (copia) and a guide to some of the principal 'figures of varying' and 'figures of amplifying' employed by Shakespeare and his contemporaries. Using a descriptive framework that mediates between the terminologies of Renaissance rhetoricians and modern linguists, the chapter aims to describe the main stylistic trends of the period and to explain the decline of classical rhetoric in the subsequent century.

Hussey, S.S., *The Literary Language of Shakespeare* (London and New York: Longman, 1992, 2nd edition)

> Of the several books devoted to Shakespeare's language this is probably the most accessible introduction for the literary reader, and the second edition takes account of recent work on rhetoric. Hussey's primary focus is on vocabulary and register variation and he offers an account both of the range of Shakespeare's styles and of their chronological development.

14

UNDERSTANDING SHAKESPEARE'S GRAMMAR: STUDIES IN SMALL WORDS

Sylvia Adamson

INTRODUCTION: CHOICE AND CHANGE

To start from a linguistic truism: *meaning depends on choice.* In other words, the less choice we have about what to say or whether to say it, the less meaning it carries. So if I write 'Dear John' at the start of a letter, it signals only that I'm starting a letter. Because it's a fixed formula, I can't use it to express affection. To do that, I'd need to replace the 'Dear' with, say, 'Darling'. Though I could express *dis*affection simply by leaving it out altogether. Unless, of course, I'm writing by email, in which case it's quite normal to begin with just 'John', or even without any salutation at all. Or so I'm told. To a member of my generation that still seems unacceptably brusque. Which is how my 'Dear John' might seem to a contemporary of Shakespeare. Or would it? Perhaps, on the contrary, it might strike him as offensively familiar?

This brings me to a second linguistic truism: *choices change.* The set of available options for any act of communication differs from dialect to dialect, genre to genre, generation to generation and, ultimately, from speaker to speaker. And unless we know the repertoire that speakers or writers are selecting from, we can't know the significance of the choices they have made. In effect, we can't tell what they mean by what they say.

Paradoxically, communication may be less problematic where the language variety is more alien. If we're reading *Beowulf* we're in no danger of forgetting that interpretation is difficult. But when we come into contact with varieties more similar to our own we are lulled into thinking we know what is meant. 'Divided by a common language' is the phrase coined by Bernard Shaw to describe conversational misfires between British and American speakers of English. But it applies equally well to our conversations with Shakespeare, and it applies particularly at the level of grammar. We're always aware that our understanding is challenged by his rich and strange vocabulary or his festive rhetoric and we are even likely to notice that his range of salutations is not the same as our own, but we are less attentive in reading his grammar because it seems to be 'not substantially different from that of modern English' (to quote from the *Shakespeare Encyclopaedia*, which consequently allots only two paragraphs to the subject).

In this chapter I will try to show that there are both pitfalls and pleasures in Shakespeare's grammar that make it worth a much closer inspection. I offer a set of case studies in Shakespeare's small words, all of them simple monosyllables and most of them still familiar parts of the grammar of English today. But they belong to a different repertoire of options now, and if we interpret them in a modern way we may be in danger of importing a meaning that Shakespeare couldn't have intended – or of missing one that he could. In some cases what's at stake is the literal sense of a passage, in others it's the messages that grammatical choices can also convey about the stylistic level of a scene or the tone of a dialogue or the social status of a character. We can't always hope to reconstruct these nuances of meaning in the language of another speaker from another time, but we can learn a lot by trying.

AND OR *AN* (MEANING 'IF')

And has a much wider range of uses in Shakespeare's English than it does today. One that causes particular problems for modern readers is illustrated in example 1 below:

(1) (Falstaff to Hal)

> now am I, if a man should speak truly, little better than one of the wicked. I must give over this life, *and* I will give it over: by the Lord, *and* I do not I am a villain.
>
> (*1H4* 1.2.92–5)[1]

The first of Falstaff's two *and*s is straightforward: he's using it to add one piece of information to another. But if we try to read the second *and* in the same way, it doesn't make sense. The *and* here means the same as the *if* which appears in the first line of the extract. For this reason I'll call it iffy-*and*. A few lines later Falstaff uses iffy-*and* again, this time in its alternative spelling *an*.

(2)

> 'Zounds ... I'll make one; *an* I do not, call me villain
>
> (98–9)

As example 1 shows, *if* and iffy-*and* were often interchangeable in terms of their literal meaning. But *if* was the more common in the literary English of Shakespeare's day, while iffy-*and* was on the decline. Forms that are going out of use often become associated with formal speech styles, but that is not the case with iffy-*and*. In Shakespeare's plays, at least, it seems to be associated largely with the range of functions of the plain or low style (as defined in Chapter 3, pp. 31–5). For example, 1 and 2 occur in a tavern setting, in prose and in a colloquial form of speech that also includes oaths (*by the Lord* in 1; *Zounds* in 2). In *King Lear*, Cornwall includes an iffy-*and* (*an*) in his parody of how plain, blunt, uncourtly speakers express themselves:

(3)

> He cannot flatter, he;
> An honest mind and plain, he must speak truth;
> *An* they will take it, so; if not, he's plain.

(2.2.96–8)

Iffy-*and* is particularly common among rustic, uneducated or lower-class speakers. There are several instances in the scene where we first meet the 'rude mechanicals' in *A Midsummer Night's Dream*:

(4a)

> *And* I may hide my face, let me play Thisby too.

(1.2.48–9)

(4b)

> *And* you should do it [i.e. roar] too terribly, you would fright the Duchess

(71–2)

(4c)

> I will roar you … *and* 'twere any nightingale

(78–9)

(in this instance *and* = 'as if')

Similar examples quoted elsewhere in this volume include Samson's '*and* we be in choler' (p. 73), Constable Elbow's '*and* it like you' (p. 122) and a servingman's '*an*'t please your honour' (p. 25). In the last two cases, iffy-*and* is part of a fixed formula of deference or politeness, and this seems to be another factor favouring its use. The formulaic quality of many instances is also evidence that iffy-*and* was in decline in the language as a whole. Sometimes it appears to need the support of *if* to make its meaning clear; so *and if* (meaning just 'if') is quite common too.

Note: Watch out for iffy-*so* as well, as in 'So they do nothing, 'tis a venial slip' (*Oth* 4.1.9). It is very common in formulaic phrases, where 'so please you' = 'an it please you' = 'if it please you'. There is also a negative counterpart to iffy-*and* in iffy-*but*, which means 'if not', 'unless', as in the following examples:

(5)

> I here do give that with all my heart
> Which, *but* thou hast already, with all my heart
> I would keep from thee.

(Oth 1.3.194–6)

(= '*if* you did *not* already have it')

(6)

> It shall go hard *but* I will better the instruction

(MV 3.1.67)

(= '*if* I do *not* improve on what you've taught me')

(7)

> And *but* thou love me, let them find me here.

(RJ 2.2.76)

(= '*unless* you love me')

HIS OR *IT* (MEANING 'ITS')

Its in Shakespeare is rather like Sherlock Holmes's 'curious incident' of the dog that didn't bark in the night. It is important chiefly because it does *not* appear in most of the plays. In English before about 1600, the three-way distinction between the pronouns *she/he/it* was not matched, as it is today, by the possessive forms *her/his/its* (as in '*her* name', '*his* name', '*its* name'). Instead, there was only a two-way contrast between *her* and *his*. *Its* is not used at all by Edmund Spenser nor in the 1611 version of the Bible. In Shakespeare's works it is first found in the 1623 Folio version of the text (prompting suggestions that it may have been added by a modernizing editor) but almost all of the few examples are in late plays (prompting suggestions that Shakespeare himself may have begun to use it late in his career as it became fashionable). Mostly, where we would use *its*, Shakespeare and his contemporaries used *his*. There are two examples in the speech, quoted on p. 42, where Agamemnon describes how the formation of a knot in wood:

(8)
    Infects the sound pine, and diverts *his* grain
    Tortive and errant from *his* course of growth.

(TC 1.3.8–9)

    (*his* = 'the pine tree's')

Another example, more proverbial in tone, is from Sonnet 95:

(9)
    The hardest knife ill used doth lose *his* edge.

(14)

If a modern writer used *his* in these contexts, we could be fairly certain that there was some intention to personify the object being described (as when Wordsworth writes 'the Sea threw off *his* evening shade'). But it is more difficult to know when this is the case in the work of those writing before *its* became fully established in the grammatical repertoire. We would probably be wrong to imagine a humanized pine-tree or knife in examples 8 and 9. But what of the candle in 10, or the lamp in 11?

(10)
    How far that little candle throws *his* beams!

(MV 5.1.90)

(11)

the lamp that burns by night
Dries up *his* oil to lend the world *his* light.

(*VA* 755–6)

Some readers may feel that there's enough purposiveness in the actions of *throw*ing beams or *lend*ing light to justify interpreting both as cases of personification. But perhaps the most useful guideline for modern readers is to err on the side of *under*interpretation: *his* should not be taken as a marker of personification unless clearly supported by other signals in the surrounding text.

The fact that *his* is the normal way of expressing 'its' in Shakespeare's English should also make us think more closely about those cases where he chooses an alternative option, since for an Elizabethan audience the avoidance of *his* must have been as striking as the use of it is for a modern audience. Occasionally, for instance, we find the form *it* (possibly an import from West Midlands dialect), as in this couplet from the Fool in *King Lear* (Quarto text):

(12)

The hedgesparrow fed the cuckoo so long
That it had *it* head bit off by *it* young

[1.4.206–7]

The motive here may be the sound-value of the form. Possessive-*it*, chiming in sound with subject-*it* and the verb *bit*, produces a fine nursery-rhyme jingle, particularly appropriate in a scene that is dominated by the Fool's sense-in-nonsense commentary.

A different motive may explain the avoidance of *his* in *Hamlet*, when Horatio describes his encounter with the Ghost:

(13)

HAMLET
Did you not speak to it?

HORATIO

> My lord, I did,
> But answer made it none. Yet once methought
> It lifted up *it* head and did address
> Itself to motion like as it would speak.

(1.2.214–17)

At this stage in the play, Hamlet has not seen the Ghost and those who have are uncertain whether it is genuinely the spirit of Hamlet's father or a hellish fabrication. It's possible that possessive-*it* is used instead of *his* because in this speech Horatio, making his first report to Hamlet, is carefully refusing to grant the apparition a human status, using *it* five times in three lines (in contrast to his later '*he* wore *his* beaver up', 229).

Possessive-*it* appears later in the same play, too, where Hamlet, seeing a funeral, infers that

(14)

> The cor[p]se they follow did with desp'rate hand
> Fordo *it* own life. 'Twas of some estate

(5.1.218–19)

At a realistic level, Hamlet's use of possessive-*it* is justified by the fact that he does not, at this stage, know whether the dead person was male or female. But there's a dramatic irony in the gap between Hamlet's ignorance and the audience's knowledge that the *it* was Ophelia, and the choice of *it*, echoing against the *her* that we might expect, acts as a poignant reminder that a corpse is the inanimate remnant of an animate being. Shakespeare seems to draw attention to this loss of human identity by following possessive-*it* with subject-*it* in *'twas* (= 'it was').

Examples such as 13 and 14 give evidence of a growing sense in the Renaissance that there is an important dividing line to be drawn between the animate and the inanimate, the human and the non-human. This feeling may have been partly responsible for the emergence of the modern form *its* as a distinctive non-animate counterpart to *his* and *her*; certainly it lent impetus to the widespread adoption of the form. Already by 1672 we find John Dryden rejecting Ben Jonson's use of *his* (to mean 'its') as an example of 'ill Syntax'.

Note: Example 13 is particularly interesting because the different texts of *Hamlet* display the whole gamut of historical possibilities, with the First Quarto (1603) opting for what would have been Elizabethan default usage, '[It] lifted up *his* head', the Second Quarto (1604/5) preferring 'It lifted up *it* head' and the later Fourth Quarto (undated) using the fully modern 'It lifted up *its* head'.

MAY

This case study and the next focus on *modal auxiliaries*. By *auxiliaries*, I mean verbs which normally occur only in company with another verb, whose meaning they modify; *modal* auxiliaries are those which modify meaning mainly by introducing indications of a speaker's attitude towards what is being said or towards the addressee (e.g. expressions of certainty, desire or power). Consider the changes we can ring on the verb *know* by coupling it with different modal auxiliaries: '*may* know', '*must* know', '*might* know', '*should* know'. These are helpful little words for a dramatist, who can use them to weave into the fabric of a character's speech the kind of information that a novelist can include in external tags such as 'she promised' or 'she commanded' or in adverbs such as 'he said *speculatively/determinedly/dubiously/threateningly*'. But auxiliaries such as *may, shall, must* are also problematic little words in that they undergo historical shifts in meaning and develop nuances which make them ambiguous. In saying 'he must know the truth', for instance, I may mean either that I am fairly certain that he already knows the truth or that I believe he doesn't and intend to force it on him.

A further complication is that these nuances can differ from one variety of English to another. So *may* in Indian English does not have the same range of meaning as *may* in American English, which in turn does not mean the same as *may* in Shakespeare's English. These mismatches between varieties are apt to cause us to misinterpret speakers' attitudes and intentions, and miscommunication is all the more liable to take place because auxiliaries are such small words, nestling unnoticed in the shade of the full verbs that they prop up.

In the passage from *The Merchant of Venice* quoted by Lynne Magnusson (Chapter 2, p. 27), Bassanio asks Shylock:

(15)

May you stead me?

(1.3.7)

Read in terms of modern English grammar, he may seem to be asking a question about *likelihood* (= 'Do you think it's possible you will help me out?') or about permission (= 'Are you allowed to help me out?'). In fact the question is about *ability*: Bassanio is asking whether Shylock has the financial resources to meet his needs. A modern Bassanio might have said: 'Are you able to help?' or simply 'Can you help?'

As used in example 15, *may* retains much of the original meaning of the Old English verb from which it descends (*magan* = 'have power to'). This type of *may* (I'll call it ability-*may*) is obsolete in modern English but still very common in Shakespeare, though already we find it in competition with *can*, the auxiliary that has since displaced it in these contexts. The equivalence between the two is shown in the Prologue to *Henry V*:

(16)

Can this cockpit hold
The vasty fields of France? or *may* we cram
Within this wooden O the very casques
That did affright the air at Agincourt?

(11–14)

The potential pitfall for modern readers is that we will tend to misinterpret all of Shakespeare's uses of ability-*may* by reading them as instances of one of the two meanings of *may* still extant today: I'll call these permission-*may* and perhaps-*may*. Both can be found alongside ability-*may* in Shakespeare's repertoire. Permission-*may* is illustrated in examples 17 and 18:

(17) (Malvolio quoting and commenting on Olivia's (supposed) love-letter to him)

'I *may* command where I adore.' Why, she *may* command me: I serve her, she is my lady.

(*TN* 2.5.114–15)

(18) (A conversation between Lady Macbeth's doctor and her waiting-woman)
DOCTOR
… what, at any time, have you heard her say?
GENTLEWOMAN
That, sir, which I will not report after her.
DOCTOR
You *may*, to me, and 'tis most meet you should.

(*Mac* 5.1.12–17)

In 17 *may* means something very like 'have the power to', but here the power is not physical ability, as in 16, or financial ability as in 15, but something closer to legal empowerment or social rights. In 18, similarly, the doctor is reassuring the gentlewoman that 'it is permissible' for his patient's secrets to be reported to him. *May* in this sense can be used either to report a permission or to negotiate it. Sometimes the distinction is an important one, as in example 19.

(19)
CORIOLANUS
May I change these garments?

SICINIUS

You *may*, sir.

(*Cor* 2.3.145)

In context, this is a highly charged exchange. Coriolanus, seeking election as consul, has been wearing the 'gown of humility' (2.3.39) as part of his (reluctant) campaign to gain the votes of the common citizens; he now wants to resume his normal clothes. He uses permission-*may*. But is he enquiring whether the rules and customs of the election permit him to change, or is he requesting his addressee to give him permission to do so? If *may I?* in 19 is a request rather than an enquiry, then Coriolanus is further humbling himself by acknowledging that the people's tribune, Sicinius, has the authority to govern his actions, and Sicinius' answer gives the actor playing the role a wonderful opportunity for combining the gratified condescension of permission-granting 'you may' with the (ironically?) deferential 'sir'. However interpreted, the exchange of *may* here is part of an ongoing power game between the two, continued at their next meeting in a battle over another auxiliary verb (see the discussion of *shall* below).

For some modern readers, especially younger ones, permission-*may* is almost as foreign as ability-*may*, since in many varieties of English it too is being displaced by *can* (or *could*), though there are still some (old-fashioned?) parents who correct their children when they ask '*can* I change my clothes?' instead of '*may* I change my clothes?'

The most common type of *may* in modern English is perhaps-*may*, where *may* is the equivalent of an adverb such as *perhaps* or *possibly*. This, too, is found in Shakespeare, as when Pompey is estimating the likelihood of Octavius and Antony combining forces against him:

(20)

lesser enmities *may* give way to greater.
                                    . . . the fear of us
May cement their divisions

(AC 2.1.44, 48–9)

Perhaps-*may* can be used either positively – something is 'very possible' – or with negative connotations – something is 'only possible'. It's the latter implication that plants a barb in Iago's (apparent) attempt to soothe Othello's jealous suspicions of Desdemona (Quarto text):

(21)

Nay, but be wise, yet we see nothing done,
She *may* be honest yet.

(Oth [3.3.435–6])

The repeated *yet* draws attention to the fact that the presumption of Desdemona's innocence is provisional and temporary.

Perhaps the most useful guidelines for reading *may* in Shakespeare are first to be alert to the possibility that *may* = 'can' (the ability-*may* that modern English has lost) and second to be aware of cases where Shakespeare's use lies on the cusp between two meanings, as in examples 22 and 23 below.

(22) (Banquo to the Witches)

Live you? or are you aught [i.e. anything]
That man *may* question?

(Mac 1.3.42–3)

(23) (Iago to Othello)

But if I give my wife a handkerchief –
. . . Why, then, 'tis hers, my lord, and being hers
She *may*, I think, bestow't on any man.

(Oth 4.1.10, 12–13)

In 22 *may* could be either ability-*may* or permission-*may*. If Banquo is asking whether man *is able* to question the witches, he is wondering about their reality or their power of human speech; if he is asking whether man *is permitted* to question them, he is raising the possibility that they are evil spirits, purveyors of forbidden knowledge. In 23 *may* slips between permission-*may* and perhaps-*may*. The primary meaning is that a wife 'has the right' to give away her husband's gift; but the meaning Iago is trying to insinuate is that it is 'very possible' that Desdemona has done so.

Note: The most common meaning of *may not* in Shakespeare's English is 'is not permitted'.

SHALL

Shakespeare has a number of ways of referring to future time. For example, *he shall go, he will go, he'll go* are all options. Of these three, the use of *shall* is likely to be the least familiar to modern readers because in some dialects it is no longer used at all and in others it is retained only in written language or in very formal speech styles. In Shakespeare's time, *shall* was as common as *will* and in many cases the two seem to be interchangeable. There was, however, an important nuance of difference between them, which Shakespeare often exploits. *Shall* can be used to signal that the future event is one that is, in some sense, *bound to happen*. How we interpret this bound-to-happen quality will depend on the particular context in which *shall* is used and on whether its subject is first person (*I/we*) or non-first person.

With *first-person subject*, where speakers are referring to their own future actions, *shall* may have the force of a promise (rather than a neutral prediction), as when in the opening scene of *King Lear*, Edmund, introduced to Kent, promises to try to deserve his good opinion: 'Sir, I *shall* study deserving' (1.1.30). Or it may signal the speaker's acceptance of a duty or obligation. So Gloucester responds to Lear's command ('Attend the lords of France and Burgundy') with 'I *shall* my lord' (1.1.33–4). Similarly, in *Antony and Cleopatra*, a whole series of subordinates accept Octavius' orders with the formula 'Caesar, I *shall*' (3.12.36; 4.6.4; 5.1.3, 68). By contrast, when Charmian replies to one of Cleopatra's orders with 'Madam I *will*' (5.2.195) we can infer that Shakespeare is signalling a different relationship. Charmian is as obedient as Octavius' servants, but she obeys with warmer feelings than mere dutifulness (*will* in contrast to *shall* often carries overtones of *will*ingness). However imperious Cleopatra may be, she is the friend as well as the ruler of her servants.

With *non-first-person subject*, when a speaker uses *shall* to refer to the future actions of others (*you* shall, *he/she* shall), it often has the force of reporting or imposing a duty (the equivalent of our 'will have to' or 'must'). In some dialects of modern English this 'laying down the law' use is retained in the framing of rules and regulations (e.g. 'Pupils *shall* be properly dressed at all times'). An example from *King Lear* shows the same ambiguity between reporting and imposing obligations. When Gloucester says of Edmund 'He hath been out nine years, and away he *shall* again' (1.1.31–2), the general meaning is that Edmund's departure is a bound-to-happen event, but the reader (or the actor) is left to decide whether this is simply because it is already scheduled (Edmund is home on leave and due to go away again) or because Gloucester is proposing to order him away (sharing Lear's belief that a father has the right and the power to dispose of his children's futures).

The issue of power is often an important one in the choice of *shall*-futures since we can only control the future of others if we are in a position of power. Hence the use of *you shall* or *she/he/it shall* is typically associated with gods, prophets, kings, army commanders and, in some cases, parents. Shakespeare contrasts a *shall*-future with a *will*-future at the end of the wooing scene in *Henry V*. Henry asks Princess Katherine '*wilt* thou have me?' (choosing *will* rather than *shall* because of its overtones of volition: he means 'are you willing to have me?'). Her reply – 'Dat is as it *sall* [shall] please le roi mon père' – characterizes her as a dutiful daughter, referring her future actions to the rule of 'the king my father'. Henry responds with: 'Nay, it *will* please him well, Kate; it *shall* please him, Kate' (5.2.243–6). This is reassurance, but not simply reassurance. The *will*-future predicts, the *shall*-future promises, and Henry is able to promise precisely because the King, Katherine's father, is in no position to refuse. What Henry is implying here by his choice of the *shall*-future is what he puts more bluntly elsewhere in the scene when he tells the French negotiator 'you must buy ... peace' (5.2.70). Other examples suggest that in Shakespeare's English *shall* was not just equivalent to *must*, but one degree stronger. In *3 Henry VI*, King Edward speaks of himself as 'their true sovereign whom they *must* obey? / Nay, whom they *shall* obey' (4.1.77–8). *Must* here points to the obligation; *shall* implies that the speaker has the power to bring it into effect.

For this reason, *shall*-futures can be particularly expressive where the question of power is in doubt. In *Coriolanus*, the power struggle between the patrician would-be consul Coriolanus and the plebeian tribunes comes to a head in 3.1.87–112, when they tell him what he 'shall' do. His outrage at their use of this 'absolute "shall"' (90), which he interprets as a violation of the natural social hierarchy, leads directly to a riot and by the scene's end he has lost the consulship and is in danger of losing his life.

In *King Lear*, Shakespeare ironically puts the 'absolute shall' into the mouth of a man who has just reduced himself to impotence:

(24)

No, you unnatural hags,
I will have such revenges on you both

That *all the world shall – I will* do such things –
What they are yet I know not, but *they shall be*
The terrors of the earth! You think *I'll weep,*
                    ... O fool, *I shall* go mad

(2.2.467–71, 75)

Lear makes use of three different first-person futures. *I'll* seems to be the most neutral, an unemphatic time indicator, used here only in a subordinate clause. *I will* is the volitional future, signalling what Lear desires to do ('have such revenges ... do such things'). In this speech it is contrasted with the first-person *shall*-future of the last line, where '*I shall* go mad' is what Lear sees as an undesired but bound-to-happen future (= 'I'm certain to go mad'). This, in turn, contrasts with the non-first person use of *shall* in *all the world shall, they shall.* This is the *shall* of absolute power, the form in which Lear has been used to issuing his kingly decrees. But here it rings hollow. Even a king cannot decree the future of 'all the world' and Lear has in any case just resigned all the power he had. Shakespeare draws attention to the emptiness of the threat by having Lear break off after 'all the world shall' (a famous example of the figure of **aposiopesis**), suggesting, as the Arden 3 editor notes, that this is an 'absurd flourish of unimaginable revenges'.

   Note: The *going to* future, now perhaps the most common for neutral prediction (e.g. 'he's *going to*/*gonna* win') has hardly come into use in Shakespeare's time. Almost all the instances of *going to* in his plays involve physical movement and are probably to be interpreted as meaning 'travelling to' or 'on the way to'.

THOU

Thou is a form of address no longer used in Standard English. To modern readers (except for those from dialect areas or religious groups that preserve it in speech) it is likely to be most familiar from the range of uses that survived into the early twentieth century: in poetry and addresses to God. These associations may predispose us to interpret *thou* as a marker of formal language or high style, which can be very misleading as a guide to Shakespearean usage. For instance, when Edward IV uses *thou* in his interview with Lady Grey (*3H6* 3.2.44) it marks a *lessening* of formality – indeed, it's a signal that he is about to proposition her; and when it occurs at the opening of *Romeo and Juliet* (1.1.7, 10) it's part of the colloquial, lower-class speech of the servingmen, Samson and Gregory. As Katie Wales says (Chapter 13, pp. 206–7), in Shakespeare's grammar the choice between *thou* and *you* is charged with complex social and emotional significance.

Originally, in Old English, the choice was simply a matter of number: *thou* was the form used to a single addressee, while *you* was used to address a group of two or more. In Middle English it became possible also to use *you* to a single individual, and the choice between singular-*you* and *thou* became a matter of social status. Broadly speaking, *thou* was used to inferiors (and between members of the lower class), while *you* was used to superiors (and between members of the upper class). Between strangers or where the balance of social power was in doubt, *you* was the default form, while siblings, intimate friends or lovers might opt to use *thou*. We can represent these social practices schematically by the following set of rules or norms (remembering that actual social practice was always much less tidy):

Thou (including *thee/thy/thine*) is the form appropriately used by:

1   monarch to subject
2   husband to wife (and male to female more generally)
3   parent to child
4   master/mistress to servant
5   servant to servant (or lower class to lower class)
6   intimate to intimate.

You (including *ye/your*) is the form appropriately used by:

 7 subject to monarch
 8 wife to husband (or female to male)
 9 child to parent
10 servant to master/mistress
11 upper class to upper class
12 stranger to stranger.

As well as status, the *you/thou* contrast was increasingly used to signal attitude. This expressive use can be seen as a metaphorical development of its social use. *You* (metaphorically) turns an addressee into a superior or a stranger, thus signalling respect, politeness or coldness; *thou* turns an addressee into an inferior or an intimate, thus signalling either contempt or affection. As a result of this development, each form became multi-valued; and the choice of one rather than the other became unstable since it no longer reflected speakers' fixed social status in relation to one another but the moment-by-moment shifts in feelings and balance of power. When both social and emotional factors are in play, the choice of address form becomes complex indeed. Each act of choice and particularly each switch of choice needs to be interpreted against a background of default usage – either the norm expected in a given social relationship (as listed in 1–12 above) or the norm established by the preceding conversation.

So, to return to my opening examples, Edward IV would be entitled to address Lady Grey as *thou* by social norms 1 and 2: she is a subject and a woman. His initial use of *you* in their dialogue ('Now tell me, madam, do *you* love *your* children?', *3H6* 3.2.36) can therefore be interpreted as an expression of kingly courtesy (a courtesy generally extended by kings to their more nobly born subjects, since it does not do for monarchs to remind powerful supporters of their subordinate status). This then sets the conversational norm against which his switch to *thou* ('What service wilt *thou* do me … ?', 44) can be seen as emotionally significant. In *Romeo and Juliet*, the opening exchange of *thou* between the Capulets' servingmen conforms to social norm 5 and also provides a contrast with their subsequent use of *you* to the Montague servants in the passage quoted in Chapter 13, pp. 205–6). In this context, *you* appears as a marked and unnatural politeness, part of each side's strategy to keep within the law while provoking the other side into starting a fight. In turn, this studied politeness provides a striking contrast with what happens next, when the nobly born Capulet, Tybalt, comes on the scene and picks a quarrel with his Montague counterpart, Benvolio:

(25)

   Turn *thee*, Benvolio, look upon *thy* death

(1.1.66)

Thou is here interpreted as an insult, because it violates norm 11 by implying that the addressee is a social inferior. The impact of being called *thou* when *you* was expected can be estimated from the fact that a verb *to thou* had been coined (probably in the early fifteenth century). In Renaissance usage, it commonly refers to the kind of deliberately provocative or aggressive use of *thou* that Tybalt demonstrates here. He might almost be following the advice that Sir Toby Belch gives Sir Andrew Aguecheek on how to challenge a gentleman to a duel: 'If *thou thou'st* him some thrice, it shall not be amiss' (*TN* 3.2.43–4). Sir Toby's own use of *thou* in this speech is, however, intended to give a different signal: it's part of the fake camaraderie by which he hopes to batten on Sir Andrew's wealth. But, noticeably, their social relationship is not symmetrical. Sir Andrew, evidently somewhat in awe of Sir Toby, never ventures to return his intimate *thou*.

There is no space here to chart the complex fluctuations of address forms that can take place in the course of an extended dialogue. But the scene between Hotspur and his wife (*1H4* 2.3.35–117), with its mixture of exasperation and affection, is well worth studying in this respect, as is the wooing of Lady Anne by Richard III (*R3* 1.2.33–228). The subtle choreography of stage space in this scene, described by Peter Lichtenfels (Chapter 11, pp. 158–60), is matched by the choreographing of emotions in the shifts between *you* and *thou*. For other relevant examples in this volume, see pp. 13 and 131–2.

The expressive richness of the *thou/you* choice is not in doubt. What I want to consider here are the problems of interpretation created by its multiple and potentially contra-dictory values. In some contexts it can be very difficult to decide which value or meaning predominates. My example is the opening scene of *Measure for Measure*, where the Duke is commissioning Escalus and Angelo to act as his deputies. Though entitled by norm 1 to use *thou* to both of them, he addresses Escalus as *you* (as we have seen, the normal polite usage from a ruler to a fellow nobleman) but he switches to *thou* for his first address to Angelo. What does this signal to the audience? It could imply a lesser rank, and hence that Angelo owes his position to the Duke's favour rather than his own noble birth. (The tone in which he is summoned – 'bid come before us Angelo' (1.1.15) – and his protestations of obedience and unworthiness, reminiscent of Dickens's Uriah Heep, might support this view.) Or should we read *thou* simply as a marker of intimacy, implying that Angelo is emotionally dear to the Duke in a way that Escalus is not? This view might be supported by the end of the Duke's speech to him:

(26)
> Old Escalus,
> Though first in question, is *thy* secondary.

> (1.1.45–6)

In fact the slightly disrespectful *Old Escalus* might indicate that the conversation is private not public. Perhaps, then, the switch to *thou* when Angelo enters is a kind of stage direction for physical closeness, indicating that the Duke takes him aside and whispers in his ear. In this case we might be meant to see 'be *thou* at full ourself' (43) as a confidential communication, contrasting with the later public announcement of the same thing, '*your* scope is as mine own' (64) which uses the *you* form to support Angelo's dignity in front of others. On the other hand, it's possible that the Duke's abrupt reversion from *thou* to *you* marks a chill in the emotional temperature caused by Angelo's reluctance to accept the commission, which prompts the Duke to say (rather pettishly?):

(27)

> No more evasion.
> We have with a leaven'd and prepared choice
> Proceeded to *you*; therefore take *your* honours.

(50–2)

It will always be productive for a reader or an actor to weigh up these different interpretations; but the very plethora of possibilities is a sign that the *thou/you* contrast was suffering from an expressive overload, and this may indeed be one reason why historically the generalized polite form *you* prevailed – leaving *thou* to Quakers, poets and Yorkshiremen.

Note: 1. Where the addressee is plural *you* is the only option. So one very common motive for *thou/you* switching is to mark changes of addressee from one to many and vice versa. This is easy to overlook in a printed play text and sometimes the signal is ambiguous. But in the Duke's speech just quoted, for instance, a director could decide that only the first line of 27 is spoken to Angelo, the remainder being addressed to Angelo and Escalus together.

2. The evidence of non-literary texts suggests that by Shakespeare's time singular-*you* was well on its way to becoming the default form in all social contexts. In general, therefore, it is the selection of *thou* that needs to be scrutinized for special significance.

THAT, THIS, THUS, THERE

In contrast to the forms discussed in my other case studies, none of those considered here has materially changed its meaning since Shakespeare's day, or at least not so far as to cause difficulties of comprehension. But they deserve an entry in a book on dramatic language because they are words with an unusually close relation to performance and stage space. Known as *deictics* (from the Greek for 'pointing'), their primary use in spoken language is to accompany an act of pointing ('pass me *that*'; 'I'll have *this* one'; 'it's over *there*') or some other hand gesture ('he's about *this* tall') or some kind of demonstrative activity ('you do it like *this*'). In written language we are more used to meeting them as devices for referring backwards and forwards in a text (you'll find many examples in the present chapter). But in a *dramatist's* text, they are often returned to their original gestural function and used as implied stage directions, as with the deictic *thus* at the end of Othello's speech (quoted in Chapter 3, p. 47), 'I ... smote him – *thus*!'. In this case the appropriate accompanying gesture is made clear by a printed stage direction: '*He stabs himself*' (5.2.353–4)

Another use of *thus* where the gesture seems clear, though this time not given in stage directions, occurs in *Richard II*, in the scene at Flint Castle where Bolingbroke meets Richard, having returned to England in defiance of Richard's sentence of exile. Bolingbroke dutifully kneels and Richard responds:

(28)
> Up, cousin, up; your heart is up, I know,
> *Thus* high at least, although your knee be low.

                                                                            (3.3.194–5)

The obvious interpretation is that Richard points to the crown, which he is wearing. Shakespeare's gestural deictic virtually forces the actor to do this and in turn ensures –

unless the actor or director is remarkably self-willed – that a crown is present on stage and is drawn to the audience's attention as a physical object (a tricky problem for modern-dress productions to get round). Its presence is important both symbolically – this is the scene in which Richard begins the process of divesting himself of royal power – and in the characterization of Richard. Defying Bolingbroke earlier in the scene, he refers to the crown repeatedly, even punning on the word (3.3.95–6); but from the moment he begins to envisage defeat he does not mention the crown directly and notably omits it from the long list of things that he will give up (145–54). It's his gesture that shows how large it looms in his mind, foreshadowing the extended play made with the physical object in the later abdication scene (4.1.181–9).

Elsewhere, the text leaves more for the interpreter to do, as when Polonius assures Claudius and Gertrude that Hamlet's strange moods are a result of love for Ophelia:

(29)
Take *this* from *this* if *this* be otherwise.

(*Ham* 2.2.156)

The third *this* is a textual pointer referring back to his analysis of the situation. But the first two are gestural deictics and the actor/director will need to decide what Polonius is pointing to. One editor suggests his hand and his staff of office (meaning 'you can dismiss me if I'm wrong'); another suggests his head and shoulders (meaning 'you can have my head off if I'm wrong'). For a fuller discussion of this ambiguous line, see Chapter 12, p. 181.

Similarly ambiguous is Antony's declaration that:

(30)
The nobleness of life
Is to do *thus*

(*AC* 1.1.37–8)

The choice of gesture here is rather important, since it must in some sense gloss what Antony means by 'the nobleness of life'. Is *thus* a stage direction for a kiss? Or does it, as one editor suggests, refer to Antony and Cleopatra's 'whole way of life' in Egypt? (in which case, does Antony gesture around the stage?) In deciding on the most appropriate interpretation here, an actor might also want to bear in mind the best way of creating a visual link with Antony's later use of the very same phrase ('to do *thus*') in his later suicide scene (4.14.103).

A whole barrage of pointings accompanies the last speech of Lear (Folio version):

(31)
> Pray you undo *this* button ...
> Do you see *this*? Look on her: look, her lips,
> Look *there*, look *there*!

(KL 5.3.308–10)

Unlike Othello, Lear is a tragic hero who does not end with a return to the grand style (see Chapter 3, pp. 47–8). It may in part be to compensate for this that the Folio text enhances the rhetoric of gesture, spectacle and tableau surrounding his death, with its insistent imperative to 'look', the question 'do you see?' and a whole series of deictics to direct the audience's gaze. But at what? whose button? what should we see? where should we look? The text leaves these questions unanswered but at the same time forces its performers to propose some answers if they are not to leave the gestural deictics as nonsense words.

NOTE

1   Italics are added in this and all subsequent quotations.

FURTHER READING

The grammatical discussion here has necessarily been both abbreviated and simplified. More detailed and technical accounts of most of the topics covered can be found in Levinson, Rissanen and Salmon; Blake and Ronberg offer more extensive discussion at an introductory level.

Blake, N.F., *Shakespeare's Language: An Introduction* (Basingstoke and London: Macmillan, 1983)

> Blake covers a wider range of grammatical topics than Ronberg, including a chapter on the nominal group and one on adverbs, prepositions and conjunctions. Of the specialized introductions to Shakespeare's language, this is the one most directly concerned with the interpretive difficulties resulting from differences between Early Modern English grammar and our own. It suffers from the lack of a subject index, but does offer a useful play-by-play guide to the passages quoted and discussed.

Levinson, S.C., *Pragmatics* (Cambridge: Cambridge University Press, 1983)

> Chapter 2 of this book offers a full and well-informed introduction to the important topic of deixis.

Rissanen, M., 'Syntax', in R. Lass (ed.), *The Cambridge History of the English Language, Vol. 3, 1476–1776* (Cambridge: Cambridge University Press, 1999), 187–331

> An authoritative, up-to-date account of Early Modern English grammar. It is fairly technical but clearly written and lavishly illustrated with examples from literary and non-literary texts. The discussion is not restricted to Shakespeare, but will enable the reader to place Shakespeare's usage in its socio-historical context.

Ronberg, G., *A Way with Words: The Language of English Renaissance Literature* (London: Edward Arnold, 1992)

> A helpful and undaunting beginner's guide, focusing mainly on grammar and rhetoric and including a long chapter on verbs and pronouns (pp. 35–98). The chapter on rhetoric includes a list of commonly used figures of speech and provides sample analyses of passages, showing how grammatical and rhetorical features combine and interact. The discussion is not restricted to Shakespeare, but he is the most frequently cited author and it can be illuminating to see how his usage compares with that of his contemporaries.

Salmon, V. and E. Burness (eds.), *A Reader in the Language of Shakespearean Drama* (Amsterdam/Philadelphia: John Benjamins, 1987)

Essays particularly relevant to this chapter are: Carol Replogle on salutations (pp. 101–15); Vivian Salmon on colloquialisms (pp. 37–70); Joan Mulholland and Charles Barber on *thou* and *you* (pp. 153–80); Piotr Kakietek on *may* and *might* (pp. 319–28); and most of the essays in Section IV, 'Shakespeare and Elizabethan Grammar'.

15

SHAKESPEARE'S NEW WORDS

Terttu Nevalainen

> Shakespeare ... was the greatest word-maker of them all. Of the 17,677 words Shakespeare employs in his plays and poems, his is the first known use of well over 1,700: one new word in every ten.
>
> Joseph T. Shipley

Although other scholars might quarrel with Shipley's numbers, there is no doubt that Shakespeare was an unusually prolific inventor of new words. However, one intriguing aspect of Shakespeare's new words is that there is something familiar about most of them. Modern readers and theatre-goers might not always be able to come up with a full definition of a word coined by Shakespeare, but they usually have some idea of what it means in its dramatic context. Out of context, some of Shakespeare's new words are clearly easier to grasp than others. The more transparent kind may be illustrated by words like *phraseless* and *rumourer*, and the more opaque, by *enactures* and *immoment*.

Modern readers are aided by the rules of English word-formation they share with Shakespeare and his contemporaries. New vocabulary items are rarely if ever invented at random, but are typically created using a set of principles shared by all native speakers of English, both today and in Shakespeare's times. If this were not the case, Shakespeare's new words would have remained incomprehensible to his contemporaries as well. New words are transparent to the extent they draw on familiar patterns. *Phraseless* ends in *-less*, and *rumourer* in *-er*.

The ending *-less* is also found in *languageless* and *spiritless*, and *-er* in *employer, murmurer* and *torturer* – all of them first recorded in Shakespeare. They are examples of a process called **affixation**. The other basic word-formation methods that were available to Shakespeare, and continue to be available to us today, are **compounding** and **conversion.**

While many of Shakespeare's new words may be transparent to modern audiences, quite a few of them will be harder to interpret, particularly if they accumulate several word-formation processes and draw on non-native vocabulary. These borrowed elements typically come from French and Latin, less frequently from Greek. In Elizabethan times, borrowing from other languages proved an extremely popular method of increasing and embellishing the English language. As Sylvia Adamson shows in her discussion of Shakespeare's grand style (Chapter 3), Latinate loans were typically motivated by specific stylistic considerations. But although the word market was flooded by these *fire-new words*, as they are metaphorically called in *Love's Labour's Lost* (1.1.176) – an allusion to money-coining – not all of them found a lasting place in English. This may be partly because new loan words and words based on foreign elements in general were often experimental, and not fixed by dictionaries and the printed word. They also posed difficulties for the less educated. In other cases coinages may not have caught on because they were intended for a given dramatic context only, not necessarily for wider circulation.

What interests us in this chapter are the various methods Shakespeare had at his disposal for coining new words. Particular attention will be paid to affixation, because it often combines with the other two methods of word-formation. These basic linguistic resources will be related to the reasons, grammatical and dramatic, that might have prompted him to use them.

COMPOUNDING

Compounding is a process which joins two or more independent words to produce a new one. It is one of the oldest native means of expanding the English vocabulary, extremely popular from Anglo-Saxon times onwards. To take an example, the medieval compound noun *lovesong* is still fully transparent to us. It consists of the native English nouns *love* and *song*. Shakespeare, too, uses it:[1]

(1)
CLOWN
   Would you have a *love-song*, or a song of good life?
TOBY
   A love-song, a love-song.

(TN 2.3.35–7)

As this passage from *Twelfth Night* illustrates, a *lovesong* (or *love-song*, as it is spelled here), is a name for a particular kind of *song* ('song of love'). As with compounds in general, no change in the grammatical function of the base-word *song* has taken place. A *lovesong* and a *song of good life* are the alternatives the Clown has to offer; both are something that he could perform. In grammatical terms, they serve as objects of the verb *have*. By means of compounding, a longer expression ('a song of love', 'song that deals with love', etc.) can be telescoped into one word, to be used grammatically in the same way as the word on which it is based.

   The conciseness associated with compounds may be desirable for various reasons besides naming entities and qualities. With limited space and the rigours of metre, economy of expression is a necessity in dramatic and poetic language. Complex poetic compounds therefore form an essential element of Shakespeare's verbal creativity, especially in his early work. Certain patterns of adjective formation are particularly favoured by him in epithets, which offer a way of packaging a lot of information in a few words. A whole clause is encapsulated in a compound adjective based on a past participle in *star-cross'd lovers* ('lovers crossed by stars', *RJ* Prologue 6). Similarly, an effective and economical way of saying 'despair which is embraced rashly' is provided by the compound adjective *rash-embraced* in Portia's description of human emotions in example 2. Sometimes a verb-based compound can be so compact as to give rise to more than one interpretation. Two are suggested for *child-changed father* in *King Lear*: 'father changed into a child' and 'father changed by his children'. (See also Chapter 3, p. 37.)

(2)
> How all the other passions fleet to air:
> As doubtful thoughts, and *rash-embrac'd* despair,
> And shudd'ring fear, and *green-eyed* jealousy.

(MV 3.2.108–10)

Another type of compound epithet that abounds in Shakespeare's poetic diction is illustrated in example 2 by the quality of jealousy, *green-eyed* ('having green eyes'). It combines compounding and affixation: the noun phrase *green eye(s)* is turned into a compound adjective by adding the adjectival ending *-ed*. Shakespeare exploited this strategy extensively in his descriptions of both the physical and the mental world. He has over twenty compound adjectives in *-hearted* alone! Some go back to earlier times, including *free-hearted* ('having a free heart', i.e. 'generous'), *hard-hearted* ('stern', 'obdurate') and *tender-hearted*, but he also created new ones, such as *maiden-hearted* ('I'm bride-habited, / But *maiden-hearted*', *TNK* 5.3.150–1), *marble-hearted* ('thou *marble-hearted* fiend', *KL* 1.4.251) and *pitiful-hearted* ('*pitiful-hearted* Titan', *1H4* 2.4.119). Overall, *-ed* adjectives based on verbs and nouns count among Shakespeare's favourite compounds.

CONVERSION

Conversion is one of the regular word-formation processes that changes the part of speech of a word, and so enables the speaker to use it in a new grammatical function. This is how the verb *bottle* 'to put into a bottle' is created from the noun *bottle*. Conversion was a popular way of coining new words in Elizabethan times, only compounding and affixation seem to have been more common. In the Middle Ages, conversion may have been facilitated by pairs of nouns and verbs borrowed from French. Loan-word pairs such as *a rule/to rule* may have served as models for other similar coinages based on both native and loan words. In Celia's speech in example 3 this word-formation process transforms the borrowed noun *silence* into the verb-form *silenced*.

(3)

For since the little wit that fools have was *silenced*, the little foolery that wisemen have makes a great show.

(*AYL* 1.2.85–7)

While the verb *silence* has been attested before Shakespeare, there are a number of instances of conversion that have been attributed to him. They include conversions of nouns into verbs (e.g. *duke* 'to act as duke' from the noun *duke*; *stranger* 'to turn into a stranger' from the noun *stranger*), of adjectives into verbs (e.g. *dumb* 'to make dumb' from the adjective *dumb*; *safe* 'to make safe' from the adjective *safe*), and of verbs into nouns (e.g. *accuse* 'accusation' from the verb *accuse*; *dispose* 'disposal' from the verb *dispose*). Modern historical dictionaries, however, suggest that the two nouns, *accuse* and *dispose*, were in fact coined earlier, but that they were becoming rare in Shakespeare's time.

The verb *dumb* was employed by Shakespeare in the passage of *Antony and Cleopatra* quoted in example 4. Both *silence* in 3 and *dumb* in 4 behave like typical verbs in that they denote the time when the action took place (the past in both cases, indicated by the past participle -*ed* forms).

(4)
> what I would have spoke
> Was beastly *dumbed* by him.

(AC 1.5.51–2)

If the sole function of conversion in Shakespeare was to enable him to use a word in a new grammatical function, we might wonder why there was a need for him to create the verb *dumb*. The existing verb *silence* had much the same meaning. Moreover, the paraphrase *make mute* is used to the same effect in Hamlet's soliloquy in the First Quarto (1603):

(5)
> Strike more then wonder in the iudiciall eares,
> Confound the ignorant, and make *mute* the wise,

[1117–18]

One of the differences between the words may lie in their connotations: the noun *silence* goes back to French and may have been associated with a higher register than *dumb*, which takes a native adjective as its base (cf. Chapter 3). Moreover, the French loan word *mute* was primarily connected with human beings, while *dumb* could similarly characterize animals, which were by nature incapable of speaking like human beings. In example 4, the messenger Alexas was *dumbed* by the neighing of a horse (*him* refers to Mark Antony's *steed*). The use of the word may therefore have been triggered in the dramatist's mind by the association with 'beastly'.

Stylistic motives of a different kind may lie behind the use of the noun *accuse* shown in the passage in example 6 from the second part of *Henry VI*. We can tell that *accuse* is a noun because it is modified by the adjective *false*. By contrast, when used as a verb, *accuse* is followed by the target of the action of accusing (the object form *me* in 'Who can *accuse* me? Wherein am I guilty?', *2H6* 3.1.103).

(6)
> And dogged York, that reaches at the moon,
> Whose overweening arm I haue plucked back,
> By false *accuse* doth level at my life.
>
> (*2H6* 3.1.158–60)

(7)
> The lady is dead upon mine and my masters false *accusation*; and briefly, I desire nothing but the reward of a villain.
>
> (*MA* 5.1.233–5)

Had he simply wanted to create a noun from the verb in example 6, Shakespeare need not have resorted to the conversion form *accuse*, which was going out of use at the time. He could equally well have turned to the current form *accusation*, which he uses in Borachio's speech in *Much Ado About Nothing* (example 7). *Accusation* is an earlier loan from French and in general use in Shakespeare's time. It often co-occurred with the adjective *false*, as is the case in 7. As the long and short nouns could appear with the same adjective, the reason for Shakespeare using the shorter form may have been primarily metrical. As in 6, he employs *accuse* only in his verse, where *accusation* would have introduced two unwanted extra syllables. *Accusation* in 7, by contrast, comes from a prose passage.

One is much less likely to find *accuse* as a noun than a verb, and *dumb* as a verb than an adjective, in Shakespeare. And because these conversion forms are considerably less frequent than their base words, they stand out from the text. This may also be more generally true of conversion forms in Shakespeare. The nouns *boy, child, coward* and *stranger*, for instance, appear hundreds of times in his drama, but their respective conversion verbs usually only once (e.g. 'I shall see / Some squeaking Cleopatra *boy* my greatness' ['boy actor take my part on stage'], *AC* 5.2.218–19); 'Why, what read you there, / That hath so *cowarded* and chased your blood / Out of appearance?' ['turned into a coward'], *H5* 2.2.74–6; 'Dow'rd with our curse and *strangered* with our oath' ['turned into a stranger'], *KL* 1.1.205).

The form *childed* derived from the noun *child* appears in *King Lear*: 'He *childed* as I fathered' (3.6.107). Edgar's compressed expression is notoriously difficult to paraphrase. Several critics interpret *childed* here as a conversion verb and give it the dynamic reading 'he (being) turned into a child' or 'behaving like a child' (cf. *child-changed father*, discussed above). Edgar's reference to Lear (and to himself) is given a strikingly different meaning by those critics who interpret *childed* as an adjective 'having (cruel) children' (and *fathered* as 'having a (cruel) father'). This reading is based on the fact that the *-ed* ending could also be used to turn nouns into adjectives (cf. *green-eyed* in example 2).[2]

AFFIXATION

As pointed out at the beginning, new words can also be derived solely by means of affixation, that is, attaching a **prefix** or a **suffix** to an existing word. Prefixes and suffixes themselves are not independent but can only appear as parts of another word. The process of **prefixation** resembles compounding in that it does not change the part of speech of a word. When in *Macbeth* Shakespeare adds the prefix *un-* to the verb *provoke* he creates the new verb *unprovoke*, which reverses the action of provoking. **Suffixation** differs from prefixation and resembles conversion in that it typically alters the part of speech, and the grammatical function, of the word: when the suffix *-less* is appended to the noun *phrase* in *The Rape of Lucrece*, the resulting word *phraseless* is an adjective; *-less* is an adjective-forming suffix.

Sometimes prefixation and compounding may be used to convey similar meanings. Take the Shakespearean neologisms *over-picture* and *super-dainty* in examples 8 and 9, for instance. In both cases it is possible for a modern reader to distinguish two independent words. Unlike *over-*, however, *super-* could not occur on its own in Elizabethan English. What makes these two items interesting are their overlapping meanings.

(8)

>   she did lie
> In her pavilion, cloth-of-gold, of tissue,
> *O'erpicturing* that Venus where we see
> The fancy outwork nature.

>   (*AC* 2.2.208–11)

(9)

> But Kate, the prettiest Kate in Christendom,
> Kate of Kate-Hall, my *super-dainty* Kate,
> For dainties are all Kates, and therefore, Kate
> Take this of me, Kate of my consolation

>   (*TS* 2.1.188–192)

O'erpicturing . . . Venus in the description of Cleopatra (8) may be taken to mean either 'surpassing the picture of Venus' or 'representing the picture of Venus in excess of reality'. In *super-dainty* ('extremely dainty') the praise of Kate is intensified by means of the Latinate prefix *super-* in example 9. In Elizabethan English this prefix is typically used to form new adjectives, as in *super-subtle* ('extremely subtle' or 'excessively subtle', *Oth* 1.3.357) and *super-serviceable* ('over-officious', *KL* 2.2.17–18). It competes with *over-*, which also has the meanings 'extremely' and 'excessively'. *Super-* was however a relative newcomer to the language at the time and therefore much less frequent than its native competitor. But although several adjectives in *over-* do occur in *The Taming of the Shrew* (e.g. *over-joy'd, over-merry,* Induction 1.119, 136) there is no *over-dainty* or *super-merry*. *Super-* and *over-* were obviously not freely interchangeable in Shakespeare.

Verbal experimentation was common in the Renaissance. English was gaining new functions as a standard language in the public sphere, and was therefore in the process of acquiring a wealth of new vocabulary. A large number of these new words were borrowed from Latin and French, also to some extent from Greek. As new loans were being integrated into the English language, new prefixes and suffixes adopted from foreign sources were applied to older loan words and the native Germanic word stock as well. There were more than 120 affixes, native and borrowed, in English in Shakespeare's time – many more than in Chaucer's period two hundred years earlier. It took some time before the affixes derived from loan words found their place in English. Just like *super-*, many of them continued to be associated with borrowed vocabulary. When affixes were added to polysyllabic loan words, these learned-looking and foreign-sounding words grew even longer.

Some common Elizabethan affixes are listed below, with their meanings given in brackets. It is worth noting that affixes usually had more than one meaning.

Note: Latinate affixes are shown in ***boldface***.

Prefixes

+ *un-*, ***in-***, ***dis-*** (not; the converse of): *unfit, inhospitable, discontent*

+ *un-*, ***dis-*** (to remove; to reverse the action): *unburden, disburden; unload, disappear*

+ *be-* (to provide with; completely, thoroughly): *bestain, bedeck*

+ ***en-***/***em-*** (to make; to put into, to provide with): *enthral, embody*

+ ***mis-*** (wrongly, badly): *mislead, misuse*
+ ***re-*** (again, back): *re-answer, reunite*

Suffixes

+ *-ing,* ***-ment, -ation,*** *-ance/ence, -ure* (the act, cause, result, state, etc. of *-ing*): *landing, retirement, education, admittance, exposure*
+ *-ness,* ***-ity*** (the condition, quality, etc. of being): *weariness, capability*
+ *-er* (someone who *-s*): *teacher, dancer*
+ *-ed* (having): *dropsied, orbed, rose-lipped*
+ *-y* (like, covered with, characterized by): *icy, dirty, healthy*
+ *-less* (without): *fatherless, matchless*
+ ***-able*** (fit for *-ing*/to be *-ed*; having the stated quality): *answerable, suitable*; *fashionable*
+ ***-al, -ical*** (relating to, having the character of): *musical, fantastical*
+ ***-ive,*** *-ing* (that *-s*, capable of *-ing*, tending to): *persistive, persisting*

Prefixation

Like *over-* and *super-*, native and non-native affixes were often found in competition, giving rise to several words meaning nearly the same thing. In the hands of an exceptionally skilful dramatist, this potential could be exploited for various purposes. This can be seen in the way Shakespeare used loan words, and in his ***nonce words*** in particular (i.e. words that were coined by Shakespeare, and only used by him).

Un-, in- and *dis-* all express various aspects of negation, undoing and deprivation. The native form *un-* was widely used, and also appeared in nonce words, as in the Porter's speech in *Macbeth* in example 10, where it introduces an immediate contrast between two actions:

(10)

MACDUFF   What three things does drink especially provoke?
PORTER   Marry, Sir, nose-painting, sleep, and urine. Lechery, Sir, it *provokes*, and *unprovokes*: it provokes the desire, but it takes away the performance.

(2.3.28–30)

Shakespeare makes creative use of the rivalry between native and non-native negative prefixes in neologisms. They are found in competition, for instance, in **un***seminared*, **im***moment* and **dis***candy* in *Antony and Cleopatra*:

(11)

I take no pleasure
In aught an eunuch has. 'Tis well for thee
That, being *unseminared*, thy freer thoughts
May not fly forth of Egypt.

(1.5.10–13)

(12)

All come to this? The hearts
That spanieled me at heels, to whom I gave
Their wishes, do *discandy*, melt their sweets
On blossoming Cæsar

(4.12.20–3)

(13)

That I some lady trifles have reserved,
Immoment toys, things of such dignity
As we greet modern friends withal

(5.2.164–6)

The dramatist glosses both *discandy* ('melt their sweets') and *immoment toys* ('lady trifles'), but expects his audience to understand *unseminared*, a coinage with the native prefix *un-*, from the context. Cleopatra's words are directed to Mardian, a eunuch, whose state of being *unseminared*, i.e. 'deprived of virility', is literally related to the noun *seminary*, originally meaning 'seed plot'. In word-formation terms the borrowed noun has first been converted into a verb and a participle, and then qualified with the privative prefix *un-*. We have no evidence for the affirmative form, nor the noun for that matter, elsewhere in Shakespeare, neither does this neologism appear in other sources. Shakespeare, too, used other words meaning 'castrated': *ungenitured*, another nonce form, in *Measure for Measure* (3.2.167) and *gelded* in *Pericles* (4.6.122). *Unseminared* was, however, particularly apt in this context: it reminded the audience of the similarities between eunuchs and celibate priests, who were educated in *seminaries*.

The reason why Shakespeare preferred the prefix *un-* to *dis-* in example 11 may be that it was the more productive of the two. *Dis-* could similarly be attached to conversion verbs to denote the lack or removal of something (*disburden*, *dishorn*), but *un-* was decidedly more common. Basically, the Latinate prefixes *in-* and *dis-* could mean the same as the native *un-*, particularly in adjectives.

It may also be worth noting that *in-* is context-sensitive and becomes *ir-* when it is followed by -*r* (*irreligious*), *il-* when followed by -*l* (*illogical*), and *im-* when followed by either -*m* or -*p* (*impossible*). The process is called **assimilation**, and can be seen in *immoment* in example 13. Shakespeare's choice of the prefix in *immoment* may be connected with the fact that *moment* was less typically used as an adjective, as it is here, than as a noun (e.g. 'An oath is of no *moment*, being not took / Before a true and lawful magistrate', *3H6* 1.2.22–3). *In-* occurred more commonly with nouns than *un-*. Moreover, this choice of a Latinate prefix was in harmony with the French origins of *moment*, and may have been connected with such existing words as *immaterial*.

Dis- is commonly attached to verbs of French or Latin origin. When coining the verb *discandy* in example 12 Shakespeare first had to convert the borrowed noun (*sugar-*)*candy* into a verb, and then reverse its meaning by adding *dis-*. He gives the native phrase *melt their sweets* as a synonym for the new verb *discandy*. A candied condition is similarly dissolved in *The Tempest* but the verb used by Antonio is *melt* ('Twenty consciences ... candied be they / And *melt* ere they molest', 2.1.279–81).

We may wonder whether *dis-Candie*, spelled with a capital C in the First Folio, was coined to make a mental link between *sugar-candy* and Candy, or Candia, as the island of Crete was known in Shakespeare's time. Crete was particularly famous for its luxury exports such as wines and herbs. Shakespeare may have coined the three negative words in examples 11 to 13 partly to enrich the exotic and sensuous language he creates in *Antony and Cleopatra*.

SUFFIXATION

Moving on to suffixations, the new words *insultment* and *fleshment* in examples 14 and 15 both show *-ment*, a suffix of French origin, appended to a verb in order to turn it into a noun.

(14)

With that suit upon my back, will I ravish her: first kill him, and in her eyes; there shall she see my valour, which will then be a torment to her contempt. He on the ground, my speech of *insultment* ended on his dead body, and when my lust hath dined ... to the court I'll knock her back, foot her home again.

(*Cym* 3.5.138–45)

(15)

> It pleased the King his master very late
> To strike at me upon his misconstruction,
> When he, compact, and flattering his displeasure,
> Tripped me behind; being down, insulted, railed,
> And put upon him such a deal of Man,
> That worthied him, got praises of the King
> For him attempting who was self-subdued,
> And in the *fleshment* of this dread exploit,
> Drew on me here again.

(*KL* 2.2.114–122)

As the passages in 14 and 15 suggest, nouns created by adding the suffix -*ment* denote action, 'insulting' in *Cymbeline* and 'fleshing' in *Lear*. In Cloten's speech *insultment* is a good example of how the form of a word was not necessarily fixed at the time. Shakespeare had various options: first, he could have resorted to the noun *insult*, a medieval loan from French, which is identical in form to the verb. Second, he could have selected *insultation*, another French loan common in Elizabethan English. In principle, he could also have made use of the Latinate suffix -*ance*, and coined the form *insultance*, which does appear in his lifetime. Most obvious of all, he could have used the most frequent suffix to make nouns out of verbs: the native -*ing*, which would have yielded *insulting*. *Insulting* does occur in Shakespeare, but only as a participial adjective 'something that insults' (as in *insulting ship*, *insulting tyranny*, *1H6* 1.2.138, 4.7.19). Similarly, when the suffix -*ing* is attached to a verb in order to turn it into a noun, it commonly denotes continuous or incomplete action. This meaning of -*ing* may have ruled out its use in example 14.

Fleshment in Osric's speech in example 15 is based on the native word *flesh*. Shakespeare has used it as a verb earlier in the same scene: 'Come, I'll *flesh* ye' (*KL* 2.2.45). The usual form for the noun created out of this verb in the sixteenth century was *fleshing*, 'baiting with flesh', 'the action of inciting (hounds) to the chase by giving them a taste of flesh'. *Fleshment* has been taken to mean 'wild excitement' or, more abstractly, 'first success'. The borrowed suffix *-ment* may have been chosen in *Lear* to refer to the mental state of being excited, instead of the physical action denoted by the form *fleshing*. Other blends of native verbs and the suffix *-ment* in Shakespeare's time include the nouns *acknowledgement* and *wonderment*. Usually *-ment* was, however, restricted to the domain of loan vocabulary.

Shakespeare also uses *-ure*, yet another non-native suffix, to derive nouns from verbs in words like *exposure* (from *expose*, *TC* 1.3.195). In example 16, taken from the Second Quarto *Hamlet* (1605), the plural noun *enactures* is derived from the verb *enact* to denote a number of individual events. It is usually paraphrased by the singular forms 'enactment' or 'fulfilment'.

(16)
> The violence of eyther, griefe, or ioy,
> Their owne *ennactures* with themselues destroy,
> Where ioy most reuels, griefe doth most lament,
>
> [1909–11]

Fulfilment would have been a perfectly possible expression in this context – the verb *fulfill* is used later on in the play. Shakespeare however chose the verb *enact* (itself an older prefixed form of the verb *act*) as the base, possibly because by doing so he could refer back to play-acting, which had been the topic of Hamlet and Polonius' earlier discussion:

(17)
> *Ham.* You playd once i'th Vniuersitie you say,
> *Pol.* That did I my Lord, and was accounted a good Actor,
> *Ham.* What did you *enact*?
> *Pol.* I did *enact* Iulius Cæsar, I was kild i'th Capitall,
> Brutus kild mee.
>
> [1821–5]

Why *enacture*(*s*) was chosen instead of *enactment*(*s*) can only be guessed at. Both suffixes are of foreign origin and overlap in meaning, but *-ment* would have been the more common of the two at the time. The word may have puzzled some of Shakespeare's contemporaries as well, because in the First Folio *Hamlet* (1623) it appears as *ennactors*, a plural form of the agent noun related to the verb *enact*. *Enactor* was an existing word at the time, and may have sounded very much like *enacture*, the new word found in the Second Quarto.

While *enactor* is related to *actor*, a Latin loan word, native means also existed for deriving people-denoting nouns from verbs, i.e. the *-er* suffix found in words like *baker* and *teacher*. Shakespeare uses *-er*, for instance, when coining *rumourer* in *Coriolanus* (18). *Rumourer* is interesting as it does not seem to have caught on, even if it is recorded in some modern dictionaries ('rumour-monger', 'rumour-bearer'). By contrast, the suffix *-er* itself, added by Shakespeare to the conversion-verb *rumour* ('spread rumours'), is one of the most productive native English suffixes both in Shakespeare's time and today.

(18)
  Go see this *rumourer* whipped. It cannot be
  The Volces dare break with us.

                                  (*Cor* 4.6.48–9)

The reasons why *rumourer* has not gained popularity must be manifold. One of them may be that although *gossip* continued to have its old senses 'god-parent' and 'close friend', 'companion' in Elizabethan English, it also came to acquire the meaning 'rumour-monger'. *Gossip* had other synonyms, too, such as *newsmonger* (*base newsmongers* in *1H4* 3.2.25). On the other hand, it is worth bearing in mind that suffixes have a double duty to perform: they name a concept and assign a grammatical role to it. An extremely common suffix like *-er* could be compared with a purely grammatical ending such as *-*(*e*)*s*, which produces regular plural forms for nouns. Perhaps

-*er* was needed in example 18 not so much to create a new word for a given concept than as a grammatical shorthand for a phrase meaning 'whoever he is who spreads this rumour'.

As -*er* was so flexible and did not have any serious rivals in general use, it is no wonder Shakespeare resorted to it in numerous coinages. Those based on Latinate loans include *appearer, confirmer, employer, enjoyer, injurer, insulter, moraler, proposer, protester, ratifier, torturer* and *undeserver*. Many of them have fared better than *rumourer*, and are perfectly valid in present-day English – not to mention all the *employers, protesters* and *torturers* that hit the headlines every day.

NOTES

1   The words discussed in the text are italicized in the examples quoted.

2   See Katie Wales, 'An aspect of Shakespeare's dynamic language', in Salmon and Burness (listed below), pp. 181–90.

FURTHER READING

Reference works

There is a large number of reference works that can be used to study Shakespeare's vocabulary. Electronic versions of Shakespeare's texts include the *Oxford Shakespeare* and the Chadwyck-Healey collection of *Editions and Adaptations of Shakespeare* (1591–1911). My research for this chapter has benefited from both of them.

The *Harvard Concordance to Shakespeare*, compiled by Marvin Spevack, lists all the words, old and new, used by Shakespeare in their dramatic contexts. Other reference works include historical dictionaries, notably the *Oxford English Dictionary* and *Middle English Dictionary*. Both are available in electronic versions, and give dates to English words recorded in writing. *The Early Modern English Dictionaries Database* compiled by Professor Ian Lancashire at the University of Toronto gives access in an electronic form to a number of dictionaries published in the sixteenth and seventeenth centuries.

Other works

Nevalainen, Terttu, 'Early Modern English lexis and semantics', in Roger Lass (ed.), *The Cambridge History of the English Language, Vol. 3, 1476–1776* (Cambridge: Cambridge University Press, 1999), 332–458

This chapter contains a comprehensive treatment of word-formation in Elizabethan English. It does not specifically concentrate on Shakespeare, but provides an overall view of the increase in vocabulary intake, loan words, word-formation processes and meaning changes in Early Modern English.

Salmon, Vivian and Edwina Burness (eds), *A Reader in the Language of Shakespearean Drama* (Amsterdam/Philadelphia: John Benjamins, 1987)

This book includes some in-depth studies on various aspects of Shakespeare's new words. See for example Salmon's article on the functions of Shakespeare's word-formation, Bryan Garner's two articles on Shakespeare's Latinate vocabulary, and Katie Wales's article on the various interpretations of 'He childed as I father'd' in *King Lear*.

16

SHAKESPEARE'S SOUNDS

Roger Lass

PROLOGUE: 'DIFFERENCE' AND VARIABILITY

Modern readers or playgoers are auditorily misled by their experience of Shakespeare, just as modern listeners are when they hear Bach played on the piano or Mozart played by a modern symphony orchestra. The sound they experience was neither available to nor imaginable by the creator. We don't *have* to play Bach on the piano or Mozart with a modern orchestra; but generally we have to (or just do) read Shakespeare in editions with modern spelling and punctuation, and hear him performed with modern English pronunciation. Even silent reading is done in one's own dialect of modern English, or – if one is a second-language speaker – in whatever dialect(s) one was taught, British (of various regional types) or American or a mixture.

The professional experience (theatre, film, radio, TV) however is usually British; the 'proper' or conventional vehicle for Shakespeare tends to be a southern English style of pronunciation of the 'classical' or 'BBC' or 'Oxbridge' type. A performance of *Hamlet* in a broad Yorkshire or Alabama or Irish accent still seems somehow incongruous; or at least that's what the mystique associated with Shakespeare causes many of us to feel. Even knowing better, I find American performances of Shakespeare rather odd; and even odder when the actors try (normally with pretty indifferent success) to sound 'English'.

If we could be transported back to Elizabethan London and actually hear Shakespeare's own speech, the experience would be totally different. A modern listener would find the (probably rather small) part of the language that was comprehensible at all both surprising and rather confusing. The impression would be something like a cross between Irish and Scots and West Yorkshire, with touches of American. For instance, the words *cut* and *put* would have the same vowel (rather like the present one in *put)*, as in northern England; *cat* and *fast* would have the same (short) vowel, as in northern England and Scotland; *law* and *lore* would be distinguished by a fully pronounced *r* at the end of *lore*, and *r* would be pronounced in all positions where it is now written (e.g. in *lord* as well, as in most American, Scots and Irish). *One* would be pronounced like modern *awn;* the *gh* in *night* would still be optionally pronounced, either as a sound like German *ch* in *nicht* or an ordinary *h*; the vowel in *night* and *bite* would be very like the modern one in *bait; ease* and *seas* would have either a vowel like that in modern *bet* but long, or one like that in modern *bees*. *Days* and *daze* would have a vowel like lengthened *bet. Bird, heard* and *word* would have distinct vowels (before a pronounced *r*) as their modern spellings suggest, namely the vowels of modern *bit, bet* and *put*, as in Scots. (These particular examples stand for etymological word-classes, i.e. words that had the same vowel in Middle English. So '*seas*' is shorthand for a large group of words also including *ease, flea, beat, leaf*, etc.)

Besides these gross differences, the pronunciation as a whole would be much more variable than we're now used to. Since 'standard' English had not been codified or fixed at this time, there were many different varieties in use in London at the same time, even by the same speaker – some rather archaic or conservative, some fashionable and 'advanced', some more 'popular' or 'vernacular' than others. There was a greater availability of forms from neighbouring dialects as well, so a

London speaker could use a characteristically south-western or Kentish rhyme if needed (a common practice at least since Chaucer).

This variation may be problematic for modern readers, who normally operate with a 'one word: one pronunciation' system. We experience – and therefore expect – variation only on a rather small scale. For instance, some people pronounce *either* with the first syllable rhyming with *see*, others with it rhyming with *eye*, and many pronounce it both ways, more or less unpredictably; similarly with *economics, evolution* (first syllable as in *see* or *set*) – but never with *revolution*. Similar variability occurred in stress patterns and syllable-count as well. Only a tiny proportion of this variation is actually represented in spelling in the original editions; but this, along with other evidence, gives us grounds for suggesting that particular variants were used in places where they are not represented, and would seem odd to a modern speaker. But since we mostly read Shakespeare in modernized versions, we can be deluded into thinking that he wrote (and spoke) a form of 'our English', rather than that of his (quite distant) time.

SYLLABLE-COUNT AND STRESS

Much of the variability of natural speech was, in the Elizabethan period, institutionalized in poetic practice; in particular the dropping of unstressed syllables (**syncope**) and shifting of the position of word-stress (**diastole/systole**) were rhetorical figures one could learn about from textbooks. But we may still feel a mild outrage or sense of illegitimate 'poetic licence' when words spelled in the modern way are obviously metrically different. *Cardinal, general, pestilence, slaughtering* scan as either three or two syllables. But if we saw spellings (usually edited out) like *card'nall, gen'rall, pestlence, slaught'ring* we'd perhaps be more willing to accept them as disyllabic – especially in verse passages where the metre provides confirmation. Such spellings, however, are usually in the minority: the original printers quite properly assumed that speakers of English knew perfectly well that it was possible to drop vowels in certain positions. These indicative spellings then allow us to think of options in syllable-count when reading modern versions, and serve as evidence that these possibilities existed for Shakespeare. In general, unstressed vowels in the vicinity of *r*, *l* and *n* are particularly prone to deletion (cf. the usual modern variants *desp(e)rate*, *bach(e)lor*, *list(e)ning*), and we find metrically different versions even of the same word in the same text: thus *natural* is three syllables in the first of the two lines below, and two in the second:

And every thing that seems *unnatural*

(*H5* 5.2.62)

How shall we then behold their *natural* tears?

(*H5* 4.2.12)

But there are also rather more surprising deletions (from a modern point of view): the italicized words in the lines below have the same (**trochaic**) rhythm as a modern disyllable like *city* (i.e. ´˘; cf. p. 55):

On *blossoming* Caesar, and this pine is barked

(*AC* 4.12.23)

And *citizens* to their dens. The death of Antony

(*AC* 5.1.17)

Tut, Lucius, this was but a deed of *charity*

(*Tit* 5.1.89)

Come, come, the cause. If *arguing* make us sweat

(*JC* 5.1.48)

Ay, night by night, in *studying* good for England!

(*2H6* 3.1.111)

Therefore, since *brevity* is the soul of wit

(Ham 2.2.90)

Variable syllable-count is not that surprising in itself; one would expect it to some degree in casual speech, and Shakespeare is using both casual and formal styles of pronunciation. But what might be less expectable is variation in stress-placement: very few words in modern English have variable stress patterns in the dialect of one speaker.

Because of its complex history (a Germanic language with an extensive input from Latin and its descendants, the Romance languages like French), English had for a long time – and still has to some extent – a dual stress system. There is a 'Germanic' one that preferentially accents the first syllable of the word (except for prefixes), and a 'Romance' one that tends to have the accent as close to the end of the word as possible (but no more than three syllables back). These have interacted and competed for nearly a millennium, and Shakespeare makes good use of this in his verse, as we can see from examples like the following (stressed syllable marked ´):

Germanic
  The *révenue* whereof shall furnish us

(R2 1.4.46)

Romance
  My manors, rents, *revénues*, I forgo

(R2 4.1.212)

Germanic
  For *éxile* hath more terror in his look

(RJ 3.3.13)

Romance
  Grief of my son's *exíle* hath stopp'd her breath.

(RJ 5.3.211)

Metrical evidence tells us something about particular cases of accentuation; but of course we have no evidence in the prose. However, we do have an extraordinary source of information on stress in Shakespeare's time, Peter Levins's *Manipulus Vocabulorum* (1570), perhaps the earliest sources of marked stressings for English words. Levins notes that stress difference may signal meaning difference; he has therefore 'commonly set the accent, which is only acute, in that place, and over that vowel, where the syllable must go up & be long' (3). Levins's material, as well as evidence from verse practice and grammarians, tells us that while the Romance stress type was by and large well established, there were still many words with Germanic stress, either as sole or alternative contours. Here are examples of the stresses Levins gives and examples from Shakespeare, the latter close to certain on metrical grounds:

1 Unexpected initial stress
   dívert, óbservance, dístribute, cóntribute, délectable, éxcusable, próclamation (Levins)
   ábsurd, cément, cónfirm, óbservant, pérspective, útensil, ácceptable, súperfluous, súpportable (Shakespeare)

2 Unexpected final stress
   legáte, diláte, parént, precépt, stubbórn, flagón (Levins)
   aspéct, certáin, comfórt, precínct, turmóil (Shakespeare)

3 Unexpected penultimate stress
   adúmbrate, embássage (Levins)
   advértise, charácter, illústrate, retínue, oppórtune (Shakespeare)

Virtually all the Shakespearean forms also occur elsewhere in his works with their modern stress patterns.

Próclamation is especially interesting: while no modern dialect uses this accentuation, words of similar shape like *dictionary* and *secretary*, with four syllables, initial stress and third-syllable secondary stress are found in American English. Compare Hamlet's 'Nor *customary* suits of solemn black' (*Ham* 1.2.78), where *customary* must be scanned *cústomàry* (secondary stress marked by `), not as the British type *cústom'ry*.

RHYME AND BETRAYAL

A pre-modern poet's rhymes (assuming that he's competent and a precise rhymer) can often tell us that two sounds that are now the same were once different, or the opposite. (Of course puns and word-play tell us only about similarity, not identity.) Unfortunately, it's often impossible to decide this issue on the basis of one poet's practice; but widespread use of particular rhyme types suggests the state of play at a particular period. For instance, consider these rhymes from Shakespeare and some roughly contemporary poets:

	A	B
Wyatt	arm	warm
Sackville	regard	reward
Shakespeare	harm	warm
Donne	are	war

Nowadays the A forms would have the same vowel as *calm*; those in B would have a different one (which one depends on regional dialect: usually the same one as in *four*). The initial *w* has had an effect on the following vowel; but judging from rhyming usage, this did not happen until some time after the reign of Queen Anne (we still find these rhymes in Pope and Swift).

Another category which poses problems is words spelled with -*oo*-, which all descend from the same Middle English vowel, but nowadays have three possible pronunciations: for example *food*, *flood*, *good*, depending on when (and whether) the vowel happens to have shortened. Pronunciations of the *flood* type did not yet exist in Shakespeare's time; but the *food* and *good* types did, in almost all members of this class. Thus we find that

blood rhymes with: *brood, flood, good, mud, mood, stood, wood*
mood rhymes with: *food, flood, good, blood*

There is no way of reading *blood: brood*, or *blood: stood* or *mood: flood* in modern English so that there is a correct rhyme; one or other of the pair will have to be 'mispronounced'. And to make it worse, since Shakespeare had both the *mood* and *good* types, we can't tell in a given instance which one was being used. We would be tempted, without further information, to view these as so-called 'eye rhymes': *good* and *flood* are used as 'rhymes' by many later poets, though we know from external evidence (phoneticians, grammarians) that they had separated by the eighteenth century. Similarly with *prove* and *love*, which were possible full rhymes in the sixteenth and seventeenth centuries, but not later, though they were still used conventionally in rhyming positions.

Rhyming then can be as variable and 'exotic' as stress or syllable count, especially in a complex society like that of Elizabethan London, when the language is undergoing a considerable amount of change. Nowadays the two historically separate categories we could call '-*ea*- words' and '-*ee*- words' (*seas* vs. *sees*) have generally fallen together, and are distinct from '-*ay*- words' (*day, play*), which have fallen together with 'long -*a*- words' (*daze*). But in Shakespearean London there were at least three distinct patterns of merger and separation:

Type I, 'fashionable': *seas* rhymes with *days*, but neither rhymes with *sees* or *daze*.

> Every thing that heard him *play*,
> Even the billows of the *sea*

(H8 3.1.9–10, 1613)

(This couplet is probably by Shakespeare's younger collaborator, Fletcher.)

Type II, northern dialects, popular London: *seas* rhymes with *sees* while *days* rhymes with *daze*.

Man, more divine, the master of all *these*,
Lord of the wide world and wild wat'ry *seas*

(CE 2.1.20-1, 1591)

Type III, 'conservative': *daze* vs. *days* vs. *seas* vs. *sees*, i.e. no rhyming pairs.

(Type III represents the original historical separation, which had disappeared by the seventeenth century.)

This short treatment of some of Shakespeare's rhymes has a disturbing consequence for the modern reader or speaker. There is no way to read or speak these rhymes without in one way or another betraying the poet's intention, and what his audience would have perceived. If the words are read in their modern forms, they won't rhyme; if they're read with an attempt at the original pronunciation, which would give a proper rhyme, there would be different implications: in the case of the *are: war* type of rhyme, all the forms would (for historical accuracy) in fact have to have the vowel of *cat*, which would sound absurd. In cases like the -*oo*- words, it would be essentially arbitrary to choose any one pronunciation, since there were at least two available for Shakespeare (those of modern *mood* and *foot*, but differently distributed among the individual words); we can't tell in any instance which he would have used, and one would sound wrong anyhow. In cases where linguistic change has disrupted an older system, we may be stuck with one or another form of betrayal, no matter how good our intentions. Another possible solution of course is to read or perform all of Shakespeare's works in a reconstructed original pronunciation; the only problem here would be getting readers and actors to learn it, and audiences to understand it. I mention this just to point out that literary and historical appreciation are not the same thing, and that something is always sacrificed no matter which option you choose.

SOME FURTHER DETAILS

There is obviously no room here for a complete sound-by-sound listing of all of Shakespeare's consonants and vowels, and their variants. I'll content myself with treating only a small number of features that would have been different from the modern situation, and are worth bearing in mind when reading, and in some cases as a guide to appreciating possible word-play.

1 – *h-* – There is ample evidence for the dropping of initial *h* from as early as the eighth century, and it was common in Middle English. Our best evidence from the Elizabethan period is informal documents. The sixteenth-century diarist Henry Machyn, for instance, has spellings like *and* for *hand*, *elmet* for *helmet*. More interestingly, he also has what are called 'inverse spellings' like *holyff* for *olive*, *harme* for *arm*. That is, since the letter *h* doesn't represent an actual speech sound, you can write it in any vowel-initial word as a kind of 'decoration'. This kind of spelling does not represent 'Cockney' pronunciation as it did in the nineteenth century (as in Dickens and Thackeray); 'dropping your aitches' was normal in educated speech. The pronunciation of *h-* was reintroduced largely through schooling in the eighteenth century and later, and *h*-dropping only became an object of derision after that.

2 – *-ng* and *-ing* – In modern English the *g* in *-ng* clusters represents a separately pronounced consonant only in the middle of simplex words (*hunger, tango, finger*), or comparative adjectives (*longer*). Otherwise it does not. Compare the above with the sound of *-ng* in word-final position (*sing*) or in words like *singer*, where it is followed by a **suffix** (see p. 253). In Shakespeare's time the *g* indicated a separate consonant in all positions; the contemporary phonetician John Hart equates the sound represented by *g* in *angry* and *things* with that in *begged* and *together*.[1] So *g* would be pronounced even at the end of *sing*, as now in the north-west of England.

The story of unstressed -*ing* (in gerunds, present participles or simplex words like *herring, shilling*) is rather different. Here, after early loss of the -*g*, the final sound becomes -*n*, attested as early as the fourteenth to fifteenth centuries in spellings like *drynkyn, hayryn* for *drinking, herring*. This pronunciation, though sometimes stigmatized, was probably the Elizabethan norm. One contemporary manual urges teachers not to let pupils 'pronounce *in*, leaving out the *g*, as: *speakin* for *speaking*'.[2] But even Queen Elizabeth wrote *besichen* for *beseeching*, and it was common in educated writing. It's likely that most if not all unstressed -*ing*s in Shakespeare were pronounced -*in*.

3 – *si* as *sh, ti* as *ch* – Nowadays the spelling -*s(s)i*- usually represents the same sound as *sh*, for example in *passion*, as does -*ti*- in some cases (*nation*); in others the latter represents *ch* (*Christian*). These pronunciations were not yet the norm in Elizabethan times, though they did occur. John Hart for instance pronounces -*si*- in these words, but his rough contemporary Richard Mulcaster[3] respells -*tion* and -*sion* as -*shon*, once again old and new forms coexisting in the same speech community.

Many words spelled with initial *s*, but originally (and still frequently) pronounced with what we could write as *sy*- (some British and southern US *suit, sue*) had an alternative *sh*-pronunciation, which was widespread and familiar. This shows up clearly in *Love's Labour's Lost* [4.1.106ff.], where there is extensive punning on *suitor* and *shooter* (both kinds of hunters; see Chapter 5, p. 74), and the First Folio spells *sue* as *shue*. There are still remnants in unexpected places: the first element of the London name *Shoreditch* was originally *sewer*.

4 – -*er* as -*ar* – Spellings of -*ar* for historical -*er* appear as early as the thirteenth century, but are infrequent until the fifteenth. The words *star, heart* and *dark* had original -*er*, and we still have doublets like *person* and *parson, clerk* (US pronunciation) and *Clark*. The -*ar* extended to more words in the

sixteenth century than it does now: Queen Elizabeth for instance not only writes *clark*, *hart* and *starre* as we might expect, but *saruant* and *marcy* for *servant* and *mercy*. There is some spelling evidence for this development in early Shakespeare editions, and a rhyme of *carve: serve* (*LLL* 4.1.56–7).

EPILOGUE

To illustrate just how different Shakespeare's pronunciation could be from ours, here's a short passage from *A Midsummer Night's Dream*. Vowels that have undergone major change in pronunciation are in **bold**; rhymes which were possible in Shakespeare's time but are no longer so are in ***bold italics***; and vowels or consonants that are no longer pronounced are in *italics* (I mark *r*s as well, since many dialects do not now pronounce them in these positions):

> Through the forest have **I** ***gone***;
> **Bu**t Athenian fo**u**nd **I** ***none***
> On whose **eye**s **I** mi*gh*t ***approve***
> This flo**w**er's fo*r*ce in sti*r*ring ***love***.
> Ni*gh*t and silence – Who is ***here***?
> Weeds of Athens he d**o**th ***wear***.
> This is he my m**a**ster ***said***
> Despis*e*d the Athenian ***maid***;
> And he*r*e the maiden, sleeping s**ou**nd,
> On the dank and di*r*ty gr**ou**nd.

(2.2.65–74)

Note finally – in case you're tempted, as so many people are, to believe that even now there's only one 'English' – that the patterns of difference are not the same for all modern dialects English. The rhyme *gone/none* would still be possible in West Yorkshire; in Scots, the *-gh* in *night* would still (variably) be pronounced, *said* and *maid* would rhyme, and the vowels of *stirring* and *dirty* would still be the same as that of *is*; and *master* would have a short vowel identical to that in *dank* in most of the North and Midlands of England, and in Scotland.

Notes

1 *The opening of the unreasonable writing of our Inglish toung* (1551).

2 F. Clement, *The petie schole* (1587).

3 *The elementarie* (1582).

Further reading

There is unfortunately no comprehensive, elementary introduction to Shakespeare's pronunciation. The major works are technical and difficult without some background in the history of English. I would recommend two main sources, which often disagree with each other:

Kökeritz, H., *Shakespeare's Pronunciation* (New Haven, Conn.: Yale University Press, 1953)

> This is the classic work, and also contains a marvellous index of Shakespeare's rhymes and accentual variants, as well as much discussion of puns and word-play.

Lass, R., 'Phonology and morphology', in R. Lass (ed.), *The Cambridge History of the English Language, Vol. 3, 1476–1776* (Cambridge: Cambridge University Press, 1999), 56–186

> This guide is fairly technical, and not devoted to Shakespeare, but it covers both preceding and following periods, as well as the Shakespearean period itself. As with Kökeritz, there is extensive use of contemporary grammarians and phoneticians.

Part III

RESOURCES FOR READERS

AN A–Z OF RHETORICAL TERMS

Katie Wales

INTRODUCTION

Many of the chapters in this book have emphasized the importance of rhetoric for the education and literary craft of Renaissance writers like Shakespeare, and have also shown how creative and powerful rhetorical devices are for specific structural and stylistic effects. The word *rhetoric* today tends to have negative connotations, associated with 'hot air' and deceitful or artificial language, especially if linked to politicians, lawyers and advertisers. It has to be said that even the ancient Greeks, who invented the skills of public speaking to which the term basically referred, worried about rhetoric's possible manipulation to conceal rather than reveal the truth, in the forum and law courts where it originated. But once rhetoric became one of the major courses of study in the European education curriculum, and once its many devices and so-called 'figures of speech' were classified in handbooks, it became a valuable intellectual training for poets and playwrights, helping them to structure and elaborate arguments, to probe into nuances of meaning, to provide a vehicle for the emotions of their characters, and to move and manipulate the emotions of readers. Rhetorical devices continue to be employed in present-day literary and non-literary texts; and indeed, as modern linguists are now strongly affirming, rhetorical figures, far from being 'unnatural' or 'artificial', are really ingrained in our minds, helping us to structure our very thoughts, not just our language.

It cannot be stressed enough how important these figures were, especially for playwrights, in oral delivery to a listening audience. The patterns and plays of language for the ear were reinforced on the stage by an equally elaborate set of body gestures, for the eye. This might appear too 'stagey' or 'melodramatic' for modern tastes, but the two semiotics together, combined with the verse form, were a powerful combination, heightening the theatrical experience by an abundance of signification. Not surprisingly, devices of repetition figure prominently in rhetoric.

One problem for us today is that we no longer study classical rhetoric in schools, although many of the terms have passed into the terminology of literary criticism and stylistics, and many are widely known (e.g. **metaphor**, **simile**, **alliteration**, **rhetorical question**). Since classical rhetoric derives from Latin and Greek models, and these languages are unfamiliar, again, to the majority of present-day students, most of the terms, it has to be said, look very exotic and unpronounceable! (If any reader wants to pronounce them, a rough pronunciation guide is given for many of them.) Of course, it is possible to recognize that some word or phrase is being used in an unusual way in literature, or (very likely) that it is being repeated in an obviously stylized manner; and clearly it is the *effect* of techniques which are 'foregrounded' in this way that is the main concern for literary interpretation. Nonetheless, to call a figure by its traditional name, to call a spade a spade, as it were, is preferable to floundering. However, using a paraphrase with words like 'repetition', 'balance', 'pun', 'parallelism', 'ambiguity', 'image', 'figurative meaning', may help you if you can't remember the correct term, since these refer to features which many of the rhetorical figures have in common with each other.

The A–Z below, therefore, attempts to introduce as plainly as possible some of the main rhetorical devices that were well used by Shakespeare and his contemporaries, with illustrations from his plays, and comments on their stylistic significance. Many of these have been defined and illustrated in the chapters in Part I; but the general aim is to encourage and stimulate your own independent study of Shakespeare's stylistic art. Some of the terms, it has to be said, were used with more than one meaning; or the same device could be called by more than one term, or a Latin or Greek synonym: hopefully the A–Z will not add to the confusion, but clarify it.

In Renaissance handbooks there were many attempts to classify rhetorical figures, to group them into different kinds, on the basis of the sort of shared features referred to above. One common division was into *schemes* and *tropes*. Schemes are easily identifiable, and can be recognized in this A–Z, since they are marked by regularity or repetition of form, whether in syntax or sound. Tropes aren't so frequent, but they usually involve some kind of 'turning' (Greek *trope*) from the usual or 'literal' meaning of a word or phrase: *metaphor* is one of the clearest examples of these. **Hyperbole**, **litotes**, **irony** are tropes which depend, essentially, on some kind of literal untruth. There is another group of figures which have a pragmatic or functional role at sentence level in the presentation or dramatization of an argument, often involving a shift of tone: **apostrophe**, **rhetorical question**, for example: traditionally labelled in some handbooks as 'figures of thought'. But it is possible to see yet other ways of classifying the figures: for example those that involve the variation of an expression or idea, and those that amplify it. The main point is to study the A–Z, to see *how* a word, phrase or sentence is being highlighted or foregrounded in some way, and *why*. Then you can find your own examples from the plays you are studying, and even later literature and present-day discourses around you. Enjoy your search!

Notes

1   Terms in SMALL CAPITALS within an entry have an entry in their own right.

2 All italics in quotations from the plays are added, unless otherwise stated.

3 References to Puttenham are to George Puttenham, *The Art of English Poesy* (1589).

TERMS

adnominatio—(1) also known in rhetoric as *polyptoton* (polyp-*toe*-ton) and *traductio*. This figure was popular in Latin and Greek as a device for repeating words in different case forms (e.g. nominative (subject) and accusative (object)). The Elizabethans used it in word-play for words derived from the same 'root'. As a means of emphasis, it seems very consciously artful to modern readers, as in Richard II's self-pitying 'A *king*, *woe's* slave, shall *kingly woe* obey' (*R2* 3.2.210).

(2) sometimes refers to the same word used in different senses: what we would now call a 'pun' (*see* AMBIGUITY).

(3) also refers to the same word used in different syntactic constructions or roles: what is called ANTHIMERIA.

alliteration—a very well-known rhetorical term, commonly used in practical criticism today, to refer to the repetition of the initial consonant in two or more words. It can be used for emphasis: so at the beginning of *2 Henry IV* Lord Bardolph underlines his joyful message to the Earl of Northumberland of their success in battle against the King (ill informed though he turns out to be):

> O, such a day
> So *f*ought, so *f*ollow'd, and so *f*airly won

(1.1.20–1)

(Note, too, the repetition of *so* (*see* ANAPHORA) in a three-part structure, a common rhetorical device.) Alliteration in poetry is frequently used for onomatopoeic effects, i.e. to suggest by the association of sounds what is being described. So the witches' incantations in *Macbeth* (4.1) are foregrounded against the rest of the verse, and therefore appear to be extra-ordinary, alien and ritualistic, by the combination of alliteration, internal rhyme and end rhyme:

ALL
>   **D**ouble, **d**ouble, **t**oil and **t**r*ouble*:
>   Fire, **b**urn; and, cauldron, **b**ubble

2 WITCH
>   **F**illet of a **f**enny snake,
>   In the cauldron **b**oil and **b**ake

(10–13)

ambiguity—double meaning. Not a rhetorical term as such, but a useful critical and linguistic term to know, and certainly relevant for many rhetorical effects. Think of it also as an umbrella term, with other terms describing different kinds of ambiguity. For example, we can distinguish the grammatical ambiguity of phrases or sentences: in rhetoric termed *amphibologia*. In *Twelfth Night* this leads to comic misunderstanding. In 1.3 Sir Andrew Aguecheek enters, just as Sir Toby Belch and Olivia's maid Maria have been discussing his designs to be Olivia's wooer; Toby's imperative is misconstrued as a proper name:

SIR ANDREW   Bless you, fair shrew.

MARIA   And you too, sir.

SIR TOBY   Accost, Sir Andrew, accost.

SIR ANDREW   What's that?

SIR TOBY   My niece's chambermaid.

SIR ANDREW   Good Mistress Accost, I desire better acquaintance.

MARIA   My name is Mary, sir.

SIR ANDREW   Good Mistress Mary Accost –

SIR TOBY   You mistake, knight. 'Accost' is front her, board her, woo her, assail her.

(46–56)

Lexical or word ambiguity arises because of what linguists term *polysemy* (words having more than one meaning), or *homonymy* (words having the same form, but different origins), and this gives rise to *punning* or different kinds of word-play (*see* PARONOMASIA; *also* ANTANACLESIS; SYLLEPSIS). There is also discourse ambiguity, where an utterance may have more than one function. So, in *Richard II* Exton interprets Bolingbroke's 'Have I no friend will rid me of this living fear?' as a command to kill Richard (5.4); Bolingbroke, however, is able publicly to claim it as merely a wish (5.6.39–40)

amplificatio—amplification; the use of devices and figures of speech such as APOSTROPHE, HYPERBOLE, SIMILE, and synonyms (SYNONYMIA) to expand or 'decorate' an argument or narrative; to suggest 'copiousness' or *copia* (see Chapters 2 and 3); and also to intensify the emotional impact. Thomas Wilson in his *Art of Rhetoric* (1553) felt it could 'win favour or move affections'. In *1 Henry IV* Sir Richard Vernon describes to the jealous Hotspur how Prince Hal and his comrades appear in battle in a series of extended, hyperbolic similes, which make him cry 'No more, no more!':

> All furnish'd, all in arms;
> All plum'd *like* estridges that with the wind
> Bated, *like* eagles having lately bath'd,
> Glittering in golden coats *like* images,
> *As* full of spirit *as* the month of May,
> And gorgeous *as* the sun at midsummer;
> Wanton *as* youthful goats, wild *as* young bulls …

(4.1.97–103)

anadiplosis—from the Greek 'to double back': the repetition of the last part of one sentence or verse line at the beginning of the next. Puttenham called it the 'redouble', after the Latin term *reduplicatio*, which gives English 'reduplication'. This both linked lines or sentences and reinforced the progression of ideas, sometimes leading to a climax. So, in Richard III's soliloquy after the ghosts of his victims appear to him in his sleep, the repetition intensifies his agony:

> My conscience hath a thousand several *tongues*,
> And every *tongue* brings in a several *tale*,
> And every *tale* condemns me for a villain

(R3 5.3.194–6)

Across speakers, it suggests a characteristic feature of conversational discourse, of one picking up the words of the other. There is an extended example in *Othello* 3.3, as Iago plants the seeds of suspicion about Cassio in Othello's mind. Othello has just said that Cassio regularly interceded on his behalf when he was courting Desdemona:

IAGO

> Indeed?

OTHELLO?

> *Indeed*? Ay, indeed. Discern'st thou aught in that?
> Is he not honest?

IAGO

> *Honest*, my lord?

OTHELLO

> *Honest*? Ay, honest.

IAGO

> My lord, for aught I know.

OTHELLO

> What dost thou think?

IAGO

> *Think*, my lord?

OTHELLO

> *Think, my lord*! By heaven, thou echo'st me
> As if there were some monster in thy thought
> Too hideous to be shown. Thou dost mean something ...

(101–11)

anaphora (an-*a*-fe-ra)—from the Greek 'carrying back': the repetition of the same word at the beginning of successive clauses, sentences or verses (also known as *epanaphora*). It can effectively underline descriptive and emotional effects. So Othello's deep sorrow for what he believes to be Desdemona's affair with Cassio is intensified by the repetition of *farewell*, in an extended rhetorical 'lament':

> O, now for ever
> *Farewell* the tranquil mind, *farewell* content!
> *Farewell* the plumed troops and the big wars
> That makes ambition virtue! O *farewell*,
> *Farewell* the neighing steed and the shrill trump ...
> *Farewell*: Othello's occupation's gone!

> (3.3.350–4, 360)

Anaphora is commonly used in oratory to give structure to an argument, or to 'hammer home' a point. So Cassius, at the opening of *Julius Caesar*, impresses upon Casca the seriousness of the unnatural weather, and other portents:

> But if you would consider the true cause
> *Why* all these fires, *why* all these gliding ghosts,
> *Why* birds and beasts, from quality and kind,
> *Why* old men, fools, and children calculate,
> *Why* all these things change from their ordinance
> Their natures and preformed faculties
> To monstrous quality, *why*, you shall find
> That heaven hath infused them with these spirits
> To make them instruments of fear and warning
> Unto some monstrous state.

> (1.3.62–71)

antanaclesis—a kind of pun, where a word is repeated with a shift in meaning: as in Othello's chilling words as he contemplates the murder of Desdemona: 'Put out the

light [candle], and then put out the *light* [her life]!'
(5.2.7)

anthimeria—the transfer, 'conversion' or shift of one part of speech or word class to another, with no change in its form. This is a very common lexical process in modern English, for example nouns being used as verbs (*to elbow, to thumb (a lift)*, etc.), or verbs as nouns, and came into popularity from the Elizabethan period onwards. Shakespeare loved the device, and many of his 'conversions' are from nouns to verbs, reflecting an active or dynamic world view (e.g. *window, monster, climate*). In the best examples there is not only a compression of meaning but also a shift from a literal to a metaphorical meaning, as in Macbeth's 'Come, seeling Night, / *Scarf* up the tender eye of pitiful Day' (3.2.46–7). (See further Chapter 15.)

antimetabole (anti-met-*a*-bol-ee)—the repetition of words in an inverted or reverse order. This figure of speech confusingly is also known by other names: *chiasmus* (key-*as*-mus) (Greek: 'cross-wide'); *antistrophe* (Greek: 'turning about'); and *epanodos*. Antimetabole and chiasmus are the more frequently used terms. The figure is often used for witty effect: as in Falstaff's 'A *pox* of this *gout*! or a *gout* of this *pox*!' (*2H4* 1.2.244); or to make pithy sayings or 'aphorisms'. Polonius, in *Hamlet*, is prone to what he considers to be worthy generalizations and rhetorical elaborations. Rebuked in 2.2. by the impatient Queen eager for news of Hamlet's condition ('More matter with less art'), he still cannot restrain himself:

Madam, I swear I use no art at all.
That he is mad 'tis true, *'tis true 'tis pity*,
And *pity 'tis 'tis true*. A foolish figure –
But farewell it, for I will use no art.

(96–9)

antithesis—the contrast of ideas through the contrast of lexical items (i.e. content words) in a formal structure of parallelism. This structuring distinguishes it from the figures of OXYMORON and PARADOX. Antithesis is often used for witty or satirical effect. Queen Margaret uses it in *Richard III* to list Queen Elizabeth's reversal of fortune:

> For happy wife, a most distressed widow;
> For joyful mother, one that wails the name;
> For one being sued to, one that humbly sues;
> For Queen, a very caitiff, crown'd with care;
> For she that scorn'd at me, now scorn'd of me …

$$(4.4.98–102)$$

aphesis—Used in rhetoric for a kind of word-clipping process, in which the initial syllable of the word is omitted. It can be contrasted with *apocope* (ap-*o*-co-pee), where the last syllable is dropped; and *syncope*, where the middle consonant or syllable is omitted. These are very common licences in poetic language, for the sake of the metrical rhythm, for example *(a)gainst*; *o'er*; *oft(en)*; but they are also common phenomena in colloquial speech (e.g. *'phone*; *temp(ora)ry*; *telly(vision)*). So Emilia's words in *Othello* 3.3. appear quite 'natural', despite the blank verse frame; speaking of the handkerchief:

> I'*ll* have the work *ta'en* out
> And give'*t* Iago

$$(300–1)$$

aposiopesis (a-posio-*pe*-sis)—a term for what appears to be a sudden breaking off of an utterance before it is completed, usually in moments of emotion. It seems quite a colloquial and 'natural' feature in speech, but in earlier literature and drama it would be rare, and therefore marked. Hamlet seems too overcome by emotion, finding his mother's hasty second marriage too hard to contemplate, in the following lines from his soliloquy in 1.2:

>   Heaven and earth,
> Must I remember? Why, she would hang on him
> As if increase of appetite had grown
> By what it fed on; *and yet within a month* –
> Let me not think on't – Frailty, thy name is woman –

>   (142–6)

apostrophe—an emotive address to an absent person, or to an inanimate object or abstraction, as if personified. From the Greek meaning 'turning away' (Puttenham's 'turn tale'), it originated in the orator's turning aside (in Latin, 'aversion') from his immediate audience to address some other person, whether physically present or not. Apostrophe is typically exclamatory (*exclamatio*) (and marked by the presence of *O*); and it is particularly striking in Shakespeare's soliloquies. The full horror of Hamlet's emotions after the revelations of the ghost of his father are emphasized by the series of apostrophes in his self-address in 1.5. Note the addresses to the cosmos, and to his own body:

> O all you host of heaven! O earth! What else?
> And shall I couple hell? O fie! Hold, hold, my heart,
> And you, my sinews, grow not instant old,
> But bear me stiffly up.

>   (92–5)

Shakespeare himself exploits the melodramatic potential for comic effect in the 'Pyramus and Thisbe' play in *A Midsummer Night's Dream*, with Bottom-as-Pyramus'

> *O grim-look'd night! O night with hue so black!*
> *O night, which ever art when day is not!*
> *O night, O night, alack, alack, alack …*

>   (5.1.168–70; original italics)

articulus—simply a list of words. Lists occur commonly in descriptions of qualities, but also in insults, as in the (affectionate) interchange between Hal and Falstaff in *1 Henry IV*:

PRINCE   This sanguine coward, this bed-presser, this horse-
    back-breaker, this huge hill of flesh, –
FALSTAFF   'Sblood, you starveling, you eel-skin, you dried
    neat's-tongue, you bull's-pizzle, you stock-fish – … you
    tailor's-yard, you sheath, you bow-case, you vile standing
    tuck!

(2.4.238–45)

asteismus (ast-e-*is*-mus)—the Greek word for a witty and sophisticated, often ironical, joke: particularly in a riposte, with a word or phrase picked up and turned back on the user; what the Romans called *urbanitas*, and Puttenham a 'merry scoff'. The speeches of Shakespeare's official fools and jesters are full of such witty ripostes, but Falstaff too is fond of them:

LORD CHIEF JUSTICE   Well, the truth is, Sir John, you live in
    great infamy.
FALSTAFF   He that buckles himself in my belt cannot live in
    less.
LORD CHIEF JUSTICE   Your means are very slender, and your
    waste is great.
FALSTAFF   I would it were otherwise, I would my means were
    greater and my waist slenderer.

(*2H4* 1.2.136–43)

(Note also the pun and ANTIMETABOLE in Falstaff's final riposte.)

bathos—*see* GRADATIO

catachresis—a kind of figure, according to Puttenham and his contemporaries involving unusual or far-fetched metaphors, like the Elizabethan CONCEIT. From the Greek meaning 'misuse' or 'abuse'. Much of the dynamism of Shakespeare's language, for example, comes from the use of words outside their usual contexts or functions, and with compressed, metaphorical meanings. So Edgar in *King Lear* plans his disguise:

> My face I'll grime with filth,
> ... *elf* all my hairs in knots

(2.2.180–1)

where *elf*, a noun, is used as a verb by the process known as 'conversion' or 'transfer', and means something like 'tie up in knots to look like an elf'. (*See also* ANTHIMERIA.)

circumlocution—literally 'about-speech', a direct translation (in Latin) of the Greek *periphrasis*, a term also used in rhetoric and modern literary criticism; and so it is a phrase which uses more words than would appear to be strictly necessary, replacing a shorter or commoner phrase. Circumlocutions have been a common feature of poetic diction over the centuries, out of the desire for elaboration or elevation. However, it is hard to see why Prospero just doesn't say 'Raise your eyelashes' or even 'eyes' in the following example:

> [*to Miranda*] *The fringed curtains of thine eye advance*,
> And say what thou seest yond.

(*Tem* 1.2.409–10)

A special kind of 'speaking round' a subject is found in *euphemism* (Greek 'nice-speak') to avoid unpleasant topics. 'He's passed away' we might say for 'he's died'; just as the Earl of Warwick attempts to tell the Lord Chief Justice of Henry IV's death:

> his cares are now all ended.
> ... He's walked the way of nature,
> And to our purposes he lives no more.

(*2H4* 5.2.3–5)

climax—*see* GRADATIO

collocatio—a special kind of lexical incongruity in rhetoric, which juxtaposes words with different levels of tone or style. A famous example is Macbeth's

> No, this my hand will rather
> The *multitudinous* seas *incarnadine*,
> Making the green one *red*.

(2.2.60–2)

where, out of emotive emphasis, the polysyllabic words in one line are juxtaposed with the basic adjectives in the next, with 'Making … red' a paraphrase of *incarnadine*.

conceit—a popular Elizabethan and metaphysical figure of speech which depended on wit or ingenuity of idea for an effect (originally meaning 'thought', as in *conceive*). SIMILE, META-PHOR, HYPERBOLE and OXYMORON could also be involved, since conceits often extended for long passages, and were very popular in sonnets, often conventionalized, but sometimes far-fetched or CATACHRETIC. A famous extended elaborate example, in dialogue rather than monologue, occurs in *Romeo and Juliet*, where in fourteen lines (like a sonnet), beginning with Romeo's 'If I profane with my unworthiest hand' (1.5.93), the two lovers play on words to do with lips, palms, palmers and pilgrims, and by their wit reveal their match.

diacope—*see* EPANALEPSIS

enallage—the technique of using one grammatical category, for example gender, person, case, number, tense, where another is expected. This is very difficult to distinguish from simple carelessness or ignorance on the part of the writer! But Chapter 8 has an interesting example of Isabella's shift of pronouns in *Measure for Measure* 2.2 (see p. 119).

enthymeme—in logical argumentation, an abridged or incomplete syllogism, where a syllogism is a form of reasoning usually involving two linked propositions and a deduction: for example 'I like animals – elephants are animals – therefore I like elephants'. Shakespeare's argumentative characters are fond of enthymemes, which work by inference, a piece of the argument 'missing'. This might sound like everyday reasoning or conversing, but an enthymeme is also effectively exploited as a tactic of persuasion. So Brutus addresses the plebeians after the murder of Caesar: 'Had you rather Caesar were living, and die all slaves, than that Caesar were dead, to live all free men? (*JC* 3.2.22–4). Here, in the *antithesis*, only one reality is presented: if Caesar had lived he would not have ever granted them their freedom.

Sometimes a whole 'chain' of enthymemes can be uttered, what rhetoricians termed a *sorites*, leading up to a climax (GRADATIO). Notice the lexical repetition (ANADIPLOSIS) in the following example from *As You Like It*, as Rosalind graphically and pithily summarizes to Orlando events that have happened 'off-stage', between the acts:

> For your brother and my sister no sooner met, but they *looked*; no sooner *looked*, but they *loved*; no sooner *loved*, but they *sighed*; no sooner *sighed*, but they asked one another *the reason*; no sooner knew *the reason*, but they sought the remedy. And in these degrees have they made a pair of stairs to marriage ...

> (5.2.32–8)

epanalepsis—a rhetorical figure of repetition, from the Greek meaning 'a taking up again'; but critics and commentators differ in their use of it: (1) the repetition of words after intervening words, effective for emphasis or emotion: also known as *diacope*, *epanadiplosis* and *ploce* (*plo*-see). Puttenham calls it the 'echo sound'. In Edmund's soliloquy in *King Lear* 1.2 his 'bastard' origins clearly rankle with him:

> Well then,
> *Legitimate* Edgar, I must have your land.
> Our father's love is to the bastard Edmund
> As to the *legitimate*. Fine word, '*legitimate*'!
> Well, my *legitimate*, if this letter speed
> And my invention thrive, Edmund the base
> Shall top the *legitimate*.

> (15–21)

(2) the repetition of words at the beginning and end of a line, phrase, clause or sentence (see Chapter 2, p. 21). Buckingham's last, rueful, words before his execution have the force of aphorisms:

> Come, lead me, officers, to the block of shame;
> *Wrong* hath but *wrong*, and *blame* the due of *blame*.

> (*R3* 5.1.28–9)

epistrophe (e-*pis*-tro-fe)—a rhetorical device of repetition, the opposite of ANAPHORA, by which the last words in successive clauses, lines, or sentences are repeated. Also known as *epiphora*. So Othello uses it for intended IRONY: 'A fine *woman*, a fair *woman*, a sweet *woman*!' (4.1.175–6).

For Henry Peacham in *The Garden of Eloquence* (1577), the repeated words would stay longer in the mind of the listener.

epithet (**epitheton**)—a qualifying or descriptive word or phrase, usually adjectival, used very commonly in poetic diction of all periods as a means of amplification (AMPLIFICATIO). Many of these are semantically redundant: for example Oberon's references to the '*nodding* violet' and '*sweet* musk-roses' (*MND* 2.1.250, 252); or formulaic: for example the '*pious* Aeneas' and '*rosy-fingered* dawn' of classical epic; but the term can also be used for striking and unusual adjectives in the 'grand style', as Sylvia Adamson reveals in Chapter 3 (pp. 40–1). (*See also* TRANSFERRED EPITHET.)

epizeuxis—a figure of repetition, where there are no words intervening; colourfully called 'cuckoo spell' by Puttenham. Giving the appearance of natural emotion, it is used by Shakespeare to suggest great intensity of feeling: as in Lear's '*Howl, howl, howl, howl!* O, you are men of stones!', on the death of his beloved daughter Cordelia (5.3.255); and his frantic 'O thou'lt come no more, / *Never, never, never, never, never*', the repetitions audaciously filling up the measure of the line, and trochaic (/ x) rather than the more usual iambic (x /) (x = unstressed syllable; / = stressed syllable). (See Chapter 4, p. 55.)

euphemism—*see* CIRCUMLOCUTION

exordium—a division of an oration which marks the opening, or introduction; also known as *proemium.* This was designed to catch the attention of the listeners, and to put them in a receptive mood, as in Mark Antony's famous 'Friends, Romans, countrymen, lend me your ears' (*JC* 3.2.74).

gradatio—commonly known as 'climax' ('ladder' in Greek), this figure of speech presents arguments in an ascending order of importance, reserving the best or the most dramatic point till the last. It is therefore the opposite of 'anti-climax' or *bathos*, where there is a deflation from a heightened level or tone.

   An artful kind of gradatio involves the linking of words between clauses, the last word of one clause echoed in the next (*see also* ANADIPLOSIS), but leading up to a climax: as in Othello's

No, Iago,

I'll see before I *doubt*; when I *doubt*, *prove*,
And on the *proof*, there is no more but this:
Away at once with love or jealousy!

(3.3.192–5)

hendiadys (hen-*die*-ad-is)—a relatively uncommon rhetorical syntactic feature, where two nouns connected by *and* are used instead of the more usual adjective-plus-noun construction. The Greeks called it 'one thing by two', and Puttenham 'the figure of twinness'. The effect is to give added emphasis or 'weight', as in Jachimo's '*The heaviness and guilt* within my bosom / Takes off my manhood' (i.e. 'the heavy guilt') (*Cym* 5.2.1–2).

hypallage—a rhetorical figure like a kind of 'spoonerism', where words are misplaced from their proper places in an utterance. Puttenham calls it 'the changeling', following the Greek meaning of the term. Shakespeare exploits the device for comic effect, most notably in Bottom's attempts to recall his vision under the spell of the magic flower-juice. The confusion of words aptly suggests his confused mind:

> The *eye* of man hath not *heard*, the *ear* of man hath not *seen*, man's *hand* is not able to *taste*, his *tongue* to *conceive*, nor his *heart* to *report*, what my dream was.
>
> (*MND* 4.1.209–12)

(*See also* TRANSFERRED EPITHET.)

hyperbaton—the reversal, or inversion, in normal word order of the major elements of a sentence, particularly subject, verb and object. From the Greek meaning 'overstep'. This is often used for emphasis or focus, as in Claudius's soliloquy: '*Pray can I not*' ('I can not pray') (*Ham* 3.3.38); although it is an extremely common device in poetic language generally before the twentieth century, to aid rhythm and rhyme. Look out also for the term *anastrophe*, to describe marked word-order variation.

hyperbole (hype-*er*-bol-ee)—popularly known as 'exaggeration' or 'overstatement' (for 'understatement, *see* LITOTES), this is a common figure or trope in speech as well as literature: we say things like 'he made my blood boil'. Hyperbole means 'exceed' in Greek; and Puttenham called it the 'over-reacher' or the 'loud lyer'. The Romans called it *dementiens*, as if it were a form of madness! There is certainly an element of chilling hysteria in Clarence's vivid description of his dream in *Richard III*:

> Methoughts I saw *a thousand* fearful wrecks;
> *Ten thousand* men that fishes gnaw'd upon …
>
> (1.4.24–5)

Hyperbole often signifies great emotion or passion: as when Hamlet tries to 'outdo' Laertes with his description of his own love for Ophelia:

> Forty thousand brothers
> Could not with all their quantity of love
> Make up my sum.
>
> (5.2.269–71)

Hyperbole distorts the truth by saying too much, of course, but in Hamlet's case the strength of his emotions is such that he himself at that moment must surely believe he is telling the truth.

irony—a commonly known figure of speech or trope derived from the Greek for 'dissimulation' (*eironeia*), alternatively known as *antiphrasis* by the Elizabethans. Like HYPERBOLE irony misrepresents the truth: the words actually used appear to differ from, contradict, or mean the exact opposite of the sense actually required in the context. Sometimes it is sarcastic, serving as an oblique form of criticism, as in 'That's very clever of you'. No wonder Puttenham called it 'dry mock'. Some examples are actually 'echoes' of previous utterances. So Gratiano echoes Shylock's frequent words of praise ('O wise young judge', 'O noble judge', etc.), once Portia has delivered her verdict:

> O upright judge! –
> Mark Jew, – O learned judge!

(MV 4.1.310–1)

But irony can be unintentional too, and the critical term *dramatic irony* covers those situations where the readers or audience know more than the characters in the play. So Duncan compliments Macbeth's castle at the beginning of 1.6, not knowing his murder has been plotted:

> This castle hath a pleasant seat; the air
> Nimbly and sweetly recommends itself
> Unto our gentle senses.

(1–3)

Irony need not only be verbal therefore, but also situational, with a discrepancy between what appears, or is believed, to be the case and the real state of affairs. Phrases like *tragic irony* when applied to Shakespeare's plays account for our realization, for example, that *King Lear* is about a father who rejects the daughter who actually loves him the most.

isocolon—clauses or sentences of equal length (Greek 'equal-member'), and therefore parallel in syntax and rhythm. (*See also* PARISON.) It was a very fashionable feature of a certain style of Elizabethan prose, influenced by Latin rhetoric, but Shakespeare uses it in his plays for very marked effects. So Richard Duke of Gloucester can hardly contain his glee at overcoming the scruples of Lady Anne, recently widowed after the murder of Edward Prince of Wales by Richard himself:

> Was ever woman in this humour woo'd?
> Was ever woman in this humour won?

(R3 1.2.232–3)

(also showing an extended example of ANAPHORA)

litotes (lie-*toe*-tees)—understatement (from the Greek meaning 'meagre'). This is a rhetorical figure or trope also common in ordinary speech ('it's not bad'; 'oh, it was nothing'), and quite the opposite of HYPERBOLE or overstatement. It typically takes the form of a negative statement or phrase used to express the opposite, and often signifies the speaker's modesty or politeness, or even intensity of feeling. So in *King Lear* Cordelia finds it quite impossible to utter the hyperbolic words of love to Lear that her sisters are capable of, impossible to 'heave / My heart into my mouth'(1.1.91–2); yet she is 'sure my love's / More ponderous than my tongue' (77–8). All she can say is that she loves him 'According to my bond, no more nor less' (93). Lear takes her words too literally, and hence the seeds of the tragedy are sown in 1.1.

metaphor—a very common term in literary criticism today, for a very common figure of speech or trope, in everyday speech as well as literature, and one of the most highly regarded by the rhetoricians of the past. Modern linguists argue that metaphor is fundamental even to our thought processes. Meaning 'carry over' in Greek, a metaphor 'carries over' one field of reference (what modern critics call the *tenor*) to another (the *vehicle*) on the basis of some perceived similarity between the two fields (the *ground*). So when Hamlet says the world 'is an unweeded garden / That grows to seed' (1.2.135–6), the features of gardens are transferred or 'translated' (Latin *translatio* means 'metaphor') to the world; and when Romeo says 'jocund day / *Stands tiptoe* on the misty mountain tops' (*RJ* 3.5.9–10), features of human beings are applied to the early morning (in a particular kind of metaphor involving PERSONIFICATION).

Metaphors are sometimes discussed in relation to SIMILES, as being more compressed: so 'the world is [like] an unweeded garden' could have been Hamlet's phrasing. Metaphors are sometimes therefore more complex for us to understand than similes, but the most interesting ones, usually literary or poetic, enable us to see the world in a different way. What a poet like Shakespeare also does, however, is to give even common, conventional or 'dead' metaphors a new twist or elaboration. So the image of death as 'sleep', for example, familiar on gravestones, is mused upon by Hamlet, who contemplates the possibility of dreaming:

> To sleep, perchance to dream – ay, there's the rub:
> For in that sleep of death what dreams may come …
> Must give us pause

> (3.1.65–6, 68)

metonymy—from the Greek meaning 'name change', a well-known figure of speech or trope by which the name of an entity is replaced by the name of one of its associated attributes or features. It is a common figure in everyday language, reflecting our knowledge of our particular society and culture: for example, phrases like *the press* ('newspapers'), *the Crown* ('monarchy'), *the White House* ('US Presidency') show how an object associated with an occupation has come to stand for the office itself.

Metonymy is easily confused with *synecdoche* (sin-*eck*-duck-ee), which is really a particular kind of metonymy, where the name of something is replaced by the name of an actual part of it: e.g. *set of wheels* ('car'); *strings* ('stringed instruments'). In the Elizabethan theatre, visual metonymy was common: a tree could stand for a whole forest, for example.

Like metaphor, metonymy works by substitution, of an expected word by the unexpected; yet there is no figurative extension of meaning involved. Nonetheless, metonymy in its apparent economy of reference clearly has the evocative power of suggestion and also symbolic power, if you think of the force of the crown standing for the monarchy as an example. This is emphasized by Isabella in *Measure for Measure*:

Well, believe this:
No ceremony that to great ones longs,
Not *the king's crown,* nor *the deputed sword,*
The marshall's truncheon, nor *the judge's robe,*
Become them with one half so good a grace
As mercy does.

(2.2.58–63)

oxymoron—the juxtaposition of apparently contradictory expressions for witty or striking effects: a kind of condensed PARADOX. *Oxymoron* means 'sharp-dull' in Greek, illustrating its very meaning; in Shakespeare's time it was more commonly called *contrapositum.*

It is commonly associated in poetic convention with the contradictions of being in love. The lament of the 'love-sick' Romeo in 1.1 is a parody of the sonnets at the time, and would clearly signal to the audience that his love for Rosaline is just a passing whim:

Why, then, O *brawling love,* O *loving hate,*
O *anything* of *nothing* first create!
O *heavy lightness, serious vanity,*
Misshapen chaos of *well-seeming forms!*
Feather of lead, bright smoke, cold fire, sick health,
Still-waking sleep that is not what it is!

(176–81)

(See also Chapter 8.)

paradox—an apparently self-contradictory statement (from the Greek 'against-opinion'), a kind of expanded OXYMORON. There is usually some philosophical point to a paradox, or an evaluation being made of a character or situation, or some attempt to describe conflicting emotions. Prince Hal, fatally wounding Hotspur, contemplates

When that this body did contain a spirit,
A kingdom for it was too small a bound;
But now two paces of the vilest earth
Is room enough.

(1H4 5.4.88–91)

parenthesis (par-*enth*-e-sis)—a term still used in grammar to describe interspersed qualifications in a sentence or utterance, in modern English writing usually marked by brackets or dashes. It can give the impression of lack of premeditation, so orators exploited it to suggest artlessness, and dramatists to suggest 'natural' speech and thoughts. So, in Hamlet's soliloquy,

Now whether it be

Bestial oblivion, or some craven scruple
Of thinking too precisely on th'event –
A thought which, quartered, hath but one part wisdom,
And ever three parts coward – I do not know
Why yet I live to say this thing's to do

(4.4.39–44)

parison—what Puttenham called 'the figure of even', since it involves parallelism of clauses or sentences side by side (*see also* ISOCOLON), and words in one corresponding to words in the other. So the Friar tries to console Juliet's family on her apparent death, with the generalizations

She's not well married that lives married long,
But she's best married that dies married young.

(4.5.77–8)

paronomasia (paro-no-*maiz*-ia)—a general rhetorical term for word-play, especially puns, involving words that sound similar, or have more than one meaning. Although the word *pun* itself did not appear in English until 1662 with the poet and playwright John Dryden, Shakespeare's plays are full of puns. Since we associate puns with joking today, we are not surprised to find many examples in his comedies; but punning or 'quibbling' was in earlier periods a sign of cleverness. So they turn up in the battles of wit between young lovers (as in *Love's Labour's Lost*, for instance). Word-play in Shakespeare's plays is therefore *not* to be dismissed merely as a means of 'comic relief' (an overworked phrase as it is), for it can appear in unexpected places. Prince Hal, believing his drinking comrade Falstaff to be dead, says

> Death hath not struck so fat a *deer* today,
> Though many *dearer*, in this bloody fray

(1H4 5.4.106–7)

playing affectionately on the sameness of sound (*homonymy*) between the words. A cynical character like Hamlet uses word-play as a barbed outlet for his bitterness: his aside 'A little more than kin, and less than kind' (1.2.65) in response to his uncle's attempts at familiarity is a particularly clever example, playing not only on two meanings of *kind* as noun and adjective, and on similarities in sound between *kin* and *kind*, but on a metalinguistic level also playing with the length of the words *kin* and *kind*. For particular kinds of word-play and puns, *see also* ANTANACLESIS, ASTEISMUS and SYLLEPSIS. See also Chapter 5.

periphrasis—*see* CIRCUMLOCUTION

perseverantia—literally our word 'perseverance' from Latin, this aptly signifies what is in essence a refrain, a phrase repeated regularly in a speech or monologue. One of the most famous examples in Shakespeare's plays must be the repetition of

> But (yet) Brutus says, he was ambitious
> And Brutus (sure he) is an honourable man

repeated three times in Mark Antony's oration after Caesar's murder in *Julius Caesar* (3.2), and echoing again in their coupling two separate propositions from the beginning of the speech. By the end of the oration the truth of these statements has been considerably undermined, the apparent praise (*laudatio*) is actually no compliment, so that IRONY holds sway.

personification—a figure of speech or trope like METAPHOR in which an inanimate object or abstract quality is given human attributes. This is very common even in everyday speech ('Time *flies*'; 'table *leg*'), but it has been a striking feature of poetic language through the centuries. A surreal example is found in Richard Duke of Gloucester's opening soliloquy, but quite appropriate for his own grotesque personality:

> Grim-visag'd *War* hath smoothed his wrinkled front:
> And now, instead of mounting barbed steeds
> To fright the souls of fearful adversaries,
> He capers nimbly in a lady's chamber
> To the lascivious pleasing of a lute.

> (*R3* 1.1.9–13)

(See also Chapter 6.)

ploce—*see* EPANALEPSIS

polyptoton—*see* ADNOMINATIO

quaesitio—several questions uttered one after the other. Characteristically they suggest anxiety or some kind of heightened emotional state, as in Shylock's defence of his race and religion in *The Merchant of Venice*:

> Hath not a Jew eyes? hath not a Jew hands, organs, dimensions, senses, affections, passions? Fed with the same food ... as a Christian is? – if you prick us, do we

not bleed? if you tickle us, do we not laugh? if you poison
us, do we not die? and if you wrong us, shall we not
revenge?

(3.1.54–5, 59–62)

Since these particular questions do not expect an answer, and
are really equivalent to statements ('A Jew does have eyes', etc.)
they can be identified individually as RHETORICAL QUESTIONS.

rhetorical question—a term still commonly used in grammar
for a question that does not expect an answer. In rhetoric it is
known as *erotema* (Greek) and *interrogatio* (Latin). Such a
question really asserts something which is known to the
speaker and listener, and cannot be denied: so it is the
equivalent of a statement. In classical oratory, as in public
speaking still, it is useful as a persuasive device to appeal to
reason, or useful emotively to suggest an outburst of 'natural'
feeling. Lady Macbeth uses a series of rhetorical questions to
taunt her husband for his lack of courage, when he changes his
mind about murdering Duncan:

> Was the hope drunk
> Wherein you dress'd yourself? Hath it slept since?
> And wakes it now, to look so green and pale
> At what it did so freely? ...
> Art thou afeard
> To be the same in thine own act and valour
> As thou art in desire?

(1.7.35–41)

When a speaker, also emotively, asks a question and gives his
or her own reply, this is known as *rogatio*. Hamlet resorts to
rogatio frequently in his soliloquies; for example:

> What would he do,
> Had he the motive and the cue for passion

That I have? He would drown the stage with tears,
And cleave the general ear with horrid speech ...

(2.2.560–3)

simile—from Latin *similis* 'like', a well-known term even today
to describe a common figure of speech, whereby two concepts
are imaginatively and descriptively compared. *Like* and *as* (...
as) are the characteristic connectives, and simile is therefore
much more explicit than METAPHOR. Yet in descriptive poetry
similes and metaphors often occur together; and in the
following example from Helena's recollection of her childhood
friendship with Hermia in *A Midsummer Night's Dream*, it is
impossible to tell whether the words italicized are a metaphor
or an elliptical simile, since they amplify the first image and
simile of a 'double cherry':

> So we grew together,
> *Like to* a double cherry, seeming parted,
> But yet an union in partition,
> *Two lovely berries* moulded on one stem

(3.2.208–11)

sorites—*see* ENTHYMEME

stichomythia—from Greek 'line-speech', a formalized dialogue in alternate lines. This was very popular in Elizabethan
drama, as a result of Senecan influence. It suggests a rapid
repartee, so it can be exploited for a variety of effects, from
witty banter to sharp rebuttal. It is used very appropriately in
Love's Labour's Lost, one of the themes of which is the 'battle
between the sexes'; so here Berowne and Rosaline:

BEROWNE   Lady, I will commend you to mine own heart.
ROSALINE   Pray you, do my commendations; I would be glad
   to see it.

BEROWNE   I would you heard it groan.
ROSALINE   Is the fool sick?
BEROWNE   Sick at the heart.
ROSALINE   Alack, let it blood.
BEROWNE   Would that do it good?
ROSALINE   My physic says ay …

(2.1.179–87)

syllepsis—from the Greek meaning 'taking together': (1) a grammatical figure of omission or 'ellipsis' where a verb has to be understood, and quite loosely; for example Brabantio's warning to Othello about Desdemona: 'She has deceived her father, and may [deceive] thee' (1.3.294). (2) a kind of PARONOMASIA or pun, where two meanings have to be understood; as in Falstaff's words to Pistol: 'At a word: *hang* no more about me, I am no gibbet for you' (*MW* 2.2.16–17).

symploce (sim-*plos*-ee)—from the Greek for 'interweaving', a figure of repetition where a set of words at the beginning and also the ending of a sentence are repeated: a combination of ANAPHORA and *epistrophe*! Where there are frequent examples of this in the same speech, it can appear quite forced to modern ears; but in *Richard III* there are many examples to catalogue forcefully the remembered woes of the royal dynasties in lamentations (*lamentatio*). So the old Queen Margaret addresses Queen Elizabeth and the Duchess of York with examples underscored by parallelism or *parison*:

I had an Edward, *till a Richard kill'd him*;
I had a husband, *till a Richard kill'd him*;
Thou hadst an Edward, *till a Richard kill'd him*;
Thou hadst a Richard, *till a Richard kill'd him*.

(4.3.40–3)

The Duchess rejoinds, in an 'echo':

> *I had* a Richard *too,* and *thou* didst *kill him;*
> *I had* a Rutland *too:* *thou* holp'st to *kill him.*

(44–5)

But she is 'trumped' by Queen Margaret again:

> *Thou hadst* a Clarence *too,* and *Richard kill'd him.*

(46)

synecdoche—*see* METONYMY

synonymia—our modern term is *synonymy,* the expression of the 'same' meaning by different words (where the connotations, however, might be different). Pairs or strings of synonyms were regularly used by Renaissance writers as a means of 'amplification' (AMPLIFICATIO); so Puttenham aptly called synonymy 'the figure of store'.

At the beginning of Hamlet's first soliloquy, however, the piling up of the adjectives signifies to the audience the extent of his depression:

> How *weary, stale, flat,* and *unprofitable*
> Seem to me all the uses of this world!

(1.2.133–4)

But with a different kind of character they can suggest garrulousness and tedious redundancy, as in the mouth of Holofernes the schoolmaster in *Love's Labour's Lost*:

> The posterior of the day, most generous sir, is *liable,*
> *congruent* and *measurable* for the afternoon. The word is *well*
> *culled, choice, sweet* and *apt,* I do assure you sir, I do assure.

(5.1.84–7)

John Hoskyn's *Directions for Speech and Style* (1599) also associates synonymia with a schoolmaster: he advises his pupils to use synonyms with care, *not* like that kind of speaker, 'foaming out synonymies'. (See also Chapters 2, 3, 5 and 13.)

transferred epithet—also referred to as a kind of HYPALLAGE in rhetoric, a figure of speech in which an adjective properly modifying one word is shifted to another in the same sentence: for example when we say 'she passed a *sleepless night*'. In Desdemona's 'Alas, what *ignorant sin* have I committed?' (*Oth* 4.2.71) her confused emotional state is aptly conveyed.

A GUIDE TO FURTHER READING

Adamson, S.M., 'The literary language', in R. Lass (ed.), *The Cambridge History of the English Language, Vol. 3, 1476–1776* (Cambridge: Cambridge University Press, 1999), 539–653

> The first half of this chapter (pp. 541–95) offers an introduction to the Renaissance theory and practice of rhetorical richness (*copia*) and a guide to some of the principal 'figures of varying' and 'figures of amplifying' employed by Shakespeare and his contemporaries. The second half explores the consciously different ideal of 'perspicuous sublimity', advocated by writers of the post-Restoration period. In a cross-disciplinary approach, Adamson draws on the terminology of both Renaissance rhetoric and modern linguistics to tell the story of one of the most far-reaching changes in the history of literary style.

Barton, John, *Playing Shakespeare* (London: Methuen, 1984)

> Deriving from a remarkable series of televised workshops Barton's book offers analysis of Shakespeare's language from the firmly pragmatic perspective of how an actor seeks to *play* the text. Discussions between leading members of the Royal Shakespeare Company (RSC) are the basis for the first half of the book, which explores how Shakespeare's text works by examining the use of verse and prose, set speeches and soliloquies, language and character. The second half concentrates on more subjective areas such as irony and ambiguity, passion and coolness. Barton, with the RSC since its beginning, is central to the way we think of speaking Shakespeare today.

Berry, Cicely, *The Actor and His Text* (London: Harrap, 1987); later retitled *The Actor and the Text*

> Berry was Head of Voice at the Royal Shakespeare Company for many years, and, with John Barton, a central influence on the way we think

of speaking Shakespeare today. The book is especially good on text, demonstrating ways of infusing life and meaning into words that are first encountered on the printed page. It is full of useful exercises, and practical strategies to making the language your own. Berry's book is widely used within the theatre profession.

Blake, N.F., *Shakespeare's Language: An Introduction* (Basingstoke and London: Macmillan, 1983)

Of the specialized introductions to Shakespeare's language, this is the one most directly concerned with the interpretive difficulties resulting from differences between Early Modern English grammar and our own. It includes chapters on the nominal group (Chapter 4), the verbal group (5), adverbs, prepositions and conjunctions (6) and word order and sentence types (7). It suffers from the lack of a subject index, but does offer a useful play-by-play guide to the passages quoted and discussed.

Brown, John Russell, *William Shakespeare: Writing for Performance* (Basingstoke: Macmillan, 1996)

Brown engages with Shakespeare's plays as the raw material for performance rather than as texts to be confined to the study. The importance of the historical context in which Shakespeare worked is acknowledged, but the dramatist's method is also examined within the context of how modern dramatists approach the business of crafting a play. Analysis consistently seeks to promote the need to study the plays with a heightened theatrical consciousness.

Cercignani, Fausto, *Shakespeare's Works and Elizabethan Pronunciation* (Oxford: Clarendon Press, 1981)

Cercignani regards the work of his predecessor Kökeritz as flawed because of his determination to prove that the pronunciation of Shakespeare's London was close to that of modern Southern English. He re-examines and re-evaluates the relevant evidence from rhymes, puns, spellings and metrical peculiarities in this comprehensive reference work, which has a useful word index and a bibliography.

Donawerth, Jane, *Shakespeare and the Sixteenth-Century Study of Language* (Urbana, Ill.: University of Illinois Press, 1984)

This book investigates how language was studied and analysed in the sixteenth century; it pays close attention to the language texts

Shakespeare might have known, and to the general controversies over the nature of language. The book continually relates these issues to Shakespeare, analysing in detail five plays: *Love's Labour's Lost*, *King John*, *The Merchant of Venice*, *All's Well That Ends Well* and *Hamlet*.

Drakakis, John (ed.), *Alternative Shakespeares* (London: Methuen/ Routledge, 1985)

This collection offers several approaches to the study of Shakespeare's plays. Of particular interest to students and teachers of language and poetics are A. Serpieri's 'Reading the Signs', which offers a semiotic study of *Julius Caesar* and *Othello*, and C. Belsey's 'Disrupting Sexual Difference', which carries out a clear and helpful close reading of several texts in the context of meaning and gender.

Elam, Keir, *Shakespeare's Universe of Discourse: Language-Games in the Comedies* (Cambridge: Cambridge University Press, 1984)

Elam makes use of modern theories taken from linguistics and semiotics alongside Renaissance approaches to language in an analysis of the dialogue of Shakespearean comedy (with particular attention to *Love's Labour's Lost*). He demonstrates that the apparently highly stylized exchanges between characters on Shakespeare's stage are to a large extent governed by the same rules and conventions as everyday conversation.

Hardy, Barbara, *Shakespeare's Storytellers: Dramatic Narration* (London: Peter Owen, 1997)

Hardy sees narrative as central to Shakespeare's dramatic explorations of human behaviour. She focuses both on the stories that characters tell and the plays themselves as stories, with useful accounts both of the various functions of narratives in the plays and of the ways in which *Hamlet*, *King Lear* and *Macbeth*, especially, use narrative as one of their central themes.

Herman, Vimala, *Dramatic Discourse: Dialogue as Interaction in Plays* (London and New York: Routledge, 1995)

Herman offers a comprehensive review of a variety of approaches developed in recent years to the study of conversation, including ethnography, which attends to the overall situation of communication; conversation analysis, which attends to turn-taking and sequencing;

linguistic pragmatics, which attends to speech acts, logical progressions and politeness; and gender studies, which examines sex-differentiated models of speech. The book suggests applications of each approach to the analysis of dramatic dialogue, with illustrations drawn both from Shakespeare and from such modern dramatists as Osborne, Pinter, Chekhov and Beckett. It also articulates some important differences between conversation and dialogue.

Hibbard, G.R., *The Making of Shakespeare's Dramatic Poetry* (Toronto, Buffalo and London: University of Toronto Press, 1981)

Hibbard argues that Shakespeare's early love for fine poetry and sensuous description is at odds with the requirements of a truly dramatic style, which must be responsive to the demands of the theatre and to the pressure to push the action forward. The book also examines how Shakespeare incorporates, critiques, parodies and transforms older dramatic styles inherited from playwrights of the 1580s and early 1590s. It traces a development to a flexible and fully theatrical language through Shakespeare's early plays to *Henry IV*, a process, he argues, that involves Shakespeare's self-conscious and constructive criticism, not only of the dramatic writings of others but also of his own earlier stylistic experiments.

Houston, J.P., *Shakespearean Sentences: A Study in Style and Syntax* (Baton Rouge and London: Louisiana State University Press, 1988)

A discussion of the chronological development of Shakespeare's style in terms of the changing relations in it between colloquial and Latinate sentence structures. Topics covered include inverted word-orders, nominal structures, syndeton/asyndeton and 'adjectivation'; the plays examined range from *Henry VI* to the late plays, with special attention devoted to the Histories and Tragedies.

Hussey, S.S., *The Literary Language of Shakespeare* (London and New York: Longman, 1992, 2nd edition)

Of the several books devoted to Shakespeare's language, this is probably the most accessible introduction for the literary reader and the second edition takes account of recent work on rhetoric. Hussey's primary focus is on vocabulary rather than syntax, but he offers an account both of the range of Shakespeare's styles and of their chronological development. Concludes with a reading of four plays: *Henry V, As You Like It, Macbeth* and *The Winter's Tale*.

Joseph, Sister Miriam, *Shakespeare's Use of the Arts of Language* (New York and London: Hafner, 1966)

Although written many years ago, this work is still a mine of information about the different elements of language in the Renaissance, and what commentators at the time had to say about them. Mainly concerned with Shakespeare's plays, but providing some material written by his contemporaries, Joseph works through the persuasive effects of grammar, argument, logic, pathos and ethos. Every device is illustrated with examples from the plays, and her index allows us to locate devices used by particular plays.

Kastan, David Scott, *Shakespeare and the Shapes of Time* (London: Macmillan, 1982)

Focusing on Shakespeare's history plays, tragedies, and romances, this book explores the relationship of the form of dramatic action and assumptions about historical time. In the ways in which the plays of each genre shape their stories, Kastan finds evidence of their distinct, though provisional, conceptions of time as the fundamental dimension of human experience.

Kennedy, Andrew K., *Dramatic Dialogue: The Duologue of Personal Encounter* (Cambridge: Cambridge University Press, 1983)

This book focuses on the interpersonal features of dramatic duologue (encounters with only two persons), offering a 'strong' concept of dialogue as transformative to character, effecting an exchange of values and 'worlds'. Kennedy argues usefully that dramatic dialogue differs from conversation in (1) developing a 'cumulative dialogue' within the totality of the play, (2) including 'counter-speech', or the counterpointing of verbal styles, and (3) providing acting and reading signals. He introduces such paired terms as *balance* and *domination, modes* and *moods, sympathy* and *alienation,* and *sincerity* and *dissembling* for the analysis of dialogue. The book draws its examples from Greek tragedy, Shakespeare, Restoration comedy and modern drama.

Kökeritz, Helge, *Shakespeare's Pronunciation* (New Haven, Conn.: Yale University Press, 1953)

This book may not appeal immediately to students unprepared for technical analyses of sixteenth- to seventeenth-century phonology, but it provides nevertheless a splendid, lucid, non-technical display of

information on homophonic puns and word-play. It also supplies IPA
(International Phonetic Alphabet) transcripts of some familiar passages
from the plays. It is worth learning the IPA – not a very difficult
acquisition – to study these. Shakespeare's pronunciation turns out to
be not dissimilar to Northern Irish.

Lakoff, George and Mark Johnson, *Metaphors We Live By* (Chicago and
London: Chicago University Press, 1980)

> Lakoff and Johnson argue that metaphor is an inevitable and
> inescapable element in everyday conceptualization and verbalization, not
> a 'literary' embellishment. They identify broad categories of structural
> metaphors ('time is money'), orientational metaphors ('more is up')
> and ontological metaphors ('the mind is a machine') which influence
> the ways in which we perceive, think and act as well as speak and write.
> They do not discuss elaborated or heightened uses of language, but their
> approach is thought-provoking for students of literature and implicitly
> illustrates the extent to which some of Shakespeare's most complex
> metaphors are grounded in everyday language.

Lanham, R.A., *A Handlist of Rhetorical Terms* (Oxford, Berkeley and Los
Angeles: University of California Press, 1991, 2nd edition)

> Lanham attractively fulfils his aim of providing an inexpensive, readily
> available beginner's guide to the traditional terminology of rhetoric.
> The terms are listed both alphabetically and by function, accompanied
> by helpful descriptions and illustrated from sources ranging from
> classical orators to modern blues singers.

Lass, R. (ed.), *The Cambridge History of the English Language, Vol. 3,
1476–1776* (Cambridge: Cambridge University Press, 1999)

> The most comprehensive one-volume history of English for the period
> between the establishment of Caxton's first press in England and the
> American Declaration of Independence. Six contributors trace
> developments in spelling and punctuation, phonology and
> morphology, syntax, vocabulary and semantics, regional and social
> variation, and the literary language, richly illustrating the turbulent
> transition from Middle English to modern English. The volume has
> been written with both specialist and non-specialist readers in mind. It
> offers an invaluable reference point for those readers of Shakespeare
> who are interested in setting the language of his plays in the context of
> the language of his period.

Lass, R., 'Phonology and morphology', in R. Lass (ed.), *The Cambridge History of the English Language, Vol. 3, 1476–1776* (Cambridge: Cambridge University Press, 1999), 56–186

> This guide is fairly technical, and not devoted to Shakespeare, but it covers both preceding and following periods, as well as the Shakespearean period itself. As with Kökeritz, there is extensive use of contemporary grammarians and phoneticians.

Linklater, Kristin, *Freeing Shakespeare's Voice: The Actor's Guide to Talking the Text* (New York: Theatre Communications Group, 1992)

> Linklater is the most celebrated of American voice teachers. The book begins by accessing language from vowels and consonants, then building into words, then into phrases. Linklater goes on to look at form: the verse and prose of Shakespeare's language. The book has many useful exercises for the reader to access Shakespeare's language; and is written in a lively and passionate style. Linklater's book is much used within the theatre profession.

McAlindon, T., *Shakespeare and Decorum* (London: Macmillan, 1973)

> An attempt to relate the concept of 'the three styles' to the analysis of character and action. Arguing that 'the doctrine of decorum was as much a part of moral as of rhetorical tradition', McAlindon aims to show how deeply it affected Shakespeare's 'understanding and representation of human behaviour'. The book includes detailed discussions of *Richard II*, *Hamlet*, *Othello*, *Macbeth* and *Antony and Cleopatra*.

McDonald, Russ, 'Reading *The Tempest*', *Shakespeare Survey*, 43 (1990), 15–28

> This is one of a series of excellent articles the author has written on Shakespeare's late verse style. McDonald is full of telling observations, beautifully described and illustrated, about Shakespeare's remarkable verbal techniques and his handling of repetitive vowel and consonant patterns, as well as his metrical dexterity. This essay is especially insightful in revealing the verbal patterning in *The Tempest* and showing how it serves the thematic purposes of that play.

McDonald, Russ (ed.), *Shakespeare Reread: The Texts in New Contexts* (Ithaca, N.Y., and London: Cornell University Press, 1994)

Some of the ten essays in this volume were conceived as contributions to a conference session on 'Close Reading Revisited', which would have been an equally appropriate title. Contributors, who include Stephen Booth, Barbara Hodgdon, Pat Parker and Helen Vendler, address issues of textual analysis in relation to current contextual (social, historical, political) ways of reading. There is no consistent ideological stance, but all the approaches are challenging and theoretically sophisticated.

Magnusson, Lynne, *Shakespeare and Social Dialogue: Dramatic Language and Elizabethan Letters* (Cambridge: Cambridge University Press, 1999)

This book opens up an interactive approach to Shakespeare's language and the rhetoric of Elizabethan letters. Moving beyond claims about the language of individual Shakespearean characters, Magnusson develops a rhetoric of social exchange to analyse dialogue, conversation, sonnets and letters as the verbal negotiation of historically specific social relationships. The book relates concepts from discourse analysis and linguistic pragmatics, especially 'politeness theory', to key ideas in epistolary handbooks of the period, including those by Erasmus and Angel Day. Arguing that Shakespeare's language is rooted in the everyday language of Elizabethan culture, it creates a way of reading both literary texts and historical documents which bridges the gap between new historicism and linguistic criticism.

Mahood, M.M., *Shakespeare's Wordplay* (London: Methuen, 1957)

This book is still a good example of a critical engagement with the richness of Shakespeare's language, primarily through the pun. Mahood argues that, while the eighteenth century disapproved of Shakespeare's word-play and the nineteenth century ignored it, the twentieth century could acclaim it as offering access to the very heart of the drama. Mahood's imaginative readings of the nuances and implications of Shakespeare's language are extremely suggestive. Individual chapters focus on *Romeo and Juliet*, *Richard II*, *Hamlet*, *Macbeth*, *The Winter's Tale*, and the sonnets.

Murphy, James J. (ed.), *Renaissance Eloquence: Studies in the Theory and Practice of Renaissance Rhetoric* (Berkeley: University of California Press, 1983)

The essays collected in this volume bring together some of the most thought-provoking writers on persuasion in the Renaissance. They range from education in schools and universities, to cultural contexts in Europe, to the issue of deceitful versus morally persuasive rhetoric, to specific work on style in sixteenth and early seventeenth-century writing. Many of these essays have subsequently been developed by the writers themselves and others, especially in the journal *Rhetorica*. Nevertheless they provide a good starting point, and represent probably the most comprehensive approach to argument and persuasion in the Renaissance.

Nevalainen, Terttu, 'Early Modern English lexis and semantics', in Roger Lass (ed.), *The Cambridge History of the English Language, Vol. 3, 1476–1776* (Cambridge: Cambridge University Press, 1999), 332–458

This chapter does not specifically concentrate on Shakespeare, but provides an overall view of the increase in vocabulary intake, loan words, word-formation processes and meaning changes in Early Modern English.

Parsons, Keith and Pamela Mason (eds), *Shakespeare in Performance* (London: Salamander, 1995)

The sixteen contributors share a commitment to the continuing life of Shakespeare's plays. After introductory chapters establishing the context in which Shakespeare worked and outlining how theatrical tastes have changed, individual essays 'say what the plays treats on' with abundant reference to recent productions. The book is recommended particularly for its lavish use of illustrations, which can encourage readers to engage with the range of interpretative possibilities that have been explored in performance.

Rees, Joan, *Shakespeare and the Story: Aspects of Creation* (London: Athlone Press, 1978)

Rees explores the relationship of story to play, focusing on the ways in which Shakespeare organizes his plots as evidence of the operation of his creative imagination. For Rees, always the most interesting aspects of the plays are those which threaten the narrative framework, where the energy of a character, for example, disrupts the shape of the story and forces Shakespeare to discover the deepest logic of his material.

Rissanen, M., 'Syntax', in R. Lass (ed.), *The Cambridge History of the English Language, Vol. 3, 1476–1776* (Cambridge: Cambridge University Press, 1999), 187–331

An authoritative, up-to-date account of Early Modern English grammar. It is fairly technical but clearly written and lavishly illustrated with examples from literary and non-literary texts. The discussion is not restricted to Shakespeare, but will enable the reader to place Shakespeare's usage in its socio-historical context.

Robinson, Randal, *Unlocking Shakespeare's Language: Help for the Teacher and Student* (Urbana, Ill.: National Council of Teachers of English and the ERIC Clearinghouse on Reading and Communication Skills, 1989)

This book is specifically aimed at high-school and undergraduate college teachers and students. It addresses the typical problems which modern students have in reading Shakespeare's language. It includes worksheets, with examples from Shakespeare's plays, to provide concrete exercises in reading 'difficult' language.

Ronberg, G., *A Way with Words: The Language of English Renaissance Literature* (London: Edward Arnold, 1992)

A helpful and undaunting beginners' guide, focusing mainly on grammar and rhetoric. It offers substantial discussions of verbs and pronouns (Chapter 3), of punctuation and sentence structure (Chapter 4) and of rhetoric (Chapter 5). The chapter on rhetoric includes a list of commonly used figures of speech and provides sample analyses of passages, showing how grammatical and rhetorical features combine and interact. The discussion is not restricted to Shakespeare, but he is the most frequently cited author and it can be illuminating to see how his usage compares with that of his contemporaries.

Salmon, V. and E. Burness (eds.), *A Reader in the Language of Shakespearean Drama* (Amsterdam/Philadelphia: John Benjamins, 1987)

A useful collection of thirty-three essays, all previously published between 1951 and 1982 in a wide range of specialist books and journals. They are arranged in seven sections: 'Shakespeare and the English Language', 'Aspects of Colloquial Elizabethan English', 'Studies in Vocabulary', 'Shakespeare and Elizabethan Grammar', 'Studies in Rhetoric and Metre', 'Punctuation' and 'The Linguistic Context of Shakespearean Drama'. The volume aims to 'explicate some of the major differences' between Elizabethan and Modern English and to show how Shakespeare 'handles the language of his time for artistic purposes'.

Sonnino, L.A., *A Handbook to Sixteenth-Century Rhetoric* (London: Routledge and Kegan Paul, 1968)

A more specialised work than Lanham's *Handlist*, Sonnino's handbook concentrates on Renaissance views, collating the definitions and examples of rhetorical figures provided by the major rhetoricians of the period. It is particularly helpful in identifying and illustrating points of agreement and disagreement in their nomenclature and classification systems.

Spain, Delbert, *Shakespeare Sounded Soundly: The Verse Structure and the Language* (Santa Barbara: Capra Press, Garland-Clarke Editions, 1988)

The author calls this *A Handbook for Students, Actors, and Directors*; it is intended especially for inexperienced actors who have trouble speaking Shakespeare's lines with a firm sense of their metrical patterning. Spain sympathetically recognizes the difficulties and offers sensible, clear and accurate advice about how to handle them. This is a very unpretentious, helpful guide to Shakespeare's verse practice.

Tarlinskaja, Marina, *Shakespeare's Verse: Iambic Pentameter and the Poet's Idiosyncrasies* (New York: Peter Lang, 1987)

A Russian linguist now living in the United States, Tarlinskaja adopts a rigorously scientific approach to metrical study. She analyses vast numbers of verse lines and makes extensive use of statistical charts and tables in order to frame precise generalizations about Shakespeare's metrical practice. By studying the correlation between positions 1–10 in the iambic line and lexical and phrasal stress, she measures changes in Shakespeare's verse style over the years and his differences from other poets and dramatists. Her book is difficult to read, but she is sensitive to the rhythms of verse, and her work deserves much more attention than it has received from literary metrists.

Thompson, Ann and John O. Thompson, *Shakespeare, Meaning and Metaphor* (Brighton: Harvester Press, 1987)

This book applies non-literary research on metaphor to a number of Shakespearean texts – *Troilus and Cressida*, *King Lear*, *Hamlet*, Sonnet 63 – and more generally to Shakespeare's use of metaphors from the domain of printing. The approaches used are drawn from philosophy, psychology, linguistics and anthropology, and the authors argue that they can illuminate Shakespearean usage even though they do not address it directly but focus on everyday language. In turn the approaches themselves are tested and illuminated by the range and complexity of Shakespearean examples.

Vickers, Brian, *The Artistry of Shakespeare's Prose* (London: Methuen, 1968)

In what is still the major work on this topic, Vickers takes a chronological approach to the canon, analysing Shakespeare's use of prose in comedy, history, tragedy and romance. He includes a 'percentage distribution' table showing the amount of prose in each play (*The Merry Wives of Windsor* has the most prose, followed by other comedies: *Much Ado About Nothing*, *Twelfth Night* and *As You Like It*). He pays special attention to characters whose dialogue makes most use of prose: Bottom, Shylock, Beatrice and Benedick, Mercutio, Falstaff, Hamlet and Iago.

Vickers, Brian, *In Defence of Rhetoric* (Oxford: Clarendon Press, 1988)

This book offers a historical context for literature and rhetoric and a summary of the main parts of rhetoric, as well as one detailed chapter on the Renaissance and another surveying a range of the figures, with useful examples found in an appendix. Vickers argues that the Renaissance brought together rhetoric, logic and philosophy, after fragmentation during the medieval period. This theory is highly contentious, but his argument is an effective demonstration of some of the issues. A later chapter on rhetoric in the modern novel offers a platform for those concerned with relevance to the present day.

Wales, K., *A Dictionary of Stylistics* (London: Longman, 1990; fully revised 2nd edition forthcoming 2001)

A highly readable and richly illustrated comprehensive glossary of useful critical, stylistic, rhetorical and linguistic terms for the study of literary texts from Old English to the present day, and also of non-literary and media discourse types.

Wilson, Rawdon, *Shakespearean Narrative* (London: Associated University Presses, 1995)

Wilson is interested in both Shakespeare's command of narrative conventions and his exploration of narrative functions. Applying the concepts of recent narrative theory to Shakespeare's plays, he analyses the narrative acts in the plays in terms of the conventions that structure them and the effects they produce.

Wright, George T., 'Hendiadys and *Hamlet*', PMLA (*Publications of the Modern Language Association of America*) (1981), 96, 168–93

> Wright discusses the importance of the 'doubling' scheme of hendiadys ('They drank from cups and gold' is a classic example) as both a frequent local effect in *Hamlet* (and other plays of Shakespeare's middle period) and a reflection of the play's thematic concern with doubleness, disjunction, misleading parallels and false relationships. This essay has become a classic example of the significance of a particular rhetorical device to a single text. (Reprinted in Salmon & Burness, pp. 407–32)

Wright, George T., *Shakespeare's Metrical Art* (Berkeley: University of California Press, 1988)

> Wright's aim is 'to describe the metrical system Shakespeare uses, particularly in his plays – the basic forms of his iambic pentameter line, its relation to other patterns (such as short lines, long lines, and prose), its changes over his career, and ... the expressive gestures and powers the system provides for Shakespeare and his dramatis personae'. Also included are discussions of the verse art of other Renaissance poets and playwrights, from Chaucer and Wyatt to Sidney, Spenser, Marlowe, Donne, Webster, Middleton and Milton.

DICTIONARIES AND OTHER REFERENCE WORKS

The *Harvard Concordance to Shakespeare*, compiled by Marvin Spevack, lists all the words, old and new, used by Shakespeare in their dramatic contexts. Notable historical dictionaries include the *Oxford English Dictionary* and *Middle English Dictionary*. Both are available in electronic versions, and give dates to English words recorded in writing. *The Early Modern English Dictionaries Database* compiled by Professor Ian Lancashire at the University of Toronto gives access in an electronic form to a number of dictionaries published in the sixteenth and seventeenth centuries.

Abbott, E.A., *A Shakespearian Grammar* (London: Macmillan, 1869)

> This book is still the standard reference work on this topic, though a new version is being prepared for Arden by Jonathan Hope. Abbott offers a systematic account of the differences between Elizabethan and Modern grammar, explaining, with due reference to the transitional

nature of the language at the time, the ways in which apparent
irregularities can be idiomatic. The arrangement is by topic, from
'Adjectives used as adverbs' to 'Suffixes'; there is a useful section on
prosody (including pronunciation) and extensive indices of quotations
and individual words.

Onions, C.T., *A Shakespeare Glossary*, enlarged and revised by Robert
Eagleson (Oxford: Clarendon Press, 1986)

This venerable text, which has run through several reprints since its
first publication in 1929, remains a valuable, indeed necessary,
companion to the study of Shakespeare's vocabulary, not only for
'look it up' purposes but also as a resource for browsing among shades
and shifts of meaning in Tudor–Stuart English. Entries are supported
by citations from the plays, allowing the user to compare contexts, to
gain an insight into the common usage of the time, and in due place
to glimpse Shakespeare's innovative power.

ELECTRONIC VERSIONS OF
SHAKESPEARE'S TEXTS

Electronic versions include the Arden Shakespeare in Ardenonline
(www.ardenshakepeare.com), the *Oxford Shakespeare*, and the Chadwyck-
Healey collection of *Editions and Adaptations of Shakespeare* (1591–1911).

INDEX

Abbott, E.A. 314
Adamson, S.M. 49, 209, 302
adnominatio 21, 274
affixiation 238, 244–54
alliteration 9, 44–5, 274–5
allusion (intertextuality) 11
ambiguity 175–6
amplification 276
anadiplosis 21, 24, 123, 276–7
anaphora 278
antanaclesis 22, 120, 278–9
anthimeria 279
anthymeme 285
antimetabole 22, 279
antithesis 123, 154, 280
Antony and Cleopatra: characters in
    151–5; description in 92,
    99–100; grammar in 221–2,
    233–4; new words in 241–2,
    244, 245, 249; persuasion in
    123–4; sounds in 259
aphesis 280
aposiopesis 226, 280–1
apostrophe 38, 45, 134, 169, 207, 281
appearance of characters:
    anonymity of 151, 155;
    disconcert/unsettle audience
    145–7; listing of 144–5;
    mistaken assessments of 147–8;
    personal focus of 148–9;

preconceptions concerning
    151–5; relationship with each
    other/audience 144, 156; shared
    experience 149–51
Aristotle 89, 114
articulus 282
As You Like It: description in 91;
    narrative in 104; new words in
    241; parody in 82, 83–4
assimiliation 249
asteismus 22, 282

Barton, J. 156, 171, 302
Bate, Jonathan 96
bathos *see* gradatio
Beckett, Samuel 174
Berry, C. 172, 302
Betterton, Thomas 182
Blake, N.F. 235, 303
body: discursive 179–82; dramatic
    177–8; historical 178–9; mean
    meaning 173–7; performative
    182–3; in the text 183–5
Branagh, Kenneth 183
Brown, J.R. 156, 303

caesura 58
catachresis 123–4, 282–3
Caxton, William 193
Cercignani, F. 303